D0934092

More Thoughts
of Chairman Moore

Also by Brian Moore

Beware of the Dog
The Thoughts of Chairman Moore

More Thoughts
of Chairman Moore

The Wit and Wisdom of
Brian Moore Vol. II

BRIAN MOORE

**SIMON &
SCHUSTER**

London · New York · Sydney · Toronto · New Delhi

A CBS COMPANY

First published in Great Britain by Simon & Schuster UK Ltd, 2011
A CBS COMPANY

1 3 5 7 9 10 8 6 4 2

Simon & Schuster UK Ltd
1st Floor
222 Gray's Inn Road
London
WC1X 8HB

www.simonandschuster.co.uk

Simon & Schuster Australia, Sydney
Simon & Schuster India, New Delhi

A CIP catalogue for this book
is available from the British Library.

ISBN: 978-0-85720-245-1 (hardback)
978-0-85720-246-8 (trade paperback)

Typeset by M Rules
Printed and bound by CPI Group (UK) Ltd, Croydon, CR0 4YY

To those brave athletes who risk body and soul in pursuit of excellence – and give those of us who cannot do likewise the chance to watch and comment

Contents

1 Even pampered players like Adrian Mutu deserve
  equal justice   1

2 Team GB's Beijing success more to do with
  professional approach than budget   3

3 BNP must not poison England's patriotism   4

4 When and why did 'old-fashioned' rucking
  become illegal?   8

5 Why the Brendan Venter saga is so ominous   11

6 A good start for Hugh Robertson   12

2010 FIFA World Cup

7 Jamie Carragher's return causes far more concern
  than Capello Index   13

8 Calm down, England, it's only the phoney war – real
  hysteria is coming   17

9 Fabio Capello should tell his players earlier, but
  keep opponents guessing   20

10 Intelligence and attitude help England confound
   the critics   23

11 World Cup 2010: English football has only itself
   to blame for its failings   26

12   English football is hamstrung by hidebound
     thinking   30

13   South Africa World Cup besmirched
     'beautiful' game   34

14   Ferrari apologists have left Formula One's
     credibility in a sorry state   38

15   'Bloodgate' doctor Wendy Chapman must be
     allowed to return to work   42

16   Paralympians should be admired for their sporting
     ability, not physical disability   46

17   The Ryder Cup is a golf tournament, not a
     superpower challenge   49

18   Corrupt players must be banned or cricket
     will reach its tipping point   53

19   Liverpool supporters cannot cry foul now –
     the damage was already done   57

20   Elite rugby ignores Asia at its peril   61

21   Wayne Rooney is another example of player
     selfishness   64

22   Quietly and phlegmatically, Phil Vickery joins
     the list of giants   68

23   Refereeing will only improve when officials get
     the respect they deserve   72

24   For the first time under Martin Johnson England
     showed some balance   76

25   New Zealand's PR for banned hooker Keven
     Mealamu has put rugby world in a spin   79

26   David Haye's farcical world title fight with Audley
     Harrison shows just how far boxing has fallen   83

27 BBC Sports Personality of the Year candidates
     can only sit and suffer   86

28 Schools given sporting chance? Michael Gove's
     management-speak doesn't fool me   90

29 Michael Gove's flawed logic is redolent of a kid
     always shoved in goal   94

30 Focus on the achievements, not the fluff that
     accompanies BBC's sport show night   98

31 Barry Hearn's big challenge – to make snooker
     the new darts   102

32 Time will tell whether John Steele's RFU revamp
     will aid Martin Johnson and England   106

33 A touch of humility could go a long way in making
     England a world player again   109

34 The IRB has finally woken up to the fact the scrum is
     causing a problem   113

35 Businesslike solution to Olympic Stadium row is
     for Spurs and West Ham to share   116

36 Admitting weakness and asking for help requires
     truly brutal honesty   120

37 Time to educate pushy parents on the futility of
     abuse from touchline   124

38 Hopefully Rugby World Cup will boost
     Christchurch   128

2011 Six Nations Championship

39 France need unity to capitalise on strength of domestic
     game for success in Six Nations Championship   129

40 There's no telling who will win Six Nations
     Championship . . . and that's fantastic   132

41 Wales need key figures to save them from Six Nations
   Championship crisis following defeat to England 136

42 Mike Tindall and Shontayne Hape at centre of
   England's development in 2011 Six Nations 139

43 Six Nations 2011: Biased? Not me, but I do fancy
   England to overcome naturally talented French 142

44 England *v.* France: After some displeasure, I will hail
   Steve Thompson for equalling my record 145

45 A subtle touch would improve England's pack in quest
   for 2011 Six Nations Championship Grand Slam 149

46 Manu Tuilagi and Matt Stevens power their way into
   England's World Cup shake-up 152

47 Brian O'Driscoll should be man enough to accept
   blame for Ireland's defeat against Wales 155

48 England need not fear any team in one-off fixture 158

49 England defeat to Ireland in Six Nations
   Championship was a painful but necessary lesson 162

50 Manchester United manager Sir Alex Ferguson
   typical of a game that fails to respect officials 165

51 Self-interested parties prevent English football's
   big issues being tackled 169

52 PFA chief executive Gordon Taylor's argument for
   inclusion on FA main board just does not wash 173

53 A victory for common sense – Rain Tax follow-up 176

54 Clock is ticking on a wonderful Games 178

55 India *v.* Pakistan match demonstrated the
   unique pressure of a semi-final 179

56 Divided FA is disastrous for football 183

57   It's all in the mind as Tottenham implode in
     the Bernabeu   186

58   Rory McIlroy's reaction to defeat was the most
     worrying part of his Masters meltdown   188

59   Sky has raised standards in sports coverage –
     but at a price for the viewer   192

60   Wales need Gavin Henson and Andy Powell –
     but they should grow up or go away   196

61   Return of Sir Clive Woodward is a gamble
     worth taking for the RFU   200

62   What price another northern hemisphere team
     in the rugby World Cup Final?   203

63   Sporting red tape and how to remove it   217

64   British tennis – where does it go from here?   226

65   'You are the worst, most biased commentator
     in the world'   241

66   Twitter: freedom of speech or freedom to abuse?   255

67   Beware of the aftermath: the repercussions of
     writing an autobiography   286

1

Even pampered players like Adrian Mutu deserve equal justice

August 2008

Some say Adrian Mutu took drugs and deserves everything he gets. This might be legitimate were it applied consistently to all, including Rio Ferdinand, given that failure to test is as serious as failing one (otherwise everyone would simply avoid being tested).

The background to the Mutu case, which stemmed from his failed drugs test in 2004 while he was still a Chelsea player, is interesting. Before it blew up Mutu was in poor form; he was in conflict with Jose Mourinho for declaring himself unfit for Chelsea, but playing internationally a few days later.

When Mutu tested positive for cocaine use (only performance enhancing in the mind of the user) Chelsea had a conundrum. If they accepted the fundamental breach of contract, they could summarily dismiss Mutu and not pay the rest of his contract. However, who then owned Mutu's registration? If not them, it was the FA and they could not withhold permission for Mutu's transfer, seeking to force a fee from a buyer.

Having failed to get money from Juventus, the club Mutu left Stamford Bridge to join, Chelsea prosecuted their claim through an arbitration clause in Mutu's contract. In 2005 they lodged an £8.4 million claim with the Premier League. They succeeded, Mutu appealed. On appeal Chelsea were awarded £9.6 million; Mutu appealed.

Chelsea were then awarded damages of £13.8 million by Fifa's Dispute Resolution Chamber (DRC) comprising two player representatives, two club representatives from FIFPro (the world body for players' associations) and a chairman. The DRC have no fixed rules of evidence and are governed by Swiss, not UK, law. FIFPro have now publicly disagreed with the decision, so it must have been a deadlocked vote with the chairman having the casting vote. The award is curious.

In 2005 Chelsea claimed their loss was £8.4 million; how could it have increased by £5.4 million only two years later? Further, Chelsea confirm they asked for no specific sum and on appeal it is not usual for any further evidence to be allowed.

Some representatives on the DRC are legally qualified, but they are not experienced civil court judges. Moreover, if the case were brought in a UK civil court, strict rules of evidence would apply. Chelsea would have to prove their loss by using an expert whose duty is to the court, not the litigant. I do not believe this is the appropriate forum for the making of a potentially far-reaching legal precedent. Although I often feel antipathy to pampered players, I do not accept that they are entitled to a lesser standard of justice than anybody else.

Finally, you wonder why Chelsea have not pursued former goalkeeper Mark Bosnich. Could this be because he had no transfer value and is now bankrupt, or am I being unduly cynical?

Team GB's Beijing success more to do with professional approach than budget

August 2008

The government claims their tripling of funding for elite sport, to £265 million, is in part responsible for the success of Team GB in Beijing. However, the claim compares funding over four-year cycles between Games. Until two years ago, extra funding was only £2 million above the Sydney cycle of £63 million; the £200 million extra funding was announced in the first budget after London was awarded the 2012 Games.

This hike in funding had more to do with having to back the London Games with solid cash, rather than a conscious effort to increase the chances of those presently competing. Not all of this extra sum has been distributed to athletes and, in any event, the long-term preparations undertaken by the members of Team GB started when funding by the government had increased imperceptibly.

The main reason for the increased success is the professionalism of those sports which have given their athletes the best possible preparation; that, and money from the National Lottery, the creation of which Labour opposed.

3

BNP must not poison England's patriotism

October 2009

Patriotism will be the watchword for World Cup 2010 and, though much improved, the behaviour of England fans will necessarily trumpet national superiority. Nick Griffin of the BNP is on *Question Time* on Thursday. He never misses a chance to tell us he is a patriot, so it is to be presumed that he will be supporting the English football team in the 2010 World Cup.

How does he square this with his party's policy of repatriation of anyone whose ancestors do not come from the earliest settlers here after the last great Ice Age, as complemented by the historic migrations from mainland Europe (the BNP's definition of indigenous Britons)? Patriotic? Rubbish. If you took his definition, hardly any of Capello's last starting XI would be playing.

Not that this point would stop the far right from hijacking football if they could. You only have to look at the way the BNP has misappropriated British military emblems to see that. As an aside, someone should ask Griffin how, in our finest hour, the Battle of Britain could have been won without the non-indigenous pilots from the Canadian and Polish air forces.

History should have taught us that movements, such as the National Socialist German Workers Party, which later formed the Nazi Party, are adept at exploiting opportunities to advance their cause as and when they occur. Political disaffection is turned into divisiveness and masked under a cynical respectability, with patriotism the core appeal.

All this threatens to undermine the huge efforts of the UK football authorities to rid their grounds of this ignorant and offensive behaviour. They must have been tempted to think that they had removed this problem for good, but that would be to misunderstand the nature of the problem.

Football has little credibility when it blames society for its ills of abusive swearing, boorishness and violence but it does have a legitimate claim to not being the author of its racism problems. Unlike other forms of unacceptable behaviour, racism is sometimes politically motivated and supported; in times past its adherents have used sport and other forms of social entertainment like books, films and TV and radio shows to propagate their divisive message.

Tribalism in football is more easily exploited than other organised gatherings because it creates 'us and them' in every game. Most people are able to see this for what it is, a necessary mindset for sporting contests, but if you have been to any ground recently you can see that the temporary 'hatred' needs not too much redirecting to make it a wholly different thing.

It is crucial that Griffin and the BNP are not allowed to poison the fans' support of what is still only a football team, however much emotion is invested in their success.

If you think that this is feigned, politically correct, offence-taking then you only have to look at the racist controversies at games involving Millwall, Cardiff, Crystal Palace, Stoke, Bolton and West Ham, to name but a few. That not all the complaints were proven does not lessen the need for proper investigation of all such matters.

And if you doubt where this can lead to, look at ethnic cleansing or, more recently, the disgraceful and underplayed violence by the far right that this year forced 40 Polish nationals and 100 Romanians to flee Belfast. It is because of this potential that it is unacceptable for football's global governing bodies to hide behind initiatives, such as Football Against Racism in Europe.

All this is ultimately futile if the punishments handed down to countries, clubs and players are not sufficiently severe to deter. In 2004, no action was taken against Spain's national coach, Luis Aragones, for calling Thierry Henry a 'black s***'. The same year, black England players suffered sustained monkey chants in a game against Spain, whose federation was fined £56,000 by Uefa – less than half a week's wages of your average Real Madrid *galactico*.

Sepp Blatter, the Fifa president, said, 'Now that the clubs and associations have an obligation to find a solution, they will find the solutions necessary to eliminate this plague.' No doubt Blatter relies on the amendment to article 55 of the Fifa disciplinary code, which sets out minimum punishments for racist behaviour.

This is not enough, certainly if you leave it up to the Spanish. Last year the Royal Spanish Football Federation fined Atletico Madrid €6,000 (£5,400) when their fans racially abused Espanyol's Carlos Kameni. In January they cracked down on Real Madrid, whose fans made fascist gestures and chanted fascist slogans, by imposing a whopping €3,900 (£3,510) fine; the club spent about £330.7 million on transfers between 2008 and 2009. No swift remedial action there; in fact no action at all. Contrast the speed of denunciation and action over minor blemishes such as the Eduardo 'dive' by Blatter and Michel Platini, the president of Uefa.

There are too many incidents from Eastern Europe to mention here, but examples like these illustrate the growing problem. Last year Zenit St Petersburg's own coach, Dick Advocaat, admitted the club's supporters were racist after they abused black French players. In March 2008, the Serbian club Borac Cacak's fans attacked Ghanaian player Solomon Opoku; two years earlier, 37 fans were arrested after racially abusing their own player Zimbabwean Mike Temwanjera. The problem of anti-Semitism in

Polish football has drawn international criticism. It was named as one of the worst offenders in British MP John Mann's report, which describes anti-Semitic incidents in 18 countries across Europe.

Fifa's invitation to the Polish FA to join the fight against racism is wholly inadequate. Playing football internationally, or indeed at all, is not an inalienable right. Why did Fifa simply not say to any country, club or player that they are welcome, but only under common standards of behaviour? Fulfil them and you play; fail them and you do not.

Finally, given that allegations of racism are easily made and always affect the person accused, the seriousness of the charge demands that if a complainant is proved to have fabricated an allegation, he or she should be dealt with as severely as would be a person found guilty of racism.

4

When and why did 'old-fashioned' rucking become illegal?

January 2010

Over the past few months I have been conducting a strange and secret test. With whispered conversations in the corners of quiet rooms; during lonely hours in the garden office replaying old VHS tapes and hours watching ESPN classics at unseemly times of night; far from the prying eyes of the International Rugby Board lawmakers and their acolytes, I have been investigating the greatest taboo in rugby.

I was trying to answer two questions: at what point did 'old-fashioned' rucking become illegal; and what was the real evidence of serious injury that led to its removal?

First of all let us be exact about what I mean by rucking. Many people I spoke to remember the injuries J.P.R. Williams and Phil de Glanville suffered during rucks, but their lacerations were not caused by rucking but by illegal stamping/raking above the neck. What I mean by rucking is the removal of prone players on the wrong side of the ball by the backward use of the foot; not stamping and not contact with the knee and ankle joints.

The further I got into my quest and the more people I talked to the stranger the whole experience became. It seems that this subject has produced a bizarre amnesia in even the most informed observers. Nobody from the lowest casual watcher to the very highest-qualified international player or coach was prepared to be absolute in their proffered answer as to the precise point at which rucking was outlawed.

There must be a point at which the practice of removing illegally obstructive players with the foot was condemned, but I cannot find it and nobody has been able to help. I remember being at a meeting when the IRB referee manager, Paddy O'Brien, stated that handling the ball in a ruck was to be allowed 'because it in fact legalised what was going on anyway' – ignoring the fact that it only happened because referees were failing to do their job.

I need your assistance to identify the similar pronouncement in respect of the rucking of players.

All the evidence available on film and from anecdote supported the fact that rucking produced quicker and cleaner ball than the present mess that is the breakdown today. Everyone could remember, and the footage is there, scrum-halves sweeping the ball off the floor in one continuous passing movement – free from interference from infringing players and without having to step over and dig in-between the legs of players in a heap.

Furthermore and of crucial importance in the world of 'space-challenged' professional rugby was the fact that far more players were committed to the ruck area and its immediate environs than is the case today.

The crucial point of injury also brought more prevarication from witnesses. Every person I have spoken to thought that they ought to be able to recall incidents whereby rucking, which looks to the outsider to be a dangerous practice, had caused a serious injury, yet nobody could cite one. As above, they could refer to incidents of foul play but then they had to agree that those acts were illegal and not proper examples of rucking.

From this comes the question: on what evidence of serious risk or injury to players was this practice removed? Was it based on hard evidence or, as I strongly suspect, was it based on perception and the fact that it might scare off would-be participants (of which there was no evidence either)?

Given the figures for injuries in the tackle and scrum areas that are deemed to be acceptable as part of a game involving repeated violent collisions, you would have expected that rucking must have produced similar or worse figures. Surely the IRB would not have simply removed an effective part of the game without reliable evidence?

Those against the return of rucking should be made to produce their evidence of its nefarious effects before they are allowed to go any further with their refusal even to discuss the return of a measure which was universally popular and remains so with the majority of rugby people.

It has to be admitted that to the average sports watcher the art of rucking looks primitive. Were similar contact allowed in football you would have nearly every player rolling around for extended periods and Didier Drogba would hardly ever get off the floor. However, just because it doesn't look nice is not a reason to kowtow to the litigation-avoidance brigade; especially when they cannot back up their claims to be protecting the allegedly vulnerable.

Finally, one thing most people said to me in hushed tones was that actually they quite liked giving and getting a bit of a 'shoeing'.

5

Why the Brendan Venter saga is so ominous

May 2010

Brendan Venter, the Saracens head coach, has been appealing against a Rugby Football Union ban for his behaviour at a recent game against Leicester. One of his submissions to the disciplinary hearing was that the behaviour of his opposite number, Richard Cockerill, was similarly poor yet brought forth no charges. This was a questionable tactic, and even if Venter had a point, it is not one that excuses his behaviour.

The pair's conduct fuelled banter between the supporters of the two sides which has subsequently turned ugly. Segregation of the fans in the Guinness Premiership final between the two clubs at Twickenham on Saturday has been seriously discussed.

Martyn Thomas, of the RFU's management board, says that nobody is bigger than the game and he is right. Let rugby be in no doubt, these sort of things are the start of a slide towards practices which blight football and which have now become so commonplace that football feels unable to do anything about them.

Both coaches say they are passionate men and thereby their excesses are excusable. They are not. I understand their behaviour but the wider good of the game is far more important. What they have to understand is that rugby is not required to accommodate them and, if it does, it creates a precedent which can develop only one way – and that way should be avoided at all costs.

A good start for Hugh Robertson

June 2010

If many of the proposed reforms announced by the new Minister for Sport, Hugh Robertson, appear familiar to readers, it may be because they were prefaced in many of my previous columns.

As long ago as last June I said that Sport England was failing UK sport, and Robertson's verdict that recently declared it 'dysfunctional' and far too politicised was correct and should have been made by the previous government. Robertson's solution of amalgamating Sport England, UK Sport and the Youth Sport Trust into one organisation, housed in the same building, was called for in my column in April this year.

Then, on 20 May, I highlighted the need to protect the 2012 London Games legacy and protect sport's share of Lottery funding. Robertson has just announced that sport is to be given National Lottery funds worth an extra £50 million a year from 2012 and a share increased to 20 per cent of such funds to secure that legacy.

Even the most insidious challenge of all, identified in the same article, posed by the Independent Safeguarding Authority and its vetting and barring scheme for adults working with children, is to be modified. I suspect this is due to budgetary constraints but why does not matter; the alteration of this potentially ruinous scheme is good news; a good start and two cheers for Robertson.

Jamie Carragher's return causes far more concern than Capello Index

May 2010

In portraying Fabio Capello's link to the Capello Index as a serious matter, the footballing media are badly out of step with the average England football fan who appears more capable than seasoned watchers of placing this issue in the correct place in the scale of 'scandals', i.e. it is a minor distraction.

OK, it need not have been there at all and is surprising given Capello's previous astuteness in handling much more difficult problems, like John Terry's demotion from the England captaincy, and it has opened a small chink for hungry scandalmongers to exploit.

However, if there is no financial link it should be greeted with a shrug of the shoulders as something that would have been better not to have taken place, but in essence is not serious, especially when set off against Capello's record since he took the England manager's job.

Compare this affair to previous events that took place before past tournaments like the fallout from Glenn Hoddle's dropping of Paul Gascoigne in 1998, the multiple controversies of Sven-Goran Eriksson's reign, David Beckham's metatarsal and so on, and England have been given a relatively free run-in in terms of negative incidents.

In any event, what does it matter about how Capello rates his players? They all know he does this every time he announces the team. Whatever way Capello assesses his players there will be room for criticism because judgement is always subjective. What should cause some concern are the 30 players Capello has had to choose for his enlarged squad and what this says about the strength of English football and England's chances of winning the World Cup.

Barring a couple of personal favourites the vast majority of fans would agree that Capello chose England's best available players. However, when you look at the options available you can see that England's challenge balances on the smallest of ledges and is dependent on the gods looking favourably on the team. That some of the precariousness is due to the structure of English football is an unacceptable state of affairs.

Capello's insistence that he would pick only players that were on form, were playing regular first-team football and were fully fit went out of the window when he surveyed the wreckage of a season where no proper rest was built in to aid players to prepare for the biggest of tournaments.

Compare this to the three-week Christmas break given to Germany's players. It is said that Germany always do well in World Cups; well, there is a reason for that and it is called preparation.

Those who champion the Premier League as the best in the world should also ask: why is it that it cannot produce just two English players in each position, both unarguably of international standard?

Defensively Capello has chosen six centre-backs, three left-backs and one right-back. Without even knowing the team or the players, that bald statistic shows that an injury at right-back leaves a problem. When you add to this the knowledge that the right-back is Glen Johnson, who is not the most renowned defender in world football, you know things are not ideal to start with.

When you add that cover is likely to be given by Jamie

Carragher you really have got issues. Carragher's case is founded on two points: firstly, the fact that he used to play there, and secondly, that he is cover for three centre-backs, Terry, Rio Ferdinand and Ledley King, none of whom you can say for certain will last the tournament.

The first observation to make about this state of affairs is that England should not have to go into any tournament without two specialist players in every position. Making do is not good enough when you compete with the rest of the world. Further, Carragher's form has not been good enough this season to justify a role as first-choice replacement for the centre-back position.

Finally, any player who refuses to play for his country should not be given the chance thereafter. Any other stance can be called pragmatism; it can also be called a betrayal of principle and what signal does it send out about the minor accolade of representing your country?

Are we now a nation that in footballing terms has no pride in what representing England means? Is all to be sacrificed on the altar of convenience? This is a widespread view among football fans and yet in this regard the media have given the point of view little or no prominence; it is a much bigger and more noteworthy point than Capello's website.

Defensively England could, with one unfortunate clash of bones, find themselves with at best a makeshift back four and behind them no goalkeeper that can demonstrate ability, form and experience; all of which have been present with previous selections in that position.

Midfield gives no similar concern, although Steven Gerrard's form has to come back for him to retain his place and without Joe Cole there is no spark of inventiveness. Aaron Lennon should be retained but the advocacy for Shaun Wright-Phillips and Theo Walcott is not firmly based. The last two mentioned have only attracted interest as to whether they will start for their clubs and neither has demonstrated anything other than flashes of potential.

Up front Capello has to pray that Wayne Rooney lasts for the whole of England's challenge because the other players are not among the world's leading strikers. Darren Bent, Peter Crouch, Jermain Defoe or Emile Heskey – none of these players has regularly gained plaudits in the Premier League, let alone at international level, and they have not been tried in combination for any meaningful number of games.

With a fit first XI, England may have a chance of winning the World Cup; with anything less they are doomed to repeat the past years of hurt and the golden generation will have been squandered.

Calm down, England, it's only the phoney war – real hysteria is coming

May 2010

It is England's football fans who need to keep their nerve not Fabio Capello and his players. From now until England either win (preferably) or get knocked out of the World Cup there will be little else in the media.

You may have forgotten, or at least tried to, that the coverage will be all-encompassing and that it has a marked effect on the English psyche. The mass hysteria that is on the way is not one in which people lose all semblance of will; it is more unusual than that. What is created is a compulsion to comment, and most of the multitude of comments will be notable only because of their stupidity. Armchair professionals and would-be/could-have-been international sportsmen will opine sagely on any and all facets of English football.

There will be a divided nation; all wanting England to win and approaching each minute piece of news with solemn consideration yet reacting in different ways.

On the one hand you will have the know-all-know-nothings. Pessimists at heart, they will become most expert on the topic on which they are least qualified to comment. Indolent lard-arses will criticise players' fitness levels; some with the tactical nous of a radish will berate Capello for his use of one system over another; with the miracle of hindsight, many more will tell you they knew it all along.

On the other side of the national divide will be those who approach their support as a faith. As is the way with zealots they will be less entertaining but messianic in their proclamations for 'Ingerland'. As a mantra they will urge, if not demand, that we 'get behind the lads' whatever the results or level of performance. They will laud quite ordinary players as 'world-clarse' and display wilful ignorance concerning anything that might suggest England are not the best team in the world – oh, and by the way, anyone not in agreement is a traitor.

The aftermath of England's laboured win over Mexico saw the beginning of the inexorable path to frenzy, with sucking of the teeth and rumblings about Steven Gerrard, which were countered by the first rallying calls to back the boys. During one phone-in on TalkSport Radio, the caller managed to say this fourteen times in a two-minute call.

The fact is that pre-tournament games tell you almost nothing about how a team will compete when the tournament starts. The absence of almost half of Capello's intended first XI against Mexico on Monday ensured that this was so. It will be the same when it comes to the final warm-up game against Japan on Sunday, even if a near-full team is selected.

For players it is impossible to shake out the knowledge that this is not the real deal and though they may say that 100 per cent attention is given, they will have reserved some part of their thoughts for South Africa. There is nothing wrong with this and nothing Capello can do anyway. The only thing you can hope for is that none of the players gets injured.

So for the media and public, let's stamp down the surges of passion and keep it for when it really counts because as certain as all the above is, there will be incidents that rightly provoke our indignation.

It is manifest that there will be another outrageous World Cup injustice that could have been avoided by the use of technology. This will be followed by Fifa's refusal to try the same and will be accompanied by the ridiculous and dull claim that 'it evens itself out in the end'. Actually, the World Cup, with its limited number of games, half of which are sudden death, is the last place where things like this even themselves out. The victim of the wrong might not qualify for the finals for another twelve years.

It is when this clamour is reaching its height that Capello and his squad need to excuse themselves, at least mentally, from the scene. It is very difficult to enforce a ban on accessing the news, given the number of platforms on which it is available and, unless a player is very strong-willed, widespread criticism will affect him, even if he believes this not to be the case. Praise is not without its possible pitfalls; self-belief is welcome, indeed necessary, but self-importance is too often the reaction to preternatural adulation. If the temptation to browse can be enforced or resisted, it would aid Capello's campaign no end.

Fabio Capello should tell his players earlier, but keep opponents guessing

June 2010

The practice of Fabio Capello and other football managers of not naming their team until a couple of hours before kick-off has been a hot topic for conversation at the World Cup.

One of Capello's England players, Wayne Rooney, has dismissed the clamour for the line-up to be named earlier, saying, 'At club level we find out two hours before kick-off so it's no different.'

Advocates of the late announcement claim that it keeps players on their toes, as they are not certain of selection, and prevents the opposition being given advance notice of the final XI, thereby preventing detailed work being done to combat that selection.

The first point should not be a consideration when it comes to international sport. Any player who needs to be kept on his toes should not be playing at that level. Moreover, if, as the policy's proponents claim, players prepare as though they are to play, why do they need keeping on their toes?

The second claim has some merit. However, it is unlikely that whatever combination is eventually announced has not been the subject of thought and preparation by an opposing manager and his staff, and the actual advantage gained is probably less than imagined. Additionally, the implication in this pretence is that a team does not have complete confidence in themselves. An advance announcement assumes that a team is confident that whatever preparation is done by an opponent, they are good enough to prevail. 'Let them worry about us' is the common descriptor.

Rooney's comments were made in reference to his club's policy. In a club season there are going to be about fifty such moments and with this is the consolation of a player knowing they will probably have another chance if they are not selected. A World Cup, where England might play only three games, is entirely different. More reliable would be a player's behaviour and reaction to whether he was picked for a cup final. Further, Rooney is an automatic choice for his club and therefore does not face the agony of awaiting a marginal decision each week. I suspect he might have a different view if each selection was in the balance for him.

Most players waiting for such a decision might also force themselves to confront the challenges provided by their opponents in the next game, but at least some of their mental energy is focused internally and laterally at their contenders for selection within the squad. It is human nature to try to lessen expectation as a way of lessening the hurt that comes with not being picked; bear in mind that a player carries not just his own hopes but those of his family and friends.

A period of time is needed to deal with rejection before a player then re-commits to the wider cause and publicly supports somebody who has been given the place the rejected player believes should be his. Some players can do this quickly; most cannot, and certainly not in a couple of hours.

All these negatives can be avoided by announcing the team early to the squad and maintaining the surprise element by handing the team sheet in at the last possible moment.

On a different note, Capello's line on criticisms from Franz Beckenbauer that England look nervous and have regressed to 'kick and rush' football seems to be to feign indifference. This is probably correct publicly. In private, it could be a useful coaching aid – it should remind players not to resort to lumping long balls into the box when things get tough.

Beckenbauer's comments about there being too many foreign players in the Premier League are right, but there is no logic in claiming this is connected with an alleged return to primitive football; the thing most foreign players do not do is kick and rush.

As for Michael Ballack's claim that German players are always totally prepared; he is right, but that this is not so with England is not the fault of any England player or manager. The blame lies with a combination of the Football Association and the Premier League and – though they will not like it – the fans of those clubs. Their unwillingness to allow a significant reduction in fixtures in a World Cup year and their inability to agree a winter break handicaps every England player and manager.

Patriotism is a temporary state for the English football fan; it is not for the German and that is the difference. It is not about what you say and how loud you say it; it is about what you do and when you do it.

Intelligence and attitude help England confound the critics

June 2010

It should not need a crisis to bring forth a performance commensurate with the rewards and talents possessed by the England football team, but whatever way they found the inspiration to beat Slovenia it was welcomed by millions of supporters, many of whom had feared the worst.

That England were not going to be as abjectly awful as in their first two group games was immediately apparent from the body language displayed when they arrived on the pitch in Port Elizabeth.

This performance exposed the supposed wisdom which has rained from all quarters on Fabio Capello for what it is – nonsense.

For a start, any system utilised by a team necessarily assumes it will be executed competently. When players do not pass, control or compete for the ball, it matters not what system is in place. The material differences between Wednesday's and the previous games show that the definitive factor in how well England play is not what formation they adopt at the start of the game. The much derided 4–4–2 system continued by manager Fabio Capello was used, as it should be, as an outline, not as a commandment set in stone.

Throughout the game Wayne Rooney, Jermain Defoe and Steven Gerrard reacted to what was happening around them and altered their positioning from left to centre, occasionally right and back again. As a result they presented easier targets for their midfield and pulled the Slovenian centre-backs all over the place. This fluidity was augmented by something that was conspicuously absent against the United States and Algeria. Selfless runs were made by all the midfield players who, while knowing that a majority would not result in them receiving the ball, also knew they attracted defenders.

The above two facts meant that easier passes were available, more space was created and crucially, in James Milner, they at last had a wide player who could deliver the ball properly. The cliché that all defenders fear pace means little on its own. It might frighten full-backs, but it does not cause a stir with central defenders if the ball sails harmlessly off target.

Further evidence of spirit within the England camp came from covering tackles by John Terry, Matthew Upson and Ashley Cole, and late in the game when defenders threw their bodies in the way to block shots. In the previous two games you would have been pushed to see anyone run an extra inch for the cause.

A sober look at what England have done thus far has to record that they failed to top a relatively easy group and scored just twice. Nothing Capello's men have shown will cause angst for their forthcoming opponents.

It is difficult to predict confidently that England will build on a much improved performance, but the fact that they have recorded a win should not be underestimated. They came into the Slovenia game with a welter of criticism – most of it justified – ringing in their ears and had heaped greater pressure on themselves than necessary. Victory means they will not have to contend with the psychological handicap of humiliation lurking at the back of their minds. If they do not progress further it will be hugely disappointing but not ignominious.

Forget about rigid systems; intelligence built on attitude is far more important.

Only those with excessive expectation will utterly condemn England if they go no further. The truth is that, while talented, most of England's players are not truly world class and it was foolish to contend they were in the first place. However, given that many England fans and much of its media seem not to concur, there may still be a lot of recrimination to come.

World Cup 2010: English football has only itself to blame for its failings

July 2010

Much of the anger accompanying the four-yearly whinge about the state of English international football is caused by the knowledge that whatever is said, nothing will be done to address the real problems. These are legion and are not limited to those arising directly out of the World Cup failure.

It is convenient that there is a foreigner, Fabio Capello, to blame. Doesn't know the English psyche; can't understand modern tactics; where is his international pedigree? He is culpable, apparently, because he assumed grown men would be able to prepare for the most important tournament of their lives without complaining of boredom. He foolishly supposed that fêted players would be able to perform basic skills and appreciate simple tactical issues.

It will be interesting to see what the players have to say. Will they be honest and accept most of the blame or will they blame Capello? Brutal self-assessment is one hallmark of the true competitor; are they sufficiently professional to endure such a searching examination?

Myriad solutions have been proffered, but while an English manager, 4–5–1 and a winter break might help, they will not solve the problems. The long-delayed national academy is needed, but football still ignores the value of insisting that its young players receive and achieve a proper education. Other countries, including Australia and France, have specialist schools and academies for many sports, ensuring their students receive good coaching and leave with genuine qualifications.

If football is serious about addressing the whole of a young player's development it should embrace the opportunity afforded in the new Academies Bill and create its own specialist schools. Not only would this create better professionals, it would greatly assist the 99 per cent of kids who do not make it and who are thrown on to the scrap heap.

Many commentators have called for more football people to be in power at the Football Association, though they do not define what constitutes such a person. But how many professional or former players genuinely want to spend their time in committee meetings? How many have the nous to succeed as administrators?

There is also the attitude of present and recently retired players to coaching. How often is it heard, 'You can't teach me anything in a classroom.' Yes, you can; you can teach how to teach, which is all that coaching is. Possessing technical knowledge is useless if you cannot transmit it effectively, and the pitch is one place where you cannot learn to do this.

To this can be added football's dismissal of almost anything proposed by anyone not considered an insider. Ideas and practices from other sports are dismissed without proper thought, and comments, even when apposite, are dispatched with idiotic phrases such as, 'What do you know about football?' and 'Show us your medals.'

Retrospective citing; zero tolerance of abuse to officials; the 10-yard advancement of free kicks – all have been ignored. Given this wilful blindness, it is unsurprising that other sports say of football's difficulties: it is your own fault.

Consider the treatment, even the language, used against the few individuals brave enough to try to bring an outside perspective to the FA. Lord Triesman and Ian Watmore, both successful people in their own right, were arrogantly dismissed as 'suits'. They were not insiders, but they did know about debt, unsustainable business practices, corporate governance – the inconvenient truths. If supposed footballing people know so much, why is the sport in this mess?

One of the demanded remedies is that the government funds more all-weather football pitches. The notion that taxpayers' cash should be provided to a sport awash with money is particularly abhorrent given the economic climate.

Football chooses to squander its wealth by over-rewarding its professionals, some of whom have just proved that they cannot deliver under pressure or when faced with something they do not like. Twickenham was built without public money and cricket takes its internationals around the country. The sight of gluttonous football with its hand out lies ill with every other English sport – save tennis – where funds are desperately needed. It seems that football is nobody else's business until it wants help, when it suddenly becomes a national treasure.

English football is hopelessly conflicted and the fundamental question it has to ask itself is which of the following alternatives does it want?

Football can have a Premier League that is undeniably exciting, has huge revenue and is a strong global brand; a league that does contribute to the financial wellbeing of the rest of the game. It is also built on debt, overpays just one section of its employees, has allowed several of its top clubs to be controlled by foreign business interests and appears powerless to prevent similar control of its remaining clubs. Most importantly, it needs continued immediate success and accepts business practices that are similarly short-term. With this goes an unsuccessful national team and an ineffective FA.

Alternatively, a more powerful FA could fight the battle for greater contributions from the professional game. It could assert its authority on disciplinary matters. There would be a face-off about internationals and the criteria under which players were picked but as the FA would control the national team, the clubs and players would have to get in line eventually, no matter how bitter their resistance. It could then take the steps that are needed to improve international performance and change the long-term emphasis from power and athleticism to skill and tactical intelligence. With this would go a more modest, though not ruinously so, Premier League with less global appeal and reduced wages, probably fewer top foreign stars and arguably a less attractive brand.

English football has to choose between the above two structures, because in their present incarnations it cannot have both. And by the way, other sports are now saying, 'Show us your international medals.'

12

English football is hamstrung by hidebound thinking

July 2010

Chris Waddle, in his admirably frank rant following England's exit from the World Cup, asked why the FA did not learn lessons from other countries.

The German model has been widely praised in the English media, and with good reason, given the considerable improvements in that country's international and club football. The focus which underpins all that the Germans have achieved is simple: it is all about preparation.

In addition to their investment at youth level, the number of Uefa-qualified coaches (34,790 against 2,769 in England) speaks for itself. The national side augmented their preparation by using a special research unit at the German University of Sport in Cologne, helpfully described by one English tabloid as a spy unit. Every player in domestic leagues and international matches, and representing all of Germany's 31 World Cup rivals, was scrutinised in minute detail to show their strengths and weaknesses.

While the FA had two people providing video analysis, it is the season-long scrutiny that would have yielded the more valuable information. Video evidence can often be unclear without statistical evidence to differentiate between a trait and an act dictated by the moment. In fact, footage of players not directly contesting the ball is even more valuable, because you can learn what runs they favour and how these work in combination with their team-mates. English rugby internationals have cameras that follow them individually for the whole game, which ensures they cannot fabricate accounts of what they were doing at a given moment.

Waddle's criticism should have been extended to the Premier League because, for all its brand success, it could learn similar lessons. In fact, why does English football as a whole not adopt successful preparation techniques used in other sports?

Perhaps Manchester United should look to the Glazer family, not for money but for information on how the Tampa Bay Buccaneers went from a position of near bankruptcy in 1995 to become Super Bowl champions. In 2002, their championship season, the Buccaneers had seventeen specialist coaches, not including the people who provided statistical and analytical support. It was the season their defensive linemen voluntarily reported for hours of video analysis at 6 a.m., before the day's practice session began.

This depth of knowledge and preparation is standard in the NFL, the most professional league of any sport in the world. Given the vast amounts of money available, these practices should be, but are not, the norm at every Premier League club, let alone the national team. In fact, if you go through the library – a novel institution to many in football – of any college football team in America, you will find voluminous footage, statistics and intelligence about the game which dwarfs anything held by England's top clubs.

In my experience, when these topics are raised with football people, they are often met by the lazy and inaccurate rebuttal that 'you can't tell anything by statistics'. In isolation this may be partially true, but applied correctly, such information is invaluable. I wonder how many of the England players had comprehensive dossiers and footage of all their potential opponents before the tournament began?

A similar objection is raised against unit coaches, namely that

football is too fluid to compartmentalise players into crude cate-
gories. However, a centre-back specialist might well have been
able to prevent John Terry and Matthew Upson being woefully
out of synch for the majority of the Germany game. Attacking and
defensive midfield specialists might have found a way to solve the
Lampard/Gerrard conundrum, and so on. How does football
know it would fail without trying it, and what harm would there
be in doing so?

Some say that football does not want over-coached players
bombarded with information, but this does not happen if things
are done correctly. And would it be any worse than what we have
at the moment – under-coached and ignorant players?

Another issue was raised by Manchester United manager Sir
Alex Ferguson's recent claim that inordinate pressure was partly
to blame for Wayne Rooney's miserable displays during the World
Cup. Pressure, stress, fear of failure, all come from inside the
player's head.

The stereotypical reaction of some in football to sports psy-
chology is scorn. There is an instinctive mistrust of its
practitioners and its validity. Part of this is because of unease at
the whole issue of mental health which, in turn, has produced the
English attitude that all you need to do is keep a stiff upper lip and
'pull yourself together'. It is also claimed that this is a job that is
done by managers, with Ferguson named as a leading example.

Behind such dismissive assertions lie arrogance and ignorance
about one crucial part of an athlete's preparation which is seen as
essential in many other sports. This neolithic attitude prevents the
Rooneys of this world being given advice which might help
combat their difficulties. You could say that truly world-class players do not need such guidance, but where does that get you if
players such as Rooney genuinely need this speciality? Surely it is
better to aid, rather than vilify, a player when he fails?

Laughably, the cost of specialists is sometimes raised, but taking
the average Premier League weekly wage of £21,000 and a squad

of 28, just a couple of weeks' spending would finance everything set out above. Unfortunately, behind this arrogant refusal to learn from outsiders is the denial of education in its widest sense: the ability and desire to learn and be open-minded. Football lauds instinctive talent above acquired abilities, when it could easily have both.

When the final response is 'how much money do you earn?' you know they are not really listening.

13

South Africa World Cup besmirched 'beautiful' game

July 2010

Both Valdir Pereira, the former Brazil midfielder also known as Didi, and Stuart Hall claim authorship of the now hackneyed description of football as 'the beautiful game'.

Whoever was truly the originator did football a great service because this phrase is now used to mask all manner of ills.

Fifa and much of the footballing media would have you believe that the recently finished 2010 World Cup deserves that moniker, but even a cursory examination of the facts shows that this is spin.

Those casting an impartial eye over proceedings can justifiably claim that this was the World Cup where football almost ate itself and showed that, at its highest professional level, it has become a grotesque distortion of the great game enjoyed by millions; the same people who appear powerless to arrest its excesses.

Perhaps it is because the World Cup was hosted by South Africa, the first on African soil, that there is a conspiracy to accentuate the positive in the reporting and analysis of the event. The fact that the competition went without any major logistical disruptions is a great credit to the South Africans, but it was patronising in the first place to assume that they would not be able to organise an event like this successfully.

Taking the wider context of the tournament first, the banal characterisations of the continent ignored a chance to examine

Africa as it really is – both good and bad – with most of the media settling for images of smiling faces and colourful dress. The real problems faced by Africa could have been drawn to the attention of billions and perhaps thereby would have had a better chance of being solved.

Africa is not a united continent, with neighbouring countries willingly cheering for their rivals. An explanation of why certain countries harbour historical enmity might have explained their inability to cohabit peacefully in the non-footballing world. The hordes of people living under corrupt regimes did and do not want their country to be seen through rose-tinted spectacles, and without their own means of objection would have welcomed a little uncomfortable scrutiny of unacceptable government. A measure of the unchallenging nature of the reporting was the fact that Robert Mugabe's conspicuous presence drew no criticism in the mainstream media.

Of the competition itself many, as did I, wanted the football to be good and the competition to be a success but in so many ways it was not.

Most of the television coverage, in particular the punditry, was execrable. The TV coverage was even infected by part of Fifa's inexorable campaign to promote the governing body as a brand in its own right and this was no more evident than with the branding of TV replays and interviews. Am I alone in objecting to the promotion of Fifa as opposed to football, because although Sepp Blatter might like us to believe they are indistinguishable, they are not?

There was, unfortunately, little either the TV or radio broadcasters could do about the infuriating drone of that 'historic' cultural African icon, the vuvuzela. It is a mystery why the fact that it is historic only as far back as 2001 and is, in fact, a plastic trumpet was not pointed out more plainly. It served only to give the general viewer a proper appreciation of what it is like to suffer from tinnitus.

As for the football, the statistic that the average number of goals per game was the lowest in any tournament bar Italia 90 is telling. Though this was partly a result of better organised defences, it was also a product of a lack of ambition by many teams – and not only in the group stages.

Given that this was the world stage, it was deeply unsatisfactory that three of the competition's leading protagonists, France, Italy and England, added nothing to the spectators' and viewers' enjoyment. Their exit may have allowed so-called lesser nations to progress, but if you analyse the tournament as you would any other product, that defect would be of significant concern.

The final could have been all that Fifa wished in terms of portraying football at its best. That it was a game filled with petulance, casual violence and disrespect was the joint responsibility of the players, managers and Fifa itself. The aftermath to Spain's single-goal win over Holland is illustrative of football's most intractable problems and is a demonstration as to why they remain so.

For all their superb dexterity, the winners won four of their matches 1–0 and, as the game's ultimate aim is to score goals, no amount of passing, however technical, is preferable to putting the ball in the net.

It is typical of football players to blame Howard Webb, the unfortunate English referee, for their own failings. Arjen Robben chose to do so despite missing two clear one-on-one chances. This is cowardly and dishonest, but what of Fifa's response? Sepp Blatter, usually keen to criticise anything that takes his fancy, particularly English, could only pathetically respond to the virulent and unjustified criticisms of Webb by saying that he had a 'very hard task'. Is that all he could say?

Blatter speciously added, 'Football is a school of life because it is based on discipline and respect. It's a combat game but in the spirit of fair play. You have to learn to win and you have to learn to lose, and should not forget the basis which is discipline and respect.'

Rubbish. By refusing to condemn and sanction the relevant players and team officials for their on and off-field excesses which resembled spoilt brattish three-year-olds, Blatter condones and encourages the same – beautiful, just beautiful.

14

Ferrari apologists have left Formula One's credibility in a sorry state

July 2010

If proof were needed that Formula One is not a sport – well, not in any legitimate sense – it comes in the fatuous row over the latest piece of chicanery, this time concerning the words, 'Fernando is faster than you. Can you confirm you understood that message? Good lad. Just stick with it now. Sorry.'

Were the above words a team order, illegal under F1 rules, or mere observations which left Felipe Massa free to decide whether he should allow team-mate Fernando Alonso to pass and thereby win last weekend's German Grand Prix?

Is there any serious dispute that can be had over this? The use of the word 'sorry' necessarily presupposes that the order to allow the pass will be effective and cannot be explained any other way to anyone.

The reasons cited to support the view that it does not matter are firstly, that it is a silly rule, and secondly, that it is broken on many occasions. Such observations were not ones which anyone thought sufficient to exculpate Dean Richards during 'Bloodgate', even though both could have been claimed with equal force. It is only when applied to a different set of known sporting facts that the flaws in such reasoning are fully exposed.

The extra insult comes because of the gibberish now being spouted by Ferrari and others to suggest that black is in fact white.

To many avid F1 fans the controversy over this incident and sub-sequent $100,000 (£64,500) instant fine for the Ferrari team is a frivolous bagatelle, something whipped up by a rabid media.

The fuss is actually about illegality. Whether those in the know, looking from what they see as a position of knowledge, believe the rule to be nonsense is not the point; it was introduced after Ferrari's manipulation of the Austrian Grand Prix in 2002 had brought opprobrium on F1, and it remains valid until repealed.

Participants cannot select which rules they wish to adhere to or else anarchy ensues. What is to stop teams taking Ferrari's lead and breaking the ban on in-season testing, something that no lesser figure than Michael Schumacher has called similarly ridiculous?

Regarding the decision and incident itself: the utter drivel being proffered by way of explanation is revealed by looking at the event logically. If Alonso was faster, and there was very little evidence that this was significant, he could have overtaken Massa anyway. Further, since the furore, there have been contradictory accounts of why Massa made the decision, including the risible claim that the passing manoeuvre happened because 'Massa made a small mistake when shifting up three gears at once'. If this was a freely made decision there would only have been one reason given, not several.

Ferrari president Luca di Montezemolo has tried to deflect flak by attacking his detractors, saying, 'Enough of the hypocrisy. This has always happened. If one races for Ferrari, then the interests of the team come before those of the individual.' Perhaps he has forgotten the fit of moral outrage shown by his leading driver only a few weeks ago when Alonso attacked the Valencia stewards for what he called manipulating the result.

Without a shred of consideration for how Massa might feel, Alonso is now lauding his win, saying it was a 'great feeling' and that 'all wins are special' – well, only if you are not a real sportsman. If you know you haven't earned it you shut up and move on.

Ferrari have effectively announced that only one driver is challenging for the drivers' title. That being so, they should face demands for the return of any bet made by a punter who put money on Massa winning the title or indeed any race. Where this leaves Massa, who last year could have been left blinded by his accident in the Hungarian Grand Prix, God only knows. If all this is *de rigueur* for F1, what does it say about the drivers who are prepared to be treated in this way?

Ferrari have cited the need to sell cars and the number of jobs involved as justification for their actions. Can anyone recall similar declarations being made by any other sport? Even if there is a connection between the two matters it should not rationalise team orders. The same could be said of motorbike sales and success in MotoGP, yet there are no team orders in that sport. The astonishing final-corner pass by Valentino Rossi of his then teammate, Jorge Lorenzo, at Catalunya in 2009 shows the spirit F1 should have but does not. Indeed in terms of excitement, overtaking and contest, MotoGP outstrips F1 every time.

Those who claim that what Ferrari did was no more than is done with the leading riders in the Tour de France are wide of the mark. The essential difference is that it is made plain that the aim of the teams is to manufacture the best position for their leading hill climbers and sprinters, and everybody knows this beforehand; they are not misled.

This incident comes after a litany of illegalities, fake crashing and threatened litigation. If F1 and all those involved, both teams and supporters, are happy for these practices to continue, they should at least stop claiming F1 is a sport like any other.

Competition without manipulation is an essential part of sport. Without it, however glamorous the trappings, it is nothing more than entertainment and, however dazzling are the accoutrements, it cannot stand alongside true sports.

It has been said in the past that F1 doesn't care about bad publicity because it is all good for exposure but this may not be the case forever. Additionally, the thing about tipping points is that they are unpredictable; if F1 tips over the point of credibility, it would have to work very hard to regain it. Then again, with so many would-be Jeremy Clarksons around, the truth may be that any manipulated nonsense will do.

15

'Bloodgate' doctor Wendy Chapman must be allowed to return to work

August 2010

Having revisited most of the media's coverage of last year's Bloodgate affair, it is not an exaggeration to say that some of the comment bordered on the hysterical. It was an opportunity to deliver a good kicking to rugby and, seen in hindsight, the speed with which opprobrium poured forth is frankly distasteful.

For some of the participants the matter is history, but not for one of the central, yet least willing, characters. The two-week hearing by the General Medical Council into the actions of Dr Wendy Chapman began on Monday; she has been suspended since news of the affair broke over a year ago, most of it without pay, and is recovering from breast cancer surgery.

The following is accepted by all parties as the true version of events during the Heineken Cup quarter-final between Harlequins and Leinster in 2009:

- The use of a fake blood capsule was initiated by Dean Richards, the former director of rugby, and was given to Tom Williams by the then physiotherapist, Steph Brennan.
- As a result of Williams faking a blood injury, Nick Evans, a player already substituted, was allowed back onto the field.
- On leaving the pitch, Williams went to see Dr Chapman, who had no knowledge of this.

- After repeated insistent requests from Williams, made more urgent by the fact that a European Rugby Cup (ERC) official and the Leinster doctor were trying to gain access to the private medical facility (which they had no right to do under the participation agreement, incidentally), Dr Chapman cut Williams's lip.
- The wound was healed using gauze and pressure on his mouth and no stitches were required. The cutting was the suggestion of Williams alone and Richards was neither present nor aware of it until later.

In response to allegations that her conduct was likely to bring the profession into disrepute and was dishonest, counsel for Dr Chapman admitted certain charges, accepting that she administered the cut because the player wanted to demonstrate a 'real injury'. She also admitted that she failed to tell an ERC disciplinary hearing three months after the incident that she had caused the lip injury.

Let me say straight out: Dr Chapman should not have bowed to Williams's exhortations and was wrong to do so, but to strike her off would be a gross overreaction; it is not necessary to ensure public safety, which should be the GMC's sole concern.

I was and continue to be surprised at the absolute nature of some of the public condemnation of Dr Chapman. Straight dismissal should be the only acceptable punishment according to some, often supporting their view with partial and inaccurate referral to the Hippocratic oath.

Many of the most vehement advocates of sacking have condemned Dr Chapman while being ignorant of all the facts. Let us look at Dr Chapman and ERC. She was wrongly charged by ERC, which subsequently admitted it had no jurisdiction over her. ERC could, but did not, ask her to be a witness but once she was a defendant she had no duty to make any statement and did not do so.

Moreover, when Chapman was advised that the correct tribunal before which to give evidence was the GMC alone, she was under an obligation from a professional indemnity insurance point of view to follow that advice or face the cost of all proceedings alone.

Further, regarding patient confidentiality, the oath is categorical. 'About whatever I may see or hear in treatment, or even without treatment, in the life of human beings, I will remain silent, holding such things to be unutterable.'

Williams's account of the incident to the GMC was strangely vague: 'I asked Wendy to make the cut. I do remember that she was not happy about it. The atmosphere was extremely tense. I cannot remember exactly – knowing Dr Chapman I would have had to be quite insistent.'

Dr Chapman did inflict a very minor wound, but it was with the fullest possible consent and although this does not excuse the act it does mitigate its seriousness.

The accounts given by many parties, including the agents of Tom Williams and the ERC, created an impression that Dr Chapman knew of the scam and cover-up and gave misleading statements; she did neither.

Even so, Dr Chapman was at the centre of intense publicity for nearly six weeks. If you have not been the centre of attention for the media you will not even have an inkling of what an ordeal it is. If you had experienced sustained exposure similar to that endured by Dr Chapman, even accounting for her culpability, you would deem that to be sufficient punishment – let alone if you considered the loss of income.

Has Dr Chapman been admonished? Yes and publicly so. It is almost certain she will not act as an unpaid volunteer rugby doctor again and thus there is no fear of a recurrence of the act.

The real question is surely this: if you find yourself in Maidstone A&E and Dr Chapman is attending, does her mistaken, yet isolated and instantaneous, act, under inordinate and personal pressure created by others, outweigh her many previous years of competent and professional service, witnessed by the thousands of patients she has treated? Do you really and legitimately feel unsafe? No? Well then, enough is enough – let the severely chastened doctor continue to help people.

16

Paralympians should be admired for their sporting ability, not physical disability

September 2010

A long while ago I attended a talk given by Doug Scott CBE, the Nottinghamshire mountaineer, who is a Seven Summitter, having climbed the highest peaks of the seven continents. In a fascinating discussion, Scott was asked about the incident in 1977 on Baintha Brakk, commonly known as The Ogre, in Pakistan, when he dragged himself down the mountain after breaking both his legs. 'Was I brave?' Scott ruminated out loud. 'No, what else do you do if you want to get down?'

This would not find common assent, but when you look at his situation without the emotion of horror at his plight and gratefulness that it was not you, Scott is undoubtedly correct. This pitfall is one that awaits anyone who attempts coverage of an event where a person combats seemingly insurmountable physical challenges, and this includes how you cover disability sport.

While Channel 4 deserves a loud and long cheer for its brave decision to put its coverage of the London 2012 Paralympics at the heart of its broadcasting, its hour-and-a-half documentary on six of Britain's top medal aspirants, *Inside Incredible Athletes*, had obvious flaws, which was a great pity, as much of the content was good.

Unfortunately it fell into the trap of describing almost everything about the featured athletes' performances, their ability, dedication and fortitude as extraordinary. In the background of each athlete's story is the way in which they came to be disabled and while it is probably necessary to cover this, the assumption of bravery because the athlete accommodates their handicap is misguided because what choice do they have? Similarly, you cannot judge whether it takes more wherewithal to cope with a disability from birth or one inflicted in an unfortunate accident.

The problem is that to the extent that each of the featured competitors was said to be extraordinary, then that must also be so for every one of their disabled opponents. Able-bodied people might think anyone competing with a physical or mental handicap deserves the accolade, but what that does is establish a different set of judgement criteria, something that disabled athletes expressly dislike because it is tacitly patronising.

The temptation to dramatise the programme because of its content, both that of the athletes and the location of the Games, led the maker into flights of artistic fantasy that simply got in the way of the more interesting features of each participant's tale. Sweeping aerial shots of London and giddying camera angles took up nearly a quarter of the programme, time which could have been spent more profitably in explaining other facets of the athlete's sport, like, what are the rules of wheelchair rugby and when are they allowed to deliberately ram their opponents' wheelchairs? Where was the explanation of the bewildering number of classes in disabled swimming?

The physiological explanations about what physical constraints faced each athlete were absorbing, as far as they went, but could have been profitably developed. In addition, they would have been better given by the various medical specialists interviewed as opposed to an overdramatic narrator.

Although certain aspects of training were covered superficially, a detailed breakdown of each athlete's preparation in terms of skill, conditioning and mental approach would have been far more interesting than the staged shots and panoramas so beloved of the programme makers.

Had this programme covered able-bodied aspirants of 2012 medals we would have been given some context to their current standings within their sport, details of their competitors and the basic statistics of progression and setback as they worked through their plan for glory. These facts and projections were absent and instead we were given a programme that was only partly about sport. What disabled athletes need and crave, and what the public have to get used to, is coverage of disability sport which is no different from any other sport. The narrator said that if you wanted to see courage and commitment this was the place to look; well, these qualities are also visible in the efforts of any other highly competitive athlete, and participation does not equal excellence.

Finally, there was one point memorably made by the athletes, and this was their willingness to continue to give all to compete in their country's colours. In the past couple of weeks athletes like Paul Scholes have been lauded for their performances; it is a pity they prefer self-fulfilment to giving similarly for their country.

17

The Ryder Cup is a golf tournament, not a superpower challenge

September 2010

After Europe thumped the US in the 2006 Ryder Cup, captain Ian Woosnam publicly slated the BBC for not awarding his men the Sports Personality Team of the Year award, which went to St Helens rugby league club. Perhaps he should have noted that, first, it was a vote by the fans which determined that award, and second, Europe that year had a far better team, were expected to win and did so; you should not get awards for doing the expected.

Behind Woosnam's displeasure lay the assumption that the Ryder Cup was such a special event that the winners, provided it is Europe, automatically deserve the accolade. That supposition appears to have evolved along with the purposeful portrayal of the tournament as something akin to war.

The structure of the Ryder Cup creates a number of interesting variables. Chief among these is that the US compete as a country outside their own borders, which is not the case in their three major sports. It is interesting to see how essentially solo performers react when asked to be part of a team. Moreover, the way in which the pairings and singles matches ebb and flow during the four days is fascinating, but let's get one thing straight: this is a golf competition, not some form of superpower challenge with attendant political ramifications.

This 2010 contest has the potential to be memorable, but for the wrong reasons. The choice of Tiger Woods in the US team has given some writers what they wanted: another chance to try to needle Woods into giving an undiplomatic reaction to a plethora of regurgitated and irrelevant questions about his personal life, many of which have the most tenuous connections to golf.

In a press conference on Tuesday, one reporter showed not a shred of respect for Woods when he sneeringly put the following question: 'You don't win majors any more, you don't win regular tournaments, you're about to be deposed as world No. 1 . . . is the Ryder Cup now your most important thing now you're almost an ordinary golfer?'

When Woods was faced with this impertinence he should have left the conference, as no sportsman should have to put up with insulting behaviour. He stayed and tried to laugh it off because he knew that had he departed he would have been pilloried.

Had something similar been put to Sir Alex Ferguson about Manchester United, the questioner would have got the answer he deserved. Had anyone mockingly asked me something similar in my playing days he would have got a righteous slap.

Nobody is asking for sycophantic toadying, but Woods is entitled to expect the basic courtesy that should be given to any interviewee. It is common decency.

Another reporter tried to generate sensation by asking what reaction Woods had seen from the US team's wives, given that they play such a large part in the Ryder Cup. A large part: are they now involved in the planning and playing? And there were we just thinking they dressed smartly and cheered on their men.

There is sufficient rivalry, both on a team and a personal level, without the need to manufacture a personal spat between Woods and Rory McIlroy. The young Ulsterman's original comment, that he would not mind playing against Woods, came after Woods had shot 18 over par at Bridgestone.

When facing the media this week McIlroy was again peppered with questions about Woods and stressed the context of his comments. When pressed, McIlroy said nothing that could justify the claim made by the media that he had continued to stoke the supposed rivalry. What this should make plain to McIlroy is that no matter how neutral he thinks he is being, anything that he says can and will be twisted to suit the ends of those pursuing their own agenda.

Meanwhile, rumbling in the background is the story that most people knew, but which has only just appeared in print, concerning Colin Montgomerie's injunction to stop an individual from making revelations in the press about his private life.

Previously unreported, the existence of the court order emerged following revelations by a paper that had not been served with the order – presenting the opportunity to destabilise Montgomerie and his team by sly innuendo and whispering.

The details of what the individual might reveal has been the source of speculation for weeks on the internet, via email and text; hardly anybody I know does not have some version to relate. If the details are ever revealed, and are in line with what is rumoured, all I can say is that this is yet another case of prurience over something that has nothing to do with sport and has no bearing on Montgomerie's suitability to be Ryder Cup captain. Will this stop another frenzy of lurid and irrelevant questions or will we be forced to endure the journalistic equivalent of a bout of third-form sniggering?

Given the minutely technical nature of golf and the added format of team play, there are ample sporting queries to make of the best players in the world, yet we appear doomed to listen to banal and petty questions about personal matters.

I do not understand why people whose lives are entwined with golf and who love the game want to wallow in this sort of nonsense. Is the psychological drama and tension not sufficient? Surely the delicate balance of proven greatness as against poor form is sufficiently absorbing as you watch Woods and Harrington try to resurrect their former brilliance.

If the media wants to serve its consumers, it should look at the way the public reacted to the golfers. It was not surprising or overly polite for them to cheer Woods and others, because they are there just for the golf.

They also understand something the media does not: that the players are human and make human mistakes, but are still entitled to human respect.

18

Corrupt players must be banned or cricket will reach its tipping point

September 2010

Only a couple of months past I discussed the questions of malfea-sance in sport and the danger of a particular sport reaching a stage beyond which its credibility is so thin that it loses support and, as a result, might implode. While it took neither a genius nor Nostradamus to identify the many dangers in sport and then to predict that this would happen to one sport in the future, it is nonetheless startling that there should be an example to hand within so short a time.

It has to be fervently hoped that the unsavoury allegations and counter-allegations arising out of the tour by the Pakistan cricket team do not constitute such a juncture. However, for cricket this is an issue far more serious than was 'Bloodgate' for rugby or any ills that exist within football presently.

The behaviour of the officials who have commented on behalf of the Pakistan players and team has been thoroughly counter-productive. It is a familiar tactic to try to divert attention from your own problems by attacking an accuser or anyone involved in the investigation of the misdemeanour but the first rule is usu-ally to have some evidence, however threadbare, on which to hang any counter-accusations. Three men holding positions of responsibility have recently availed themselves of this tactic but because of the lack of substantiating evidence or because of plain exaggeration they have made matters worse.

Pakistani High Commissioner Wajid Hasan's ludicrous and uncorroborated claim that the three cricketers, Test captain Salman Butt and fast bowlers Mohammad Asif and Mohammad Amir, were innocent because the video footage from the *News of the World* was shot after the event was sufficient to damn any further words that he uttered. Further, his evasiveness when talking to Radio 5 Live's Garry Richardson was so pronounced that even if his claims had substance, the manner of his delivery denuded them of any credence.

The chairman of the Pakistani Cricket Board, Ijaz Butt, has made the serious and unsupported allegation that the England team had received huge sums of money to lose last Friday's one-day international at the Oval. His evidence was the mere assertion that, 'There is loud and clear talk in bookies' circles that some English players have been paid enormous amounts of money to lose the match.' On the back of this notably unattributed talk Butt has demanded an International Cricket Council investigation into the England team. Much easier to make the case against Pakistan if another team is also being investigated. Following his appearance before the International Cricket Council in Dubai two days ago he called for the resignation of the ICC chairman Haroon Lorgat for his handling of the match-fixing investigation.

Even the incident at Lord's where Jonathan Trott was said to have held Abdul Riaz by the throat was undermined as a vehicle for sympathy by Shahid Afridi, dubiously claiming the high moral ground by saying 'we showed a big heart' by not pressing the matter with the police.

Every piece of dirt that is hurled by these representatives of Pakistan makes things worse and leaves those uttering the statements with no credibility at all, even when they make otherwise salient points.

It also removes another vestige of sympathy from those previously trying to help Pakistan by pleading the mitigating circumstances of naivety, poor education and a background of poverty and threats of violence.

Even the cries of entrapment are illegitimate because the essential trait of that practice is that it is an action by a person in authority, not a newspaper. Moreover, the tests of whether there was good reason to suspect criminal activity and whether the act was initiated or aided cannot properly be made against the reporters in question.

I have an instinctive dislike of set-ups that border on entrapment, whether they are technically such or not. Against the maxim that a person must have the propensity to sin in the first place you can set another axiom – that every man has his price.

It is possible to seduce someone in unique personal circumstances to do something that, but for those peculiarities and the temptation presented by a newspaper, he would not do ordinarily. However, this matter is not such.

The public reaction to these events has been curious but any positives probably do not come from the best of motives. The minds of many outside cricket and even some ardent fans have irredeemably been soured against any contest involving Pakistan.

The fact that the final one-day international at the Rose Bowl sold out came off the back of the Lord's confrontation and had the hallmark of the playground huddle ready to chant 'fight, fight, fight'.

For the authorities there are no easy answers. If found guilty, a team ban of any reasonable length could finish Pakistani cricket and who knows what allegations may be made or action taken if such a ban is made.

Nevertheless no country can be bigger than a sport and cricket has to stem the steady stream of invective and indictment because it threatens to engulf the 2011 World Cup (50-over) which is being held on the Indian subcontinent.

The $30 billion (£19 billion) illegal betting industry in India can easily reach Bangladesh and Sri Lanka, the other two host countries. Calls for the Indian government to allow betting on sports other than horse racing will not work now the criminal interests are well established. In the light of previous scandals and given that it is impossible to prove a negative, how can the ICC reassure anyone that the games are not fixed? Anything out of the ordinary will be suspect and in cricket there are scores of such variables by the nature of the game.

If this taint is not removed by rapid and firm action, which unfortunately will mean Pakistan and/or its players being banned, cricket could find the public has no faith in nearly half of its Test teams; that will be a tipping point.

19

Liverpool supporters cannot cry foul now – the damage was already done

October 2010

Between 1975 and 1990, Liverpool dominated English football in a way that it is almost impossible to comprehend today – they won the old Division One title ten times. That hegemony probably explains many Liverpool fans' assumption that, in football matters, they have a right to a better viewpoint than the rest of us.

On Merseyside the outcry has swelled to include the nonsensical allegation that the Royal Bank of Scotland has some responsibility for the club's present debacle. Since when does a lender take responsibility for footballing decisions? One talk-show caller pointed out that publicly owned RBS has Liverpool fans as shareholders. Yes, it does, but it has millions more who are not who would undoubtedly object to one club being given special treatment.

The latest act in this farce is the refusal of the owners to leave quietly and without taking the usual profit that investors rightly expect when they trade shares. Americans George Gillett and Tom Hicks are likely to fail in their legal bid to block any sale on the basis that the board of directors are failing in their legal fiduciary duty to act in the best interests of the shareholders.

This is a difficult argument to win as it depends on them being able to show that the proposed acceptance price is demonstrably undervalued. The argument that usually prevails is that a company is worth what someone is willing to pay for it, not what share-holders think they should.

Since the Americans bought Liverpool in 2007, they have made available close to £170 million to spend on new players, compared to Manchester City (£426 million), Tottenham Hotpsur (£177 million), Manchester United (£142 million), Chelsea (£112 million) and Arsenal (£71 million), according to figures from Transfer League. Whatever the Americans have done and however it was financed, the fact is that Liverpool have not been kept short of money to buy players.

The issue of net transfer figures does not alter the fact that only two clubs have paid out more, and the club's present position of 18th in the Premier League, in the relegation zone, is not the fault of Gillett and Hicks. It is the fault of the scouts, former manager Rafael Benítez and anyone else involved in player acquisitions. That amount of spending should not leave a club in the relegation zone and the members of the fraternity 'In Rafa We Trust' were misguided in their support of the now departed Spaniard.

The legitimate complaint against the Americans, that they have not financed a new stadium, is the only one that holds water. However, even this betrays a lack of business scrutiny back in 2007 when few supporters were pointing out that the wealth of Hicks and Gillett was not liquid. In normal business circles, the promises of expansion would have been scrutinised properly to see where the money would come from.

The recent announcement that a bid from New England Sports Ventures LLC has been accepted threatens to repeat this lack of scrutiny. NESV has within its portfolio the Boston Red Sox baseball club, a baseball park in Boston and a sports marketing agency. None of these interests is easily liquidated. They may be assets against which banks will lend, but that is the same position as before, it is just a different set of assets.

Much has been made of the personal wealth of the figures

behind NESV but they have not pledged any personal spending and anyway that would again depend on the willingness
and ability to turn capital into cash; the only alternative would
be to use equity as collateral for borrowing. It is said that the
Red Sox have done well under NESV's ownership and that the
key to their success is leaving the baseball decisions to the
people that know baseball. They do not interfere with the
everyday running of baseball operations. Additionally it is said
that the brand has been developed and scouting systems have
been improved.

In reality, the success is more likely due to the fact that they
own a large stake in the regional sports network that carries the
bulk of its games and annually generates hundreds of millions of
dollars in revenue. New England Sports Network, the network
cable arm of NESV, has a subscriber base in New England of
about 3.8 million. One view in an American business publication
is that the Red Sox are a media company masquerading as a professional baseball team. The money the network pumps into the
team is one reason the Sox are able to pay for top baseball talent
and finish at or near the top of the standings year after year.
Structured properly, the cable operation is also a way to shield
earnings from baseball's revenue-sharing system.

The size of the United States and regionalisation of broadcasting enables NESV to generate this money but it cannot do
that in England as Liverpool's television rights are ceded to the
Premier League. It may leverage broadcast rights to the club's
American fans but whether this is possible, and how much it
might produce, is very difficult to predict and it certainly is no
basis for budgeting for a new stadium, a raft of new players and
a bright new future. The Red Sox made a profit of about £25 million last year but is it likely that club will pass any of this to
Liverpool, and what happens if the Red Sox make losses?

What all this points to is more borrowing. Unless personal cash
is introduced for development or there is a rights issue (which will

be resisted because it dilutes the value of the original equity) it may be from frying pan into fire.

Liverpool fans cannot complain now; the right time to protest was in 2007 when David Moores was urging his fellow shareholders to sell to the Americans.

20

Elite rugby ignores Asia at its peril

October 2010

Having recently visited Asia for an HSBC Hong Kong Sevens Long Lunch, I was intrigued to learn some interesting facts from several people outside rugby's comfortable top tier. Though these facts are not in themselves notable, their wider significance for the global development of rugby cannot be underestimated.

The International Rugby Board, with its home firmly in Dublin, Europe, is capable of recognising their import, but whether the cosy club (the founding members on the IRB main board) has any genuine desire to take action to accommodate the uncomfortable truths is a different matter.

By 2016, 80 per cent of the planet's population aged twenty and under will live in Asia, including the Indian subcontinent.

The Asian Rugby Football Union, formed in 1968 with eight members, now has 26. Its premier tournament, the HSBC Asian Five Nations, will be seen in 90 territories worldwide, reaching millions of new fans. Though the competition sits atop four subsidiaries, all with promotion and relegation, and crowds are growing, it isn't even listed in the IRB's website tournament section.

If you ran a global business and 80 per cent of your future market was similarly situated, where would your concentration be in terms of development? Thus far the geographical spread of IRB funding has committed relatively little to this region and this must change if the IRB believes – as opposed to saying it believes – in globalising the game.

This would also repay the debt owed to the Asian nations whose votes were decisive in admitting rugby into the Olympics, a progression that gives opportunities for growing rugby for which other sports would kill.

What also has to change is the access to the four major world tournaments: the Six Nations, Tri-Nations, Pacific Nations Cup and the Nations Cup. It is in gaining access by guaranteed promotion to such competitions that Asian countries can attract more sponsorship and develop rugby without IRB money.

If those competitions are not opened up, all the development money in the world will not help rugby achieve its potential because a country's growth is proscribed beyond a minor level.

At present, the concept of automatic promotion and relegation to the top tournaments is resisted by the cosy club, not least because one or two fear they would be candidates for the drop. This will not change unless the IRB puts in place some form of automatic entitlement to an increased voting capacity commensurate with a union's playing population.

Automatically rotating its presidency and periodically moving its head office would also help; then again, that would be democratic and such idealistic notions are not fashionable at the IRB.

Stephen Jones, in another newspaper, rightly claimed that minor countries are tempted to concentrate on sevens, when rugby needed challenges in the 15-man game; even suggesting IRB aid should be tied to a promise to focus on the full game.

How can these countries reach the required standard if they cannot, as of right, compete in the top tournaments between World Cups? How can they attract the commercial funding without this exposure? It is disingenuous for the IRB to want smaller countries to feature the full game without giving them the path to so do.

The IRB's concentration is skewed towards the elite and there is a danger that it will become populated by people who have little experience of the rugby played by 98 per cent of players. It is equally legitimate to view absolute increases in participation as success.

The playing of rugby by millions of Asians would be a truer expression of rugby's soul than reinforcement of the elite game, irrespective of whether the Asian nations achieve global power status. That the majority of those players were never seen on TV or went unnoticed by traditional supporters would not alter the fact that the rugby fraternity would be enhanced.

As an example of what such idealistic aspirations can bring, at said lunch I met an ordinary rugby man with an extraordinary story. While working in Rwanda he had seen twelve boys throwing a rugby ball about and decided to help them learn the game. From his own resources he got them some kit and persuaded other Rwandans to form a rugby club. With the help of contacts in Hong Kong this year he was able to bring his team to participate in the opening games before the 2010 Hong Kong Sevens in front of 40,000 people.

Nearly half of his team had, through rugby, escaped the life of poverty to which their contemporaries had been condemned, had gained higher education and employment. Is that not the true spirit of rugby? Is that not a more laudable aim than an ever bigger elite game?

21

Wayne Rooney is another example of player selfishness

October 2010

Sportsmen deal with in-play frustration in different ways. Some shout at team-mates; some fade into the background; some, like Wayne Rooney, become over-aggressive and reckless.

Though Rooney has mitigated his irresponsibility, his ill-judged comment about fans booing after a dismal World Cup performance against Algeria shows that this character trait has merely found an alternative outlet. Rooney's stated desire to leave Manchester United is consistent with his reactions when everything is not going his way – saying 'f*** it' without giving sufficient thought to the consequences.

This summer, Rooney had the psychological pressures of a High Court case brought by a former agent, a dreadful World Cup, and – although the allegations about prostitutes came later – he would have known of the attentions of the *News of the World* far earlier and known that at some point he would have to face his wife and the world's media.

Whether Rooney or his agent, Paul Stretford, first raised the possibility of a move is unknown but it is not difficult to suppose that these unhappy factors, exacerbated by advice which highlighted the possibility of his club being in decline, produced this decision.

This sort of situation often gains its own momentum, stoked by comment and suggestion. When the pressure is heightened by something like Sir Alex Ferguson's comments on Tuesday the player is likely to set his face against the world even if deep down he has misgivings.

Rooney's statement on Wednesday, complaining about United's level of spending, had all the hallmarks of being drafted by a lawyer and was framed in the only way that could leave him with a scintilla of credibility, if it was believed at all.

We need to hear from David Gill about the several meetings that Rooney alleges he had and what was said. Rooney also has to clarify what he would have accepted as a sufficient assurance because, if he does not, that phrase is a meaningless catch-all excuse to leave. If he does so, and United give that assurance, presumably he will stay?

Important players have left without being replaced but Ferguson's record proves that he does not rebuild by buying five or six players already considered world class. Cantona, Schmeichel, Keane, Tévez, Ronaldo and Rooney – none of these players was even established on the European stage before they achieved with United. Furthermore, if we are talking about achievement, while Tévez and Ronaldo have won nothing since they left, Rooney has won further medals.

In spite of his claim to world-class status, Rooney has failed in the last two World Cups and most recent European Championship, and if you look at the list of teams against which he has scored for England it does not feature many of the world's best.

He has not been a consistently dominant force in United's Champions League games, and since the Bayern Munich game at the end of March he has scored just once from open play. Flat-track bully, anyone?

Former Chelsea winger Pat Nevin made interesting comments this week on Radio 5 Live. Nevin stated that the competitive desire that should be directed to matters on field had been allowed to extend to peripheral things such as money. Being top dog in the wages stakes was as much a medal of honour among players as those given for sporting achievement.

Nevin also, rightly, identified the restrictions sought by Monsieur Platini over clubs spending beyond their means, which, if enforced as planned, will force wages to fall, and Rooney and his agent were perhaps taking advantage of what may be the last period when preternatural salaries can be extorted from clubs frightened of losing ground to rivals.

In his defence many have forwarded that clichéd question: if you were offered four times the money, what would you do? Another former player, Stan Collymore, pointed to Sir Alan Sugar and Bill Gates, saying that they didn't say what amount of wealth was enough but carried on accumulating.

There are simple distinctions to both these simplistic points.

The decision for an ordinary man to accept an increase which will secure his and his family's future is not the same as that made by a man whose future is secure many times over.

Furthermore, the business of Sugar and Gates is to make money and by this are they measured; a footballer's business is to play football and money is an adjunct to this – nobody ranks a player's greatness according to wealth.

Rooney may by now be realising that his move is by no means the panacea that might have been painted for him. Unfortunately for Rooney, his future is not ineluctably rosy because there are restrictions about which he can do little and whose removal would bring added angst.

A move abroad, especially to Madrid, would be culturally challenging; Madrid and Barcelona are a world away from Torremolinos and the way of Spanish life is focused on the extended family.

Another point that Rooney cannot solve without significant fallout is that his wife Coleen has a young sister Rosie who has the brain disorder, Rett Syndrome. Not unreasonably, she has publicly stated that she does not intend to move far away from her sister.

Manchester City would delight at, as much as United would hate, the symbolic purchase of Rooney, but that doesn't mean anything to the player. For Rooney, the questions remain. Would he get into City's team? At present he would not replace Tévez and although City could play 4–4–2, or Rooney just behind Tévez, only a few months ago experts claimed that Rooney's best position was as a lone striker. It is far from certain that City would be prepared either to alienate Tévez or to amend their systems and more importantly their whole wage structure for Rooney.

The Wayne Rooney saga is merely another manifestation of agent influence and player selfishness; another step down the road to football being a game where all managers compromise rather than control.

22

Quietly and phlegmatically, Phil Vickery joins the list of giants

October 2010

The World Cup-winning prop made a huge contribution to England rugby throughout his career. What do you do when the man with whom you are about to lock in mortal combat has an oriental tattoo which, translated, means 'I'll fight you to the death' and when you know he is a qualified cattle inseminator? You feel nervous.

Ever since his earliest playing days with Redruth, Philip John Vickery, MBE, has been posing problems for opposition props. On my last visit to Redruth the club was quick to remind me of Vickery's association and there was nothing but praise for his contribution and attitude while he was growing through their Colts team. That is what you hear from people when you talk about Vickery – praise.

Was it obvious that he would one day reach the highest heights? Yes, if you ask the Redruth faithful. Vickery's sheer power and size were different from the rest, as was his quiet determination and unwillingness to compromise when the tough stuff started.

After gaining England Under 16 and Colts caps, Vickery's move to Gloucester was logical on both geographical and psychological levels. Gloucester rugby back then had an earthiness that brooked no pseuds, no posers and accepted only with reluctance backs. Vickery was naturally attuned to the prosaic approach of Gloucester.

The names of former great Gloucester props are not the distant echoes to a bygone age at Kingsholm. Cyril Harris, Alan Townsend, Tom Price, Mike Burton, Phil Blakeway and Malcolm Preedy are not West Country mythical figures, but giants who battled in the cherry and white jersey. That Vickery's name is now included in that list on merit and without a shred of sentiment is as fulsome a tribute as you can get from the notorious Shed supporters.

Within three years of playing for his first senior club, Vickery had progressed almost ineluctably to challenge for full international honours. After his debut game Vickery must have wondered what all the fuss was about playing international rugby. In February 1998 he came on as a substitute for Leicester's Darren Garforth and joined five of the forwards that were later to play in the 2003 World Cup-winning game. No doubt he smiled not just because of his achievement but also when he looked at the scoreboard which read: England 60 Wales 26.

If any false notions of comfort entered Vickery's head, he was roundly disabused of these when later that summer he went on England's post-season tour from hell. The ambitious fixture list would have tested the best of England squads and savage beatings came from Australia and New Zealand as well as losses to the New Zealand Rugby Academy, New Zealand Maoris and South Africa.

After that tour many players sank without trace, but not Vickery. The following year he overcame a neck injury, the first of a number of significant injuries that interrupted his career, to play in the 1999 World Cup.

However, two years later and after overcoming a shoulder injury he achieved that most cherished of goals: a British Lions place. Not only that, he took part in all three Tests in a dramatic series that was lost 2–1 to Australia. That series was effectively lost in the two 10-minute spells either side of half-time in the second Test, with a less than accidental injury to Richard Hill and the fact that the Lions conceded tries either side of the whistle. What did emerge from the losing tour was the conviction among the English forwards that played in the Test matches that in the scrum Australia were there for the taking.

Two years later Vickery was a member of the England pack that dominated both Australia and New Zealand in an end-of-season tour that took place just before the 2003 World Cup.

The degree to which the English forwards bested their Anzac counterparts was no better illustrated than when reduced to only six men in the Wellington Test, the English scrum repelled repeated attempts by the All Black pack to score a push-over try.

Having won a Grand Slam and beaten their southern hemisphere rivals, England went into the 2003 World Cup with well-placed confidence. The rest is history. Vickery and Trevor Woodman, England's two starting props, dominated their opposite numbers throughout the tournament and their contribution, in terms of points won from penalties and ball spoiled from pressure, should not go unattested.

However, the pair fell foul of the South African referee Andre Watson in the World Cup final. Despite Australia fielding two second-choice props it was Vickery and his mate that were adjudged to have dived earthwards on five occasions, including one occasion in the last minute of normal time. It is typical of Vickery that he publicly made no issue of what was, to everyone else at least, eccentric refereeing; he quietly took his winner's medal and enjoyed the inner satisfaction of knowing he had done his job and was part of a team that was the best in the world.

The accolades did not stop there as Vickery went on to captain England in Argentina and in the 2007 World Cup. Much has been written of the way in which England improbably reached another final against South Africa.

The stories of player revolt and power have been exaggerated but Vickery's influence and his part in resurrecting a beaten team was seminal. Without his understated but determined approach to prove us all wrong England would not have gone beyond the quarter-final.

It was disappointing that Vickery's last Lions tour in South Africa saw him shot skywards in the first Test by Tendai 'the Beast' Mtawarira. The ignominy was then compounded by referee Bryce Lawrence somehow penalising Vickery for standing up. The reason for this was Lawrence's tolerance of illegal scrummaging but, as with the many triumphs, Vickery took this phlegmatically.

The general public may not know much about Phil Vickery, but the rugby public and, more importantly, his team-mates do know just how much he contributed to English rugby.

23

Refereeing will only improve when officials get the respect they deserve

November 2010

Football is a simple game with simple laws – as per the Football Association's website – and these have changed only marginally since 1886. Barring the unnecessarily complicated offside rule it is clear what a player can and cannot do in any given situation; what a player has or has not done should be for the referee to decide.

When you look at the infinitely more complex and sometimes bewildering laws in cricket and rugby it is difficult to see why there is so much controversy in football over the laws and referees. Many claim this is because referees have not matched the advances of the past decade whereby the game has moved to a different level in terms of skill and speed.

There is some truth in asserting that referees do not always see what they should, even when ideally positioned. However, there are numerous factors which make refereeing far more difficult and prominent than it should be and they are not the fault of the men in black.

What must first be said is that allowing a margin of human fallibility, referees make far fewer mistakes than alleged and certainly fewer than players. Many alleged errors are no such thing when seen in replay and with the benefit of slow motion. The perception that a referee has made far more mistakes than is the case is aided by the partiality of many fans who howl whenever a decision goes against them. If fans were more objective their protests at real mistakes would carry more weight and validity.

Exacerbating matters is the invariable blame-shifting criticism from managers seeking to charge the referee for any reversal of fortune suffered, when the real responsibility lies with their players. How many times do you hear a manager highlight one decision but fail to admit his striker missed several chances or his defenders were asleep?

Again, if managers did not seek to shift blame continually their legitimate gripes would be treated differently. While they show no inclination to accept responsibility and continue to act without integrity they should not expect to be heard. This managerial dishonesty condones, if not positively encourages, players to act similarly. If players did not dispute nearly every decision, their reasonable protests might make a referee consider whether the points being made were pertinent. If they did not cheat and dive they might get more referees to officiate without viewing their every act with a justifiable degree of cynicism. When referees even get abused over simple throw-in decisions they inevitably become immune to player protests. Why do players not comprehend that when they continually confront referees, they simply add pressure to an already pressurised job and in doing so make mistakes more, not less, likely?

This behaviour remains widespread whatever the FA, with its Respect campaign, claims. The power to deal with it exists and you could condemn referees because they refuse to penalise instances of abuse and dishonesty.

The reality is that all referees know they would never referee at that level again if they exercised zero tolerance and that, scandalously, their professional organisation, the Professional Game Match Officials Limited (PGMOL), would not protect them from the inevitable, but erroneous, bleating from managers, players and some fans.

People need to remember that PGMOL's board is made up of the chief executives of the Football Association, Premier League and Football League with a non-executive chairman. Thus, when Premier League and Championship managers bemoan what they claim is the poor standard of refereeing, they should be haranguing their own representatives who are responsible for that standard.

If football was serious about eradicating this behaviour it would deduct points from a team once a specified number of cautions were received for abusive acts. See how swiftly things would change once managers and players could not offend without consequence.

Referees are also hampered by football's aversion to technology. From Fifa to the fans – sorry, some fans – the stupid refusal to try measures adopted by many other sports leaves an unsatisfactory but deserved situation. When Sepp Blatter and Michel Platini, the heads of Fifa and Uefa respectively, make ludicrous statements about this subject it emboldens the 'you might as well' tendency, those who splutter 'you might as well . . . get rid of tackling; have robots refereeing; be playing PlayStation . . .?'

Where will it all end? Well, it will end where you say it should, but the fact that you cannot decide does not invalidate the technology, which is inert, not some malign artificial intelligence intent on taking over the game.

The aforesaid leaders should be prevailing upon the International Association Football Board, responsible for football's laws, to remove the subjectivity around the offside law. Ruling offside any player whose foot is beyond that of the second-last defender would be simple – and would get rid of the contentious active-player clause that forces a referee to make a snap judgement on a player's intentions. This would penalise players who may be standing on the opposite touchline and nowhere near any action, but there is no perfect solution and at least there would be certainty.

Referees are sometimes inflexible and unwilling to accept their faults and reverse decisions, but when you consider that they contend with all the above is it any wonder they tend towards an insular mentality? It takes courage to admit errors but for referees to be candid they also have to believe they will be given a fair hearing.

There is every reason for referees refusing to attend post-match press conferences because they will not be heard objectively and they have no responsibility to feed us in the media with further copy. There is possibly a case for a PGMOL spokesman to speak about incidents, but only if managers and players are prepared to be questioned and held to account in a similarly forthright manner for their errors, acts and omissions; they can only expect referees to apologise if they do likewise.

The standard of top-level refereeing needs to rise, but until everyone else in football assists any increase will be necessarily limited. Those who will not own up to their role in this, will not accept responsibility and will not change have no right to whine about officials.

24

For the first time under Martin Johnson England showed some balance

November 2010

Martin Johnson's managerial record got worse on Saturday as his charges went down to New Zealand by 26–16. He will know that ultimately the stark recitation of statistics will be sufficient to justify either his deification or decapitation. For Johnson as a person and England as a team there can be naught else, unless we are going to wallow in another bout of that most invidious of English traits – accepting defeat if we came near and tried jolly hard.

The above legitimately stated, it should also be recognised that for the first time under Johnson, there emerged a semblance of balance, both in terms of age and experience, and power and creativity. In losing England at least looked coherent and, if we are making hard calls about Test rugby, this was more than South Africa did in the recent Tri-Nations.

Johnson's frustration was apparent through his now trademark fits of simulated violence in his seat in the stand, which is not a criticism by the way, and his interview with Radio 5 Live yesterday morning. He is well aware that of the twin tasks of creating and finishing opportunities, the former is the harder, yet England failed at the latter.

Several passages of play had pace, momentum, ambition, any of the newfangled monikers so beloved of pundits, but they ended when backs and forwards had not the ability simply to draw a defender and pass at the right time to exploit an overlap.

The question exercising many aficionados in the Twickenham hostelries post-game was which of the following accounted for the uncharacteristic sloppiness of the Kiwis: complacency, decline, inattention or English pressure.

The answer may well be a little of all of the above. And lest this be dismissed as wishful thinking, it was the view of six former All Blacks, who, assured of confidentiality, were for the first time recognising at least the possibility that their country might have to prepare for triage rather than triumph next year.

Yes, it is premature to dust down the choke collars just because the All Blacks have had two relatively poor games, but, with the exception of Dan Carter and Richie McCaw, there were some unfathomable options taken by forwards and backs. Furthermore, having scaled the highest of heights, New Zealand have to accommodate that most uncomfortable of feelings, that the vista from there is only downwards.

If you took the best two players out of any side there would be a material effect. However, such is the importance of those two individuals to the why/where/what/when of All Black rugby that the loss of either would have a disproportionate effect on their forthcoming World Cup challenge. There will be no repeat of the 2007 delusion that New Zealand possessed three teams that were world class; the replacements are not there and they know it.

Carter's almost silent accumulation of a match-winning 16 points was redolent of 'King' Wally Lewis, the Australian rugby league legend; giving the impression of a player doing very little, yet when seen with a keener eye, doing everything that counted.

Behind every successful monarch walks an equally effective Machiavelli and two sublime pieces of subliminal suggestion from McCaw showed his brilliant perception. If footballers want to know how to win referees and influence them they should study two brief exchanges between McCaw and the very competent French referee Romain Poite.

Following repeated uncomfortable scrums, when England's front row was starting to dominate and draw penalties, McCaw took the opportunity afforded while his opposite number, Lewis Moody, was prone receiving treatment. In a polite but graphic manner McCaw advocated the New Zealand case for this discomfort which, according to him, was the binding of England tight-head Dan Cole. After acknowledging this suggestion, yet making it plain he could only penalise something he had seen, Monsieur Poite then quietly spoke to Cole about his binding even before the next scrum engaged.

Later, McCaw took a cheap shot from England replacement hooker Dylan Hartley, which equalled out the earlier and even cheaper butt by the All Black hooker Keven Mealamu on Lewis Moody (why are all hookers psychopaths?). Instead of ranting or whinging or acting as though he had been shot, McCaw simply asked Poite if he had seen it; Poite said no and McCaw suggested a scrum, knowing well that the first offence had been committed by one of his team-mates.

At a time when the All Blacks were under pressure and the home crowd increasingly vocal, the referee could easily have given a couple of penalties because of pressure. By helping to lessen this McCaw helped keep Poite on an even keel, which was crucial when his side were down to 14 men for the last 10 minutes.

If England find the same maturity they could do some damage.

25

New Zealand's PR for banned hooker Keven Mealamu has put rugby world in a spin

November 2010

The All Black propaganda, sorry, public-relations machine is a long-standing adjunct to the success of the New Zealand rugby team and particularly the All Black brand. Until Tuesday of this week it had been in overdrive since recognising the threat of Kiwi hooker, Keven Mealamu, being banned for headbutting the prone England captain, Lewis Moody, last Saturday.

The PR battle was lost by the Kiwis and Mealamu was banned by an IRB disciplinary panel for four weeks for 'striking with the head'. Unless his appeal is successful, he will take no further part in the tour.

For Mealamu, and rugby generally, it was fortunate that the incident was not shown on the stadium screens at Twickenham and his cheap shot was left for the consideration of the few hundred thousand viewers watching on Sky. Had the act been replayed several times, as happened with a headbutt delivered by Springbok Bakkies Botha on Kiwi Jimmy Cowan this year, there would have been an outcry with Mealamu being barracked for the rest of the game. Had it been live on the BBC, the PR battle would have been even harder because the outcry would have also come from a few million casual watchers, thereby tainting the image of rugby in general.

From the video evidence and to anybody who has played rugby, this was a simple case of nastiness. That said, the background factors are worth looking at because they are generally unknown and demonstrate the way in which subtle issues affect the aftermath of an incident and the problems they pose for those trying to manage the fallout.

The first mistake was for the Kiwi press liaison officer to harangue any reporter having the temerity to ask Mealamu about the incident as he left the field. The media-friendly Richie McCaw was incongruously available and while you could say this was no more than an attempt to limit potentially prejudicial comment, the availability of only certain players and only allowing certain questions is a PR error as it draws attention to the issue and adds the further charge of spin. In this case it was backed by unpleasantness which taints the attitude of any journalist witnessing the confrontation.

Advice to highlight Mealamu's disciplinary record might have been correct if it had been religiously adhered to, but 'he is not that sort of player' was the line taken. This was amplified by coach Graham Henry, who said, 'He's probably the cleanest player in the world, isn't he? It was purely accidental as far as I know.'

In law the prosecution is not allowed to present evidence of previous nefariousness by the accused solely for the purpose of tarnishing reputation, but the PR arena has no such precise distinctions; it is all about perception. Once the issue of character in general was raised, most non-Kiwi fans were free to aver that Mealamu's previous innocence would not have been maintained had the Scottish verdict of 'not proven' been open to the tribunals. Mealamu was cited for his involvement in spearing Brian O'Driscoll in the first Lions Test of 2005. (It wasn't a spear tackle because that involves the technicality of someone having possession of the ball.) Although the citing commissioner found insufficient evidence, the IRB later issued a statement calling the act 'unacceptably dangerous'. Technically innocent; publicly otherwise.

In the same series Danny Grewcock was banned for two months for biting Mealamu's fingers and there was insufficient evidence to prove Grewcock's allegation that Mealamu was trying to hook his mouth. Thus Mealamu was again innocent, but the public were left wondering why his fingers were in Grewcock's mouth in the first place. When you are suspiciously seen standing in the crowd at several fires it is only a matter of time before you become the suspected arsonist. The stressing of Mealamu's Christianity was also ill-advised because it is irrelevant. Anyway, didn't Christians administer the Inquisition?

Anyone of middle age, which is most of the IRB and its officers, will remember the attempted PR spin and resultant furore after the 1993 game when Kiwi flanker Jamie Joseph was not punished for stamping on England scrum-half Kyran Bracken's ankle in the first few minutes. Joseph was pictured acting as a friendly waiter in a subsequent photo opportunity and it would be human nature to relate the two events when confronted by any form of media-control tactics.

No doubt the Kiwis thought they were on to a winner in hiring solicitor Owen Eastwood to represent Mealamu; also a Kiwi and involved in the reduction of sentence achieved by Harlequins' Tom Williams for his part in Bloodgate. They should have realised there was widespread unease about Williams's reduced sentence and unanswered questions about it.

The man who heard Mealamu's case, Lorne D. Crerar, was in charge of the Bloodgate hearings for European Rugby Cup Ltd. There are similarly unanswered questions about the decision to release the Williams judgement eight days before the other judgements. Thus, Crerar's stewardship of this matter would attract much attention and he would be keen to avoid further controversy.

Thankfully, the right verdict was reached. As for the length of the ban, McCaw is unhappy England hooker Dylan Hartley was not charged for a forearm cheap shot on him. We should thank him for raising the issue of inconsistency. Hartley was lucky and could not have complained about a two-week ban, but McCaw failed to mention Mealamu's ban was half the usual sentence and that Botha got nine weeks for butting.[1] However, we should note that McCaw stressed, 'I don't like to be bitching and moaning about it.'

1 It should be mentioned that Mealamu's ban was later further reduced to only two weeks, on appeal.

26

David Haye's farcical world title fight with Audley Harrison shows just how far boxing has fallen

November 2010

Last weekend I re-watched the third world title fight between Muhammad Ali and Joe Frazier – the 'Thrilla in Manila'. After the non-fight between David Haye and Audley Harrison it afforded a valuable perspective; though both were world heavyweight title bouts, they were a universe apart.

You could not ignore the contradiction between the astonishing brutality and courage shown by the two Americans and what had just been delivered by the two Britons. More punches were landed in the first twenty seconds of the former than the two and a bit rounds of the latter and this savagery continued for fourteen rounds, only ending when Frazier could not come out for the final round, immediately after which Ali collapsed from exhaustion. Both fighters had given absolutely everything they had.

When the totality of the two events is considered you see many differences, each an example of the steep decline in quality and integrity of the heavyweight division.

Preceding the Haye *v.* Harrison fight the manufactured hype was so implausible and vulgar it stretched even the bounds of what is now accepted in boxing. There was little either man could legitimately find offensive about the other's career. Harrison was rich because of an ill-judged multi-fight contract with the BBC, but whose fault was that? In any event, Haye had earned well from his fights and that Harrison was more widely known was a consequence of his Olympic gold medal bout and his fights being on terrestrial TV; and whose decision was it to keep Haye's fights on satellite TV?

In contrast, the enmity between Ali and Frazier was real and based on taunts by Ali that Frazier was an Uncle Tom; this despite Frazier's help with Ali's boxing licence. The whole of the American sporting public divided in their support of the fighters along racial lines, even though both were black, and the political and social significance of their battles is now difficult to comprehend.

The comparative sight of Haye and Harrison swapping hollow insults, more suited to the playground, cheapened last weekend's event with each utterance. The British bout was extraordinary in only one respect: it was almost absent of scoring punches. On radio, had there not been commentary, it would have resembled a Marcel Marceau performance. The inevitable capitulation of Harrison could only disappoint those ignorant of his record, and anybody who fell for the farcical promotion and paid to view has only themselves to blame.

The final insult has been Haye's remarkable volte-face from bragging about his winning bets to absolute denial. It was not as if Haye made a brief quip immediately after the fight when he referred to his betting and it is inconceivable that as a professional he did not know about the British Boxing Board of Control's rules on the same. If, as Haye later claimed, it was not he, but a lot of his friends and family who bet on the fight, why did he say that he 'had put a lot of money on the third round'? It defies credibility that an intelligent man, which Haye is, would have used those particular words if he meant something different.

The British Board of Boxing Control, however, seems happy to accept Haye's nonsensical explanation that 'There was no online betting. It did feel like I'd bet on myself because a lot of people had put money on it, family members and what not,' but then again we are talking heavyweight boxing, which appears intent on allowing itself to continue at the bottom of the sports credibility league.

Even if Haye did not bet himself, his fighting for the interests of his entourage as opposed to the sport in general is a gross insult and should be a lesson for anyone stupid enough to consider betting on any of his future contests.

Now that a public indication has come from Vitali Klitschko that he will fight Haye if the worldwide take is split evenly there is no excuse for Haye not to sign for the fight. Any wrangling about rights can only be an excuse because, as Haye said, he made enough money out of the Harrison fight not to have to argue over a bit more.

Unfortunately, as we come to the 20th anniversary of the monumental series of fights between Nigel Benn and Chris Eubank, we are faced with yet more devalued fare.

Unlike nearly every other sport, heavyweight boxing has not become faster and more exciting despite advances in human physiology and the detailed knowledge now available through sports science and the sad truth is that, as presently organised, it will not do so.

27

BBC Sports Personality of the Year candidates can only sit and suffer

December 2010

One of the defining characteristics of sport is the fact that competitors can and do definitively win or lose. There are many variants throughout the world, both local and regional, of the irrefutable retort to on-field sledging or off-field whingeing: 'Look at the scoreboard.'

It is the ultimate debating point because not only does it reiterate the factual difference between the teams or opponents, it also contains the implicit submission that whatever comes by way of response, this is a conclusive reply.

Whatever happened to produce the conclusion, however unfair it was or undeserved, history will not record those incidents – the outcome will never be altered. In sport, results are objective and final.

For competitors the possibility of publicly succeeding or failing creates the addictive tension that occurs on the day of the event and heightens with every approaching minute. The hunger for victory is balanced by the dread of defeat and depending on the experience and psyche of the player one or other invariably becomes ascendant.

Although an athlete has to face and accommodate this, at least his performance is in his own hands. The challenges posed by opponents have to be met but this is what the athlete knows will come and he has the opportunity to respond and successfully answer the questions raised.

In the end the athlete's fate is self-made. When the contest is over, the astute athlete does not look to blame others, even though he may have partial justification, because deep down he ought to accept that had he performed sufficiently well any extraneous factors would not matter. If he cannot be honest about what went wrong and why, it is impossible properly to address the necessary remedies.

The most successful athletes are those who can lay themselves open to failure and take the risks involved, because only by accepting the possibility of failure is it possible to play to the limits of ambition. The average performer will, at the end of the day, seek the comfort of conservatism and the lessened chance of failure and criticism.

Another corollary of striving for extraordinary achievement is that there are people, including many in the media, who are waiting for, possibly longing for, an athlete to fail and to heap derision from the comfort of their armchair. It is so easy to scoff at the efforts of others, rather than recognise that their imperfect attempts are far worthier than the sniggers of those who never dare to step into the arena in the first place.

Being familiar with the above tribulations, athletes who find themselves thrust into the limelight by being listed for an award such as the *BBC Sports Personality of the Year* will experience tensions that probably outweigh any they felt prior to a race or game, and for a number of reasons.

The first issue is that usually their inclusion on the candidates list is involuntary; the decision to put them through the stress of anticipation and probable rejection is made by someone else. Of course they have the choice to ask that their name is removed from the list, but the repercussions are not pleasant; they know the sort of headlines that would accompany such a request. In reality they have no choice but to participate.

Once the deliberations start, the candidates know that the debate about their worthiness will be public and will inevitably draw some unflattering comments in various parts of the media. About such comments they can do nothing and have no right of reply. They also have no control over the way in which their case is advocated and have to rely on the articulacy of their proponents, who may or may not highlight the salient points of their case.

Within the consideration of the relative merits of the candidate there will also be the issue of which sport they represent and whether that has an intrinsic value over another.

This year Phil Taylor, who in darts is utterly imperious, will still face the accusation that his is not a sport at all. The most extreme view of this claim came from a colleague who said, 'It can't be a sport if you can play it in a pub.'

Although not as extreme as this, there inevitably will be those who consider that a sport whereby supreme physical effort and fitness is a necessity is always more meritorious than those that have no such stipulation. Sports involving a greater degree of physical danger always appear to rank higher than those in which the chance of serious injury is slight.

There is no accepted way of differentiating between such factors and the extent to which they influence the voting is unknown, and the frustrating thing for the candidate is that a person's opinion cannot often be altered.

It is this powerlessness that is at the heart of the anxiety that candidates will feel before, and especially during, an awards ceremony. While they are familiar with competition stress in all its various forms this is something alien to them. Moreover, when they compete in their sport they at least have the opportunity to directly influence the result. With these sorts of awards all they can do is sit there and accept their fate.

The best way to survive such an ordeal is for the candidate to take the view that whatever the verdict it is not a personal reflection on them and does not diminish whatever they have achieved in their own sport.

However, all the candidates are by dint of their achievements highly competitive people and passive acceptance is not familiar, nor is it pleasant. For this reason if you asked the sportspeople who made the top ten for *Sports Personality* whether they felt more nervous before the announcement of the award or before an event in their own sport, the probability is that the former is far more difficult to handle.

28

Schools given sporting chance?
Michael Gove's management-speak
doesn't fool me

December 2010

Monday 20 December 2010 should be noted by those who campaigned against the decision of Michael Gove, the Secretary of State for Education, to end the ring-fencing of the £162 million per year used to fund Schools Sports Partnerships (SSP). As David Cameron announced revised plans to invest £112 million in a network of 3,600 sports teachers until the London Olympics in 2012 there were accusations of an about-turn, countered by claims that 'We have listened to the people'. From campaigners there appears to be an unjustified sense of relief and triumph, but if any victory has been gained it is similar to getting a death sentence commuted to life imprisonment.

In truth, the actions of the government and Gove represent huge cuts in spending. But just as important, if not more so, is the fact that the organisation and monitoring of school sport is to be revised to the point where it is possible that there will be a disastrous reversal of ten years of gains and we will have no way of proving it.

You know the government has made a purely ideological decision when it starts double-speaking on what was, is and will be. Seeking to set a favourable context for this ill-judged action, Cameron called the SSP scheme a complete failure despite the

D of E showing that the proportion of schoolchildren doing at least two hours of sport per week rose from 25 per cent to 90 per cent in the past seven years and the average number of sports offered rose from 14 to 19.

While £112 million has been trumpeted as a massive investment in school sport, it immediately needs to be set against £486 million that was guaranteed investment. Depending on what proportion of the previously sports and now general funds are spent, this represents up to an 80 per cent cut in funding and organising school sports.

The revised plans look like what they are: a desperate, last-minute compromise between ideologues and civil servants, overseen by a prime minister desperate not to fall foul of allegations that he does not really care because of his public school background.

Gove's department said that 'time-limited funding' would 'help schools embed this good practice'. The £47 million will pay for SSPs to carry on until the end of next year's summer term and 'this will ensure the partnerships and their service can continue until the end of the academic year'.

Gove insists that it is time to 'move forward to a system where schools and parents are delivering on sports with competition at the heart'. What the hell does this mean, other than more management-speak?

What Gove is suggesting, without explaining precisely how it will happen, is that in the next few months all the gains of the SSPs should be permanently incorporated into schools and then run by heads and parents' groups.

How many of the people to be charged with this responsibility have the expertise, time and will to replace professional and full-time providers? Furthermore, what about after 2011 – will this run itself? How will we monitor its efficiency, the quality of instruction, any falls in funding, drops in numbers participating?

This is not a party political issue. If SSPs in some areas are overly bureaucratic and their work can be improved by private sports providers, so be it; the crucial thing is that funds hitherto guaranteed for sport are not spent on other things.

Perhaps the more sinister aspect of Gove's plans is that we will not be able to scrutinise them, as he is removing the elements which might have produced evidence with which critics could protest.

The further £65 million promised to the end of the 2013 academic year is for 3,600 PE teachers to spend one day a week on school sport, a cut from the two days presently, and they will no longer have the support of a unified organiser for their and their colleagues' efforts. As there are almost 18,000 primary and secondary schools in the United Kingdom, this brave new world is going to rely on the goodwill of an awful lot of people without supporting them in any proper manner. This is the same sort of thinking that characterised the marketplace approach to the National Health Service whereby it is assumed that things will automatically happen without the proper structures being in place.

One of Gove's previous criticisms of the system, which he and Cameron have been forced to acknowledge has delivered major progress, was that the results were uneven. How uneven will things be when they are left up to individual school heads under academic and fiscal pressure?

The fact is that Gove cannot guarantee that one penny of the money outside that specified above will now be spent on school sport. It could be close to that spent previously or, as anyone in the real world of education will tell you, it could be a small fraction of this. Suffice to say that without going through the accounts and timetables of every single school, nobody will be able to tell.

Astonishingly, what has survived is the plan for an annual 'School Olympics', although tellingly the amount promised from government, via Sport England, to establish and run this has not been specified. Does Gove have an idea how big a project and how much administration will be required for a School Olympics? How much money it will take for it to be a success? Presumably private funds will be sought as sponsorship, thereby taking away potential funds from already established events.

School sports already have their own national championships and they are timed to suit the individual sport's needs. How and why will those sports switch to a fixed period for what is to be presumed is expected to be the new pinnacle of achievement nationally?

The complete lack of detail for this concept illustrates that this is blue-sky thinking of the worst kind, dreamed up by people ignorant of how school sport works and the economics involved.

When we look back at this in ten years' time, Michael Gove could well be seen as the man who wrecked school sport in the UK.

29

Michael Gove's flawed logic is redolent of a kid always shoved in goal

December 2010

Sometimes the comments left by readers cut to the heart of the matter. The following post was made in response to an article on the Secretary of Education Michael Gove's decision to end the ring-fencing of the £162 million used by schools to fund Schools Sports Partnerships (SSP): 'If you look at the way Michael Gove walks you can tell sport means nothing to the man. He is simply a disgrace.'

This prosaically evidences why Gove took this decision and why he ignores the overwhelming evidence from all sides that he is wrong.

If David Cameron's promise to review this is genuine, he should start by looking at Gove's flawed reasoning. If he does so he can do nothing but shake Gove warmly by the throat and order that this idiocy is reversed before it wrecks the Olympic legacy and school sport in general.

SSP funding is used to run PE classes in schools where there are no trained staff, to organise sports clubs and hold competitions.

Although their performance is variable, nobody involved with the scheme doubts that it has been a success and does good work, including the Department of Culture, Media and Sport and the Department of Health.

In public Gove has criticised SSPs for not delivering enough competitive sport in schools. In seeking to justify his decision Gove cynically and selectively offered statistics which he claims back his stance. He told BBC1's *Andrew Marr Show*, 'What we're decreasing is prescription. It's up to head teachers to decide how they want to spend that money. We haven't seen an increase in the number of children playing competitive sport. Just one in five plays against another school. The number of children playing rugby or football has gone down in some cases.'

He conveniently overlooked the fact that the average number of sports offered by schools has increased, as has participation, and while pupils may not play inter-school matches that does not mean they are not competing, as is the case when one class makes up two basketball/netball/football teams. In any event, the important thing is that they participate in some sport and derive all the concomitant benefits.

This disingenuous approach continued in the debate of an Opposition Early Day Motion on 30 November when Gove stated, 'In 1,280 secondary schools not a single pupil takes part in an intra-school competition. That equates to nearly one in three secondary schools where not a single intra-school competition takes place. Similarly, as to the proportion of pupils who regularly take part in inter-school competitions, in 710 schools not a single pupil takes part in such competitions.'

Gove gives no context. Is this measured solely by reference to how many take part in inter-school matches? What about the secondary schools outside the 1,280 mentioned?

He continued by stating, 'In ten schools, 100 per cent of pupils regularly take part in inter-school competitions, and in 320 they regularly take part in intra-school competitions. There are massive variations and disparities.'

Yes, similar to the disparities in Gove's logic, because those statistics are not comparable. Delivery is uneven and it always will be because some people are more effective than others and some areas have greater problems to deal with. The stated examples cannot, to any rational and disinterested person, be conclusive proof that SSPs do not work.

Gove has simply chosen figures that suit his case and ignored countless personal testimonies from other government departments and those at the sharp end of delivering school sport, that SSPs are crucial to organising it and that their removal will effectively end sport in many schools.

His sophistry continued: 'We know that £2.4 billion was spent by the last government on delivering their sport strategy. Our contention is that although much good work was done, that money was not spent as effectively and efficiently as it should have been.'

He then queried the job descriptions of some people in the SSPs and criticised the school sport partnership self-review tool, which he said has 115 boxes to tick. 'Every moment spent looking at the self-review tool is a moment that could be spent coaching, inspiring and acting to ensure that more children take part in sport, but unfortunately there is too much bureaucracy.'

Gove should know or find out what people in the SSPs do before he makes a decision to throw them out of work. Additionally, how can he make any assessment of value and performance without data collected from the very exercise he decries?

At one point in the debate Gove answered a question about raising the number of hours per week of sport played by children by saying, 'For me, the most important thing is outputs, not inputs.'

This is the language of an accountant, not someone who cares about school sport. It is redolent of the kid always picked last for a team and then shoved in goal. Anyway, if we must use management-speak – how does Gove expect to improve outputs without properly funding and organising inputs?

Gove's cunning plan to improve school sport by releasing allocated sports funding into the general school budget will not work.

Under-pressure budgets and insufficient time means that many heads cannot do what Gove states, even if they wanted to. When that money is released it will be put to academic use because that affects a school's Ofsted report and its league table standing. Sport does not.

Gove's claim that an annual 'School Olympics' would be better at driving participation is a fantasy that not even Gazza, in his wildest moments, would think realistic. How will pupils reach the necessary standard to compete in that tournament if he removes the expertise and organisation that trains them? How will an annual jamboree increase competition and participation?

The six men who effectively control this decision – Messrs Cameron, Clegg, Osborne, Gove, Hunt and Robertson – all went to public school and five went to Oxbridge. There is nothing wrong with this but when their school sports department had plentiful funds and ample facilities they may not appreciate how hard it is for many state schools to play even a modicum of sport; that or they collectively don't care about the oiks.

30

Focus on the achievements, not the fluff that accompanies BBC's sport show night

December 2010

BBC's *Sports Personality of the Year* is a two-hour live show covering a multitude of sports. It hosts the best of sporting talent and allows the public to enjoy the drama of the past year's sport and elect the winner. Unfortunately, its comprehensive and inclusive nature leaves the programme vulnerable to critics, some of whom have undeclared personal or corporate reasons for antipathy.

The fact is that this show will always be criticised. The number of sports covered invariably produces complaints from certain sports that they have not been given due prominence; an impossible point for the programme-makers to address, because editorial decisions can never be objective. Whatever the content or result there will be some angry or disappointed fans and a vocal body of detractors, but that should not mislead us into questioning the programme's intrinsic worth; it is unique in broadcasting.

This year's preview show, which set out the case for each of the ten contenders, was a marked improvement on last year because it reversed the fashionable but stupid policy of having celebrity advocates. The merits of each hopeful were better served because their proponents had sporting gravitas and the points made were thus likely to be given weight by the public.

The programme's anachronistic title should be amended and

not just because it sustains the hackneyed jibe that certain contenders do not have a personality. The word personality must be
removed, because this has nothing to do with sporting excellence.
Its inclusion distorts the vote by introducing a criterion that
should play no part in a voter's decision.

Though the short list is compiled by collating the votes of thirty
sports editors, that cannot prevent criticism of its composition,
because the opinions of sports editors are subjective. Nor does it
prevent glaring errors being made: last year, A.P. McCoy did not
even make the top 10 despite winning his 15th Champion Jockey
title.

Every year a number of difficult factors have to be considered
when voters choose one aspirant, but this year there are more variables than usual and choosing the winner is more problematic.

It will be interesting to see what effect TV exposure has on the
vote. Half of the contenders come from sports which are exclusively or mostly covered by satellite broadcast and therefore their
success will have been seen by far fewer than those whose triumphs were covered by terrestrial TV.

One factor that has huge influence will not be present because
2010 was not a summer Olympic year. The games are the high-
est-watched sporting event in any year they take place, with
obvious beneficial exposure for medallists. Further, the fact that
competitors represent Great Britain means that national and club
allegiances are temporarily forgotten by voters and the fact that
athletes win for the flag is often an extra point in their favour over
those perceived to win for themselves, even though logically the
latter, by virtue of their nationality, also implicitly win for their
country.

Inevitably a team sportsperson cannot escape their colleagues'
contribution to their achievements and the fact that of the past
winners the large majority came from individual sports proves
that it is harder to win this award if you play a team sport.

Other aspects which affect the vote are so disparate that it is impossible to predict which have the greatest effect; suffice to say that they include the voter's allegiance to a sport, the degree of danger involved, the level of physical prowess, the degree of dominance over the athlete's contemporaries and the status of any particular title or event won. Also, has the athlete had to compete over a season or win just one or few event(s) to be short-listed? Is the athlete's achievement in a sport at which British success is frequent or uncommon? Other aspects include the manner in which the athlete has triumphed and the longevity of the athlete's success. Also, and wrongly, such things as personality, post-event humility, conformity to the British notion of sportsmanship (whatever that is) and even whether the athlete is 'likeable' will count for or against a nominee.

Though Graeme McDowell has been tipped, it is likely that he and Lee Westwood will divide the golfing vote, while Tom Daley's youth and the minority status of diving will probably put him out of the running.

Why David Haye is included is a mystery given that of his two fights in 2010, one was against an ageing fighter [John Ruiz] and the other against a man who wears boxing gloves for no apparent reason [Audley Harrison].

Graeme Swann has been crucial in English cricket's advancement but has not been sufficiently dominant to emulate Sir Ian Botham.

Jessica Ennis does not have the Olympic goodwill this year, unlike Amy Williams whose bravery and rare success ought to put her in the top three.

The brutality of the Tour de France aids Mark Cavendish's case and his stage wins have been over an extended period, but though he is heavily feted, the likely fight for top dog will be between McCoy and Phil Taylor.

McCoy and Taylor have dominated their respective sports for many years and this year they have both swept the board to win almost every available title. In truth, such long-standing achievement should be recognised in a separate category as this would also allow team sportspeople to be recognised more easily.

The debate over whether darts is actually a sport is otiose in the face of Taylor's brilliance, but given the danger, required fitness, lifestyle and unpredictability of horse racing the award should go to McCoy. The fact that his Grand National triumph was an event that captured the nation's imagination and was on terrestrial TV may just be decisive.

Whatever your choice, focus on things that genuinely show sporting greatness and ignore the trivial.

31

Barry Hearn's big challenge – to make snooker the new darts

January 2011

Darts polarises the opinions of sports fans. With its recent rise in profile, increased crowds and prize money and visibility on both terrestrial and satellite television, it no longer occupies the position of a pub pastime; it demands serious consideration.

While the public persona of darts was that of the *Wheeltappers and Shunters Social Club*, sports aficionados did not have to think beyond mimicking Fred Trueman's catchphrase 'Ahl si thee'.

With Phil Taylor, darts unearthed that rarest of breeds: a sportsman who transcends his sport by dint of sustained extraordinary performance. Taylor's astonishing hegemony of his sport, allied to the above factors, rightly saw him take second place in this year's *BBC Sports Personality of the Year*. Unfortunately for Taylor and darts, the welcome publicity also exposed them to the criticism that comes with success in Britain.

The clichéd question as to whether darts is actually a sport is relevant only when it comes to sporting awards. Until you try objectively to compare different sports, the definition is purely semantic; not that this stops some of sport's surprisingly unsporting followers making this point in as derogatory fashion as possible.

The fact that darts has its roots in the saloon bar allows critics to add the issue of class to their detractions. Why these despisers cannot allow others to enjoy an event that they are free to ignore, without making known their dislike, is a mystery but it is indubitably a British trait.

Taylor's unusual failure to reach the final of the recent PDC World Darts Championship led to erroneous claims that the event thereafter would be sub-standard. This could only be so to those ignorant of darts or anyone watching purely because of Taylor's celebrity. Anybody who understands and enjoys sport knows that what defines a sporting contest is the product, not the producer. Monday's final between Adrian Lewis and Gary Anderson forcibly demonstrated this point. An average contest might have proved the predictors of gloom right; but it was anything but. From the defiant waving of the Scottish national flag by Anderson before either player had stepped to the oche; through Lewis's astonishing first set, which included a rare nine-dart finish and had a three-dart average of 123; to the Stokie's final arrow – this was a tremendous sporting encounter. First Anderson, then Lewis, fought savagely to reverse potentially match-winning momentum created by their adversary.

Barry Hearn is the man credited with elevating darts to the sporting mainstream and creating an almost unique atmosphere of drink-fuelled fervour that nevertheless remains civil. Barring a few pantomime boos, both sets of non-segregated supporters were passionate, without feeling the need to chant obscenities or abuse their counterparts – and remember this was England v. Scotland. For any real lover of sport, this contest had all the essential elements. Those who said or wrote different are either biased or blind and anybody present could not honestly account otherwise. When you experience such spectacle, what matter its description?

A more difficult challenge faces Hearn as chairman of the World Professional Billiards and Snooker Association. Hearn plans to crack the European snooker market by hosting new ranking events throughout Europe, starting in February in Berlin. His belief is that the basis of snooker is good but that it needs more of darts' razzmatazz and he said recently, 'It just needs a few simple things to freshen it up.'

In line with Hearn's thinking came the staged introduction of the players to music and the adoption of colourful nicknames. Snooker should ignore disgruntled traditionalists, as they are, literally, a dying breed. These small features attract a younger and more affluent audience without detracting from what was already present, unlike the maddening fad of having a celebrity singer lead a national anthem, thereby drowning out the crowd.

Some believe it is simply a matter of making celebrities of snooker players, à la Phil Taylor, but they forget that Taylor's fame comes through atypical brilliance over a prolonged period. You can temporarily make anyone famous, but if there is nothing behind the hype, it will not last and snooker needs a lasting realignment.

The introduction of a defined world tournament and bigger prize money will help Hearn, but although he is right when he says that they must not lose track of the strengths of the game, he has to be brave and alter certain fundamentals. Snooker is simply too slow and the unlimited time given to players to make a shot allows prevarication by players and it bores people unnecessarily.

Attempting to ape cricket's Twenty20, snooker is looking to introduce two amended games; one with fewer reds and Power Snooker. In the latter there is a 20-second limit per shot; each game is 30 minutes long, with the highest points total winning. Potting the middle red activates a two-minute PowerPlay during which points are doubled, but missing a shot stops the clock and the opponent gets to use the remaining time.

The important thing is that these amended versions do not diminish the skills required. Indeed, players do not have to rush their shots, they simply have to choose them quicker. Furthermore, tactical play may be even more valuable, as opponents have less time to work out how to play recovery shots. As important, if not more so, is that they reduce the number of frames. Once players agree on what total removes the element of luck and gives both players sufficient opportunities at the table, there is no need to have a single frame more.

The immovable obstacle for Hearn and snooker is that players need to have silence when they take their shots. Unlike a dart throw, which has almost a set distance and weight, snooker shots are played in myriad ways and are more technical. It is difficult to see how the enjoyable, yet raucous, crowd noise of darts could be sustained if it has to be turned on and off.

32

Time will tell whether John Steele's RFU revamp will aid Martin Johnson and England

January 2011

What's in a name? Well, you cannot but think that the Rugby Football Union's new chief executive, John Steele, lived up to his surname in his powerful assertion of authority last week. He managed to achieve a unanimous positive vote from his management board for his vision to streamline the organisation's structure and anyone who knows the slightest thing about post-war RFU politics will agree that it was no mean feat in abolishing a number of roles such as competitions director, community rugby director and head of planning.

Steele has moved decisively away from a horizontal management structure where each of the said directors had to deal with elements of operation, strategy and finance that were relevant to their compartmentalised area. In its place is a linear structure in which the areas of operations, development and performance are each given a director who will be responsible for ensuring that a consistent approach is taken irrespective of the level of rugby concerned or in what structure it is played.

As this was a major overhaul of the RFU management process, its effects will take some time to assess, but what should be one highly desirable result is that those in positions of responsibility will know more clearly what they do and do not have to do. As such, when it comes to evaluating their performance there should be agreed judgement criteria. This, in turn, should stop any manager/director effectively evading responsibility by claiming that mistakes were within someone else's purview, a classic survival tactic employed by a succession of people within the RFU.

Much of the focus of the media and rugby supporters has distilled to the point that they see the changes as negative judgement on Rob Andrew, whose post of director of elite rugby is abolished. Convenient though it is to frame this personally, the debate should be wider because Andrew's authority was fatally compromised by the RFU management board when they overruled his recommendation to retain then-head coach Brian Ashton. The moment when Martyn Thomas, chairman of the management board, instructed Andrew to dismiss Ashton and engage Martin Johnson, was the time when Andrew's post became superfluous and Andrew should have walked or been made redundant.

Inevitably, the speculation is rife as to who will get the position of performance director. Eddie Jones, Jake White and Sir Clive Woodward all have impressive credentials, but Woodward's position with the British Olympic Association means that he has overseen the performance plans for elite athletes in a multitude of sports.

Leaving aside his role in winning the 2003 World Cup, which has to be balanced with his stewardship of the disastrous 2005 British and Irish Lions tour, Woodward will know what is best practice in the rest of British sport. As such, Woodward is by some margin the best choice for the post. Though he has publicly disavowed interest in the job – openly touting himself for the role would probably breach his BOA contract – privately he may have a different attitude.

It is widely known that Woodward and Andrew do not like each other, but if Andrew moves to operations there will be separation; if then they cannot co-exist neither is sufficiently professional to merit appointment.

Although Steele succeeded in implementing his plan, he failed to avoid the mistakes made by his predecessor, Francis Baron, when it came to human relations. Though there was a possibility of agitation by those sacked, demanding that they leave the premises immediately is an inhuman practice and Steele should have had nothing to do with it; not least because those left with a job have reason to believe that they will get no better treatment under the new regime.

It is precipitous to gauge whether all this will aid Martin Johnson and England. Of more immediate concern to the manager is the form and fitness of the squad he has in mind to challenge for the Rugby World Cup. More than anything, Johnson needs his players injury-free when they board the plane for New Zealand.

Johnson will be annoyed by Dave Attwood's nine-week ban for stamping and injuries to Tom Croft, Courtney Lawes and Chris Ashton. And he cannot be happy that Riki Flutey is playing at fly-half for Wasps instead of his normal position of centre.

As the Six Nations approaches, Johnson will watch with fingers crossed as his charges play in the Heineken Cup. He needs a bit of luck to allow his team to develop properly and be successful in Steele's new order.

33

A touch of humility could go a long way in making England a world player again

January 2011

The incredulity and anger that resulted from the ignominious denouement to England's 2018 World Cup bid threatened, just for a heartbeat, to spill over into rebellious action. The Football Association resigning from Fifa was mooted, campaigning for corruption to be rooted out got a mention. Pushed a bit further, we might have got to the point of considering burning lorries on Swiss soil.

Now that, in the paraphrased words of Alex Horne, the FA's general secretary, we have calmed down, the strategy has changed from action in the streets to action in the corridors of power.

It may come as a shock to the FA, and indeed to football and sports supporters in general, but there is one fact that any English governing body must consider when it negotiates internationally: when it comes to sport, nobody really likes England. They may credit the country's contributions in many spheres of life but that will not alter the view that England is an arrogant nation and the English an arrogant people.

You may say that, with our history and position, we are entitled to state proudly our achievements and that we should not demur from saying that which is only fact. On a micro level, in the pub or in the office, you may well be right, but this is not so when it comes to global matters and every utterance reinforces this stereotype.

This issue goes beyond football. Rugby of both codes and cricket demonstrate that the desire to beat England makes allies of countries that might otherwise harbour enmity. How often do you hear the statement that 'we invented football, rugby, cricket' – usually within a rant against the latest failure to achieve our national objective in the international arena? What must be realised is that each reminder that we invented something implicitly states 'you didn't', which is a tacit evocation of superiority, even if inadvertent. Further, while it may be a legitimate source of pride, this point carries no weight today beyond the listings on Wikipedia.

Why else do you think Fifa has gone to such extraordinary lengths to disavow the English claim to have invented association football? No other global ruling body has embarked on such a course of revisionism and the only reason for this can be to prevent the English making this claim in future. In keeping with previous statements of dubious accuracy, Sepp Blatter's pointed statement that China invented football masks the suspect logic behind Fifa's alleged research into this. China's claim as the mother of football only arose because of Fifa extending the previously accepted historical definition of the game. Moreover, having revised the definition, Fifa inexplicably ignored the claims of the Greeks that their ancestors were playing a game with a ball that fits Fifa's description of football 1,500 years before the Chinese played cuju.

How football's laws and rules are fashioned causes further resentment and here you have to concede the rest of the world has a justified gripe. The International Football Association Board first convened in 1886 and its present-day composition varies remarkably little from the original.

The original members, the football associations of England, Wales, Scotland and Northern Ireland, retain individual votes, balanced by four granted to Fifa. Thus, the three-quarters majority needed to change any law cannot be obtained without the agreement of at least two UK nations. When you consider the relative strengths of club and international football in Spain, Germany and Italy alone, this situation is indefensible and the FA's desire to see Fifa restructured is disingenuous if it refuses to call for similar change to the IFAB.

Although the following point may be trivial to the English, the very name of the governing bodies provokes resentment in some quarters. There are historical reasons for the FA, the Rugby Football Union and the Rugby Football League using the definite article in their titles, but, again, the implication is that thereby is conferred some special status. When we claim that this is an unimportant point that is not worth debate, the counterpoint is: if it is thus, why do we so resolutely refuse to change to the English FA/RFU/RFL?

Remembering the above points, look at a number of the things said by Horne and you can see how ill-judged his comments are:

'We are disappointed that we are arguably the most successful commercial organisation on the planet but don't have the clout in Fifa and Uefa.' Ergo, the rest of you are less successful.

'There's a long-term plan to try to move the right people into position in Uefa and Fifa and try to clean it up, try to resolve some of these process issues from within.' Would it not be wiser to just do this and not forewarn any corrupt Fifa member?

'I would hope we can lobby for those changes carefully, appropriately, politically, over the next three to six years.' The lobbying has begun.

'I've spoken to the general secretaries of four national associations,' said Horne. 'I've spoken to Gianni Infantino at Uefa and we've got the IFAB meeting coming up. I'll spend some time with Jérôme Valcke, of Fifa, at that.' Using the IFAB, that gives three minor footballing nations an utterly disproportionate influence, inevitably meaning those excluded will resist its influence.

All these worthy aims are no substitute for a public fight with Fifa and a sustained campaign for root and branch reform. The attendant media pressure would be enormous; it is the one thing that indisputably prompts at least some action by Fifa.

When Horne and David Gill, the chief executive of Manchester United, sit down to 'work out how we tackle the international relationship', they would do well to think about the oblique factors that work against their aims. If they find that task thereby becomes too daunting, there is always the chance to resurrect the 'commercially successful', but practically useless, Home Internationals. We cannot be undermined there.

The IRB has finally woken up to the fact the scrum is causing a problem

January 2011

A number of games over the past two weekends demonstrate the continuing importance of a facet of rugby some would like consigned to the bin. The scrum continues to be the bane of elite rugby, and the Heineken Cup, habitually the best of European club rugby, has been unable to escape. There are a number of ways to look at the issues surrounding the scrum and we should be glad, but not expectant, that the International Rugby Board assure us that it is a top priority.

In the Scarlets *v.* Leicester game on Saturday, the power of English Tigers' pack subjugated their counterparts in a manner not seen since Edward I, overcoming the considerable inventiveness of the Welsh team. The Tigers scrum would probably have out-scrummaged their opponents whatever way they had to do the task, but they benefited greatly from the ignorance, purposeful or otherwise, of referee Alain Rolland. Martin Castrogiovanni is without doubt a better scrummager than is Iestyn Thomas. Even more reason, therefore, not to give the Italian the extra advantage of illegally binding on the arm persistently. At one penalty won by Leicester, Castrogiovanni twisted Thomas so far round the Welshman almost ended up staring at the face of his hooker and captain Matthew Rees. This occurred with the Irish referee only two yards away after he had come round to the non-put-in side of the scrum to see what was going on.

Given we are repeatedly told that the engage sequence is supposed to be for referees to check distance, body angles, binding etc. (so much so they allegedly cannot watch the straightness of the put-in), it is bewildering Rolland did not see this blatant illegality and penalise it. Still, Rolland should not worry: enforcing the laws of rugby appears to be only one of the assessment criteria for refereeing at elite level and not a very important one at that.

Belatedly, it is dawning on the IRB that what some of us have been saying for nigh on five years is correct: the scrum is important and retains popular support from fans who do not want its defenestration, in whole or part. However, as managed by elite referees and the IRB, the scrum is a constant source of frustration; it is boring and very possibly dangerous. Weekly, this continues and needs to – and will – be highlighted at whatever cost to patience or sanity because this goes to the heart of rugby: what sort of game it is and for whom it is run. It is too important to be left to bureaucrats.

What is also happening in the modern-day scrum is that because of the demise of proper hooking most beaten packs cannot find a way to resist annihilation.

In both this game and the game between Munster and the Ospreys in the previous round, the dominant scrum won a series of penalties and you would have put serious money on the referee awarding a penalty try had any scrum been near to the try-line. Moreover, any infringement that resulted in the award of a scrum and a put-in to the weaker pack drew dismay from the non-infringing side, which knew that not only were they likely not to get possession, they would quite probably end up conceding a penalty.

Why is it that packs in trouble do not know how to cope with superior opponents, beyond diving earthward with fingers crossed and in silent entreaty to Saint Patrick (O'Brien), the Patron Saint of Arbitrary Scrummaging? It is because packs cannot settle their feet and lock their legs as referees allow their opponents to drive immediately on engagement. Additionally, modern hookers are not required to hook the ball properly. Thus, when they cannot step over the ball as part of an advancing pack nor have it fed straight to their No. 8, bypassing them, they find they cannot get out of trouble in retreat.

When scrums were refereed properly and there was a skill to hooking, it was always possible for the ball to be struck quickly into channel one. Any modern players unaware of this now mythical passage should ask their grandfathers. Use of this technique meant the ball was in and out of the scrum faster even than a broken policy commitment from Nick Clegg.

As there was a way of limiting the dominance of a better scrummaging pack, a side always had a chance of getting decent ball, provided it had the necessary skill. Due to inadequate refereeing and a consequent demise in the technique of players, we now have a situation where any side achieving a significant edge in the scrums is extravagantly, and arguably disproportionately, rewarded.

35

Businesslike solution to Olympic Stadium row is for Spurs and West Ham to share

January 2011

The disposal of the Olympic Stadium post the 2012 Games and the rival bids of Tottenham Hotspur and West Ham United to occupy the site have led to accusations of broken promises and legacy denial. With these have come bluster, half-truths and righteous indignation.

If we start at the very beginning, a very good place to start, the predominant reason for the International Olympic Committee awarding the Games to London was the promise of a legacy. The official government definition is published in its legacy plans via the Department for Culture, Media and Sport's Legacy Promises document of 2007.

The five promises were to: make the UK a world-leading sporting nation; transform the heart of east London; inspire a generation of young people to take part in local volunteering, cultural and physical activity; make the Olympic Park a blueprint for sustainable living; demonstrate the UK is a creative, inclusive and welcoming place to live in, visit and for business.

Note that there is no mention of athletics inheriting a permanent London base at the Olympic Stadium. There were references to this in the London 2012 bid document and this has led to an assortment of people making various pronouncements.

European Athletics president Hansjörg Wirz stated recently,

'Keeping the athletics track must be part of any future plans for the Olympic Stadium.' To support the viability of a multipurpose stadium, he pointed to the success of the Stade de France in Paris, which has hosted international athletics, football and rugby events. Whatever was in the bid document, it was not akin to the legacy promises specifically accepted and made by the government. The details cannot form binding covenants, as there have already been changes in event locations and other details in light of the economic reality and the need to save money.

What is not in the interests of athletics is to have the responsibility, even in part, for the running of a venue that is oversized and expensive. Wirz's reference to the Stade de France is misguided because at that stadium both football and rugby internationals are held as well as other events. London already has Wembley and Twickenham so no Football Association or Rugby Football Union-organised events would be lured to the Olympic Stadium.

Even if the legacy is not what was originally proposed, the fact that something was left of lasting value would be a stark contrast to what has happened in Sydney, Barcelona, Athens and Beijing, where much of what remains is disused, barren or bankrupt.

The only sport that can realistically hope to make use of the Stratford site is football, but no supporter wants to watch games on a pitch surrounded by an athletics track – with some justification given the dilution of atmosphere that ensues.

Locally, the only club of sufficient size to make a commercial success of the site is West Ham United, but their plan to share an adapted stadium with athletics does not satisfy anyone. Football fans get the track they do not want and athletics gets a 60,000-seat stadium that it cannot fill. Further, can West Ham guarantee their stadium would be full for each home game? And, given their treatment of their manager, Avram Grant, would you have faith in the present board running the whole thing successfully?

The relatively recent bid by Tottenham to take the site,

demolish the stadium and rebuild a purpose-built football stadium has drawn criticism from all quarters, most of it flawed by being illogical, emotional or unrealistic commercially. Ken Livingstone, the former Mayor of London, has come up with the tangentially relevant claim that the Spurs plan has an unacceptably high carbon cost. Since when did this issue become paramount in his assessment of proposed developments? It did not feature in a host of building works undertaken during his time in office and it was not the prominent feature of his transport policy.

David Lammy, the MP for Tottenham, and Haringey Council have claimed that a Spurs move would devastate the area near White Hart Lane. Their sudden interest in Spurs is surprising given the years of inaction over infrastructure improvements and their placement of numerous planning obstacles to Spurs' initial relocation plans.

Depending on what you read, anywhere between 50 to 70 per cent of Spurs fans oppose the move, but the crucial question is how many objectors would really refuse to go to Stratford, given their proclaimed unconditional love for the club? Once fans experience the comparative benefits in respect of facilities and travel, the actual number who turn their backs may well be far less than feared. Moreover, if the claimed figure of a waiting list of 25,000 fans for season tickets is accurate, there is every chance that Spurs could make up any shortfall.

Much has been made of Spurs being a north London club: but what is special about this? Additionally, the proposed move is approximately 4.7 miles as the crow flies and 7.2 miles by road. Yet no similar furore ensued when Bolton moved 4.9 miles (as the crow flies, or 5.7 miles by road) from Burnden Park to the Reebok Stadium. Against all of this come cries of a betrayal of ordinary fans and allegations of a sellout to corporate interests. But these are a fact of Premier League football and there is no point pretending otherwise.

What most fans assume when they rely on non-commercial

arguments is that their club will never fail; which is easy when these supporters do not have the responsibility financially.

If this situation were viewed in a proper business way, Spurs and West Ham would share a purpose-built football stadium. The £50 million of public money which will be given to the new occupier should go to athletics, along with a donation from the clubs to redevelop Crystal Palace.

Thereafter, an agreed and small percentage of annual revenue from the former Olympic site would be given to athletics. However, none of this will happen, because although it is often claimed that modern sport is a business, it is not.

36

Admitting weakness and asking for help requires truly brutal honesty

February 2011

'It's so ****ing obvious' is a phrase that every fan or pundit, from every sport, has said or thought as they have watched their favourites labour with a game or race plan that has not and will not work; not even if play went on for another week.

From this thought comes another: if it is so apparent to us watching minions, how is it possible that elite sportspeople, some professionals, some extravagantly paid, cannot also see this; nay, as alleged experts, ought they not to have seen it before us?

We may, sometimes, be charitable and recognise that in the midst of battle players cannot always discern the obvious. That said, surely the coach or manager, with his professional detachment, should have identified the issue and done something about it – what else are they paid for? This question is actually two-faceted.

We should separate what might be called 'Where was plan B?' which has been the criticism levelled at teams and managers too numerous to specify, from the failure to defend a well-established lead like the 4–0 advantage surrendered by Arsenal to draw 4–4 against Newcastle United last weekend.

So why do teams and coaches persist with what, to us, is a patently ineffective plan A? It is better for a team that any plan they had initially is comprehensively shredded from the outset, because if it is so obviously wrong there may be recognition and change. The more difficult and common conundrum comes when the plan shows initial signs of success. The ball that nearly got through, the shot that missed narrowly, the ball that nearly went to hand; all narrow misses create a General Haig mentality of 'one more push'.

Sometimes it is precisely that, just a lack of precision. That is what players and coaches naturally assume because, after all, they, to a greater or lesser extent, were responsible for creating the plan. If it turns out to be unsuccessful, their analytical and planning skills have also been awry and they have not only wrongly assessed the challenge, they have wasted all the preparation time. Nobody likes to admit error and any sign of potential achievement gives false succour.

From a player's on-field perspective, the problem is slightly different, although it has, at its root, the same fear of embarrassment. If the pivotal point of the team's strategy rests on a player or unit performing in a certain way or achieving certain things, those so tasked have the added burden of knowing that their team-mates can, and often will, shift blame to them for their own inadequacies.

'I didn't get the service' could be because a player did not get into realistic and correct positions for delivery. A back row's failure to compete at the breakdowns can be caused by their front five not delivering sufficient quality possession from first-phase line-outs and scrums.

When this occurs players are instinctively reluctant to ask for help. Who wants to admit he cannot handle his opposite number? One sign of a mature team, one that has deep foundations of trust and sodality, is that any player, no matter how good, feels able to ask.

It goes against every grain in a competitive player to admit weakness and then to confirm it by openly requesting assistance. It requires brutal honesty and selflessness that is difficult to summon, especially if you are a recognised star of the team. Not only do you not want to admit fallibility to possibly younger and less talented team-mates, you become angry with yourself because you believe that you should be able to sort this without help.

If the team are lucky, they overcome this innate refusal to face the truth when the performance is debriefed, at half-time or later during the week. One sign of an unsuccessful and immature team is where players try to point the finger elsewhere, either because they are dishonest or for fear of ridicule and deselection. Any coach who does not create a secure environment where blame can be apportioned and accepted, without fear of consequence, will not find the remedy.

When I first came into the England set-up as a fringe player, there had been so many OCWs (one-cap wonders) that the post-match analyses were worse than useless, they were positively misleading. I once overheard a conversation between two selectors at the bar where this astonishing piece of corroboration was cited: 'It must have been his fault; he even admitted it.'

All this is different from occasions when a once-thought-beaten opponent overturns a seemingly hopeless position. How can the previously imperious suddenly become useless? Why are they not doing what they did in the first half, the things that got them the lead?

No half-time team talk includes an instruction to go out, forget everything you did well and play rubbish. Instead, what has happened is that the opposition may have had a frank and useful honesty session that allowed the right changes in formation or tactics. What once worked is now redundant and unless this is recognised, the leading team face the above problem.

Sometimes players do become blasé, but often they are bewildered by the fact that things that were so fruitful do not now work. Further, as the opponents start to claw back the deficit, they panic and this is not just because they are unable to cope with, or are unfamiliar with, the experience.

It is also that they have had proof that their plan A was correct.

How else did they establish their lead? How much more difficult is it for them and their coach to then admit that for the second half or whatever period remains, plan A is wrong?

The reason that comebacks like the one France managed against the All Blacks in the 1999 World Cup semi-final – when New Zealand were leading 24–10 but lost 43–31 – often succeed is that momentum can be all in sport and, unlike a poor first half, a poor second leaves no possibility of sorting it out.

37

Time to educate pushy parents on the futility of abuse from touchline

February 2011

Earlier this week Jodie Williams's coach, Mike McFarlane, defended his decision not to send the 17-year-old world junior champion sprinter to the World Championships in Daegu, South Korea, this summer. In doing so, he clashed with UK Athletics' head coach Charles van Commenee, who said he was keen to get Williams competing at senior level. McFarlane and Williams's father stressed the fact that they were focusing on her long-term development, which included concentrating on forthcoming A levels. Van Commenee highlighted the necessity for Williams to go to Daegu as part of preparations for the 4x100 metres relay team, saying, 'You need team players. It's a team event so I select the best team.'

Both parties have legitimate points but, in the end, those with more intimate knowledge of the athlete, physically and mentally, have to have the final say and bear final responsibility for Williams's career. National coach versus personal coach is a specialised facet of the unavoidable dilemma facing anyone trying to both aid and progress his or her child's sporting career. Unfortunately, while there are many booklets offering advice, a parent assuming this position faces a difficult task.

Wanting to avoid accusations of duress, I deliberately did not indulge my eldest daughter's casual request to take up mini rugby

Brian Moore   125

last year. When she repeated it, more forcefully, at the beginning of this season, I helped her enrol in the mini section of a local rugby club.

We have all seen parents living their dreams through their off-spring. I remember vividly the parents of boys against whom I competed in trial games and the resentment I felt as they bellowed to highlight anything their son did better than I did. I also recall my sympathy for the boys chided over mistakes not made purposefully.

As I had a reasonably successful sporting career, I thought that I would easily cope with the potential problems of spectating. I was wrong.

I had already read the guidelines issued to parents by the Football Association as part of their Respect campaign and those framed by the Rugby Football Union and the England and Wales Cricket Board. While each set differs slightly, they stress the same important points of positivity, support, not taking it too seriously, focusing on skill rather than winning, maintaining confidence with helpful analysis and respect for officials.

Bearing all this in mind, my only words before my daughter's first training session were, 'Enjoy yourself, listen and try your best.'

The possible problem of her coach not meeting what I thought should be an appropriate standard thankfully did not arise, as he was admirably dedicated and skilled. Therefore, I settled down to enjoy vicariously a nine-year-old's first experience of a game I love. Then it all went wrong.

All the youngsters made mistakes, but they and she had a par-ticular problem with the offside line, not surprising given that internationals, elite referees and some opinionated co-commentators have similar difficulties. I tried to help by shouting – and I promise in a gentle way – for them to make a line behind the pile-up (break-down) and saying 'Well done' when they did. As it seemed to help, I repeated the advice at the next breakdown and the next and so on. I was mortified when my daughter suddenly yelled, 'Stop shouting at me.'

I had not appreciated that, although I only mentioned her name once during this general advice, she interpreted it as personal criticism on each occasion. Prickling with automatic defensiveness, I choked my protest that I was only trying to help and instead mumbled a quiet 'Sorry' as the other parents stared at me.

Reading deeper into this shows you the fine line between helping and hindering. All children are aware of a parent's presence and this creates some pressure, whatever the parent's behaviour. Children discern far more than we think and often infer things from the slightest word or gesture. They do not always recognise a general expression of disappointment and believe it is directed at them. Head shaking, rolling of the eyes, looking away, kicking the ground – any of these can discourage children, and exhortations like 'Come on' and 'Sort it out' are as practically useless from the touchline as they are on the pitch.

There is a school of thought, subscribed to by many parents, that kids need to learn to live with this and that it will toughen them up to face bigger challenges, but the evidence refutes this. It is not about giving unqualified praise; this is wrong, especially when the child knows they have not played well. It is about being aware of all the above points and discussing performance at the right time, offering only constructive advice.

All this is counselling perfection; parents will always fall short because they are human. However, when you note the subtlety of the matters, you must wonder why a number of parents still openly threaten and abuse their own and others' children, genuinely believing that they do nothing wrong. It is astounding that these parents cannot see that their example may embarrass and subliminally condone similar behaviour from their child in the future.

Make no mistake; this sort of behaviour happens in most sports. The factual accounts of the behaviour of certain impossibly expectant, middle-class tennis parents are the equal of anything coming from Hackney Marshes.

Parental aggression led the FA to introduce the spectator zone in kids football, which ropes parents away from the pitch. While this may seem silly, we should applaud the FA for recognising the problem and attempting to solve it. They and every other sport should not tolerate even a small degree of these dangerous and damaging actions.

When you read the evidence, you have to concede that parental attitude and action play at least an equal part in a child's sporting development as does coaching. This being so, it is difficult to resist the proposition that we should invest as much money into educating parents on these issues as we do into formal coaching.

Hopefully Rugby World Cup will boost Christchurch

February 2011

After arguing that the Rugby World Cup should never have been awarded to New Zealand for 2011, the recent earthquake in Christchurch and the ensuing deaths and damage suddenly make rugby matters appear trivial.

Although the following point is solely emotional, the forthcoming tournament will, I hope, go at least a small way to restore Christchurch and its citizens' mood after this catastrophe. Though presumptuous, I do not think I am out of order in offering sympathy on behalf of the rugby and sporting world.

France need unity to capitalise on strength of domestic game for success in Six Nations Championship

January 2011

Reading the runes created by the last Heineken Cup games before the 2011 Six Nations is a favourite pastime for rugby's media folk. Is it a reliable indicator; after all, does it not show the form of those likely to represent their country in the last formal tournament before the World Cup? Yes, it does show form but no, it is not a reliable indicator.

The presence of four French quarter-finalists, Perpignan, Toulouse, Toulon and Biarritz, is no accident and you cannot say any of them have been fortunate to progress this far. This year's Heineken is a reflection of the strength of the French domestic league and its powerful purse.

Whether any of this form translates into a coherent and consistent Six Nations campaign is anybody's guess. Not only have you to consider the French occasional penchant for performing as if they don't care, there is also the question mark about the relationship between France coach Marc Lièvremont and his squad. The whispering from the French camp about the atmosphere during the autumn internationals was more than the understandable gripes from unfavoured players; it was specific about aspects of training and man-management.

The shambolic way France capitulated against Australia made

no sense until this point became known, because hitherto France were the closest of all the northern hemisphere nations to matching the power and pace of the Tri-Nations sides. If, and only if, the rumours are wrong, or the causes are removed, can you have faith in France topping the table. The Six Nations is a sufficiently difficult tournament and the unusual pressures of geographical proximity and historic enmity do not need exacerbating by internal discord.

Another reflection from the Heineken is the mirroring of this year's Aviva Premiership. Leicester and Northampton apart, the remaining clubs are inconsistent and show little progress from their previous season's performance. There has been chronic dissatisfaction with the amount of English-qualified talent that is coming from the English clubs, only part of which is justified.

England do not have, as in previous years, a number of seasoned club players who can be used to perform a specific job in times of need. When they had this resource, it meant that young talent could be introduced without it being a huge risk. Presently England have a group of experienced players, a similar group of promising but relatively green colleagues and not many players in between. When you add the medium-term injuries to the players who were a probability for the back five of the England scrum, you are forced to conclude that any further bad luck will effectively ruin England's Six Nations hopes and with it their preparation for the World Cup.

The Irish challenge for honours at club level has shifted away from Munster after their exit at the pool stage. The consequences of this for Irish international hopes are not good because the way in which Munster were bullied up front was as disappointing for their followers as was the fact of defeat. Traditionally Ireland's forward effort has been able to rely on the Munster grunt to fashion enough possession for their talented back division to exploit. It is clear that at best the depth of ability within the Irish pack has diminished and, like England, only a couple of injuries could see Ireland fatally compromised.

At least the Irish have the form of their Leinster players from which to derive optimism; what is to be said about the state of mind and body of both players and supporters alike across Offa's Dyke? The quality shown by the Welsh Heineken Cup representatives was poorer this year than for many previous. Every region had at least one gutless performance. The regions must do more to engender passion within their operations because there is a feeling they stepped away from the soul and spirit of club rugby when they embarked on professionalism.

It is not impossible for non-club sides to recreate this spirit, but it cannot be immediately gained and with insufficient attention it becomes ineffably difficult. Sir Clive Woodward managed it with his side who won the World Cup in 2003 and Andy Robinson has managed to do it with Scotland which, given the relative lack of talent at his disposal, is his biggest achievement yet.

40

There's no telling who will win Six Nations Championship . . . and that's fantastic

February 2011

The imminent Six Nations tournament will differ little from most of its predecessors; it will not turn out as expected by pundits and fans. This chronic ability to surprise is one reason that the northern hemisphere's premier international competition remains popular, even though it only sporadically produces rugby of true quality. Self-appointed aficionados of top-class rugby scorn this enduring regard, often by comparing the standard of rugby displayed with that of the Tri-Nations. Such criticism fails to appreciate properly the position of the Six Nations in both sport and rugby in this part of the world.

Since the demise of football's Home Internationals, there is no other regular opportunity for expression of national identity and good-natured enmity in the three most popular team sports, football, rugby and cricket, in Great Britain, Ireland and France. This, and the natural edge present in all versions of the local derby, adds millions of occasional fans and viewers yearly, without hugely expensive promotional campaigns, and in this rugby is extremely fortunate.

For the Home Internationals broadcasting committee, the body charged with selling the rights, protective listing removes the need to address the divisive and difficult problem of balancing the need for widespread coverage to drive participation and the basic need for cash to fund participation. Terrestrial TV provides much more of the former; satellite TV much more of the latter.

Last year, thirty million people, half the population, watched at least fifteen minutes of the Six Nations and that is why it interests broadcasters. Of all available worldwide rugby rights, the Six Nations remains the most coveted and this includes the RWC. Though not widely known, it regularly delivers a higher percentage of A and B-classified viewers than almost any other major sport.

It is probably only its current designation as a 'crown jewel' that has prevented a satellite broadcaster securing the live broadcast rights. Were it removed from the protected list, it would be fascinating to watch the ensuing, tortured discussion. All the participating countries refuse to limit their number of paid players, thereby wasting revenue sustaining too many professional and semi-professional clubs. Increasingly large amounts are required to finance expanding international operations and support intermittently profitable senior clubs and a number of ruinously ambitious aspirants.

The requirement for cash, a Murdoch-friendly government and the expiration of the existing contract in 2013 suggest that a Satellite Six Nations next time round would be a decent punt.

Acknowledging I am not disinterested, I nonetheless believe such a move would be right only if it was, in effect, financially unavoidable.

Past and present viewing figures prove satellite TV will not deliver anything like the mass audience presently enjoyed for the Six Nations. Critical in understanding this is consideration of the millions of viewers whose only rugby watching is this competition. It is inconceivable that they will pay to view given the casual nature of their viewing.

Sky TV own nearly all the worldwide live rugby rights and their coverage is good, but if they capture the Six Nations they would be able to put down a monumental bid for exclusivity. Would you bet large against the subsequent introduction of a dedicated rugby channel by subscription or at least the compartmentalisation of the RWC, Six and Tri-Nations and club league and cup rugby as separate pay-per-view events if they achieve hegemony?

Although theoretically reversible, the ineluctable consequence of accepting such a huge cash bid would mean the Six Nations would be very unlikely to appear free-to-air again. Rugby's spending horizons would increase and its present wastefulness would continue because more cash avoids the need for financial and administrative reform. If you doubt this, look at the way the ECB (England and Wales Cricket Board) subsidises the 18 first-class counties when there is only the talent and demand for half that number.

Given the unpredictability of the Six Nations, only a fool would make firm predictions about how the teams will perform, so here goes.

No team has an injury-free squad and, to a large extent, the final standings and certainly the opening games will be determined by which countries are able to shore up their units and mask the unavailability of key players. The opening game tomorrow night at the Millennium Stadium in Cardiff amply demonstrates the above point. England have Courtney Lawes, Tom Croft and Lewis Moody out and Wales are without both first-choice props.

The English absentees weaken their line-out; the Welsh wounded weaken their scrum. As there are more of the former than the latter, an advantage in the line-out usually turns out to be more decisive, unless the dominance in the scrum turns into annihilation. Watch out for the opening exchanges because any weakness in the set pieces could be conclusive.

Thereafter, you need to look at which half-back pairing makes the better tactical decisions. Phillips and Jones, for Wales, have more experience than their counterparts, Youngs and Flood, and for England to succeed they need the Leicester pairing to make calm, correct decisions. If pressed, and asked for an impartial punt, I believe that playing at home, an underestimated advantage, may help the Welsh win a very close match.

The French desperately need to beat Scotland to erase the memories of an awful autumn series of internationals and they must settle the discord that exists between their players and coach Marc Lièvremont. Scotland go into the game as the improving team, albeit still hampered by an inability to regularly score tries. Again, home advantage should be enough for France and the fact that Scotland have a poor record on French soil, but, as the rugby world knows – you can never second guess the French.

Ireland have the look of champions, on paper. They have the perfect opening game in Italy and England and France have to go to Dublin this year. Their team contains a spine of highly experienced players and the performances of their Leinster and Ulster players in the Heineken Cup suggests an opening win that could set them fair.

41

Wales need key figures to save them from Six Nations Championship crisis following defeat to England

February 2011

Popular wisdom after the opening round of the Six Nations is that only two teams are in it, France and England. The popular view is wrong. Everything is plain, after the fact. So, that an increasingly confident England beat a strangely disjointed Wales at the Millennium Stadium was no surprise. That was not the opinion of either set of supporters before kick-off. For them, it was too close to call and, while England's 26–19 victory suggests a marginal contest, it was not so.

Injuries suggested that England's line-out and the Welsh scrum might be vulnerable. The exact reverse occurred. Wales went nowhere near England's line-out and the Welsh front row made life uncomfortable for Andrew Sheridan and co.

England are not the finished article, but they know that and this opening win was not insignificant. One sign of their developing character was the way they withstood the manufactured hwyl. Warren Gatland contributed via the media. The Welsh Rugby Union commissioned a stirring pre-match video, urging the crowd and players to honour the legends and history of Welsh rugby. Both failed.

Only in the opening ten minutes did Wales dominate yet, having missed two penalties, they were seven points behind when

Toby Flood clinically exposed a dogleg in the Welsh defence and Chris Ashton scored under the posts. Ashton's second try, after half-time, forced Wales to play catch-up rugby and Morgan Stoddart's try added only respectability.

With statistics and damn lies you can construct any scenario, but the conclusions wrought by the following are irrefutable. Time in possession – Wales 27 minutes 11 seconds, England 27:26; ball won in opponent's 22 – Wales 1, England 30.

Gatland's team are close to the edge and their established stars are misfiring badly. A lack of precision from hand and boot and lateral meandering obliterated much of Wales' positivity. Their talented centre pairing was anonymous.

Wales could study France, who threatened to eviscerate Scotland in Paris on Saturday. Having witnessed at first-hand a French team flowing atop their crowd's baying, I know that at times the Scots felt bewildered by the pace and dexterity of what appears to be a team with five extra men.

The three rules when playing France: don't give them loose turnover ball, don't kick loosely and don't be loose. The Scots broke all of these and only heroic defence prevented France from making them pay for every transgression.

Aspects of the French performance were exemplary, especially the way backs and forwards ran at the inside shoulder to fix defenders, passed into space and to men hitting the line flat and at pace.

Watch how the French pass in close contact. The slight dip of the hands before releasing the ball creates a brief delay that fixes defenders and prevents them from drifting. It also disguises the short pop pass to a straight runner. This enables them to work narrow channels profitably, without ceding possession by drifting into touch.

The French scrum terrorised the Scots and it was good to see the scrum laws more rigorously applied. Once Euan Murray – this applies to all tight-heads – had to bind on the shirt and not the arm, his job became considerably harder. As he had to stay square and his binding with hooker Ross Ford was loose, the Scots splintered, conceding a penalty try.

A note of thanks to referees for beginning to referee the scrum properly, but also a caution. It is crucial that the side not putting the ball in cannot drive before the feed. France did that twice and wrecked the Scots. If you allow this, you return to both packs trying to push on impact, as Andy Robinson said in his post-match interview.

The sometimes breathtaking nature of the French display has left their flaws overlooked. Though they punished three Scottish gifts of possession, they looked fragmented once Scotland got beyond the first defence line and, when not given the run of the park, they struggled. That Scotland buckled but did not break is to their credit. Three tries, given their recent scarcity, shows further progress. No side will consider a game against Scotland as straightforward.

For Italy, all that was missing against Ireland was the ability to close out a game they should have won. Snatching their final attempted dropped goal let the Irish off the hook. Nevertheless, they face France and England at home and will not be caught cold again.

There is a long way to go yet. The possibilities, as Alice said, grow 'curiouser and curiouser'.

42

Mike Tindall and Shontayne Hape at centre of England's development in 2011 Six Nations

February 2011

Another bout of revisionism occurred in the aftermath of England's demolition of Italy. Italy were obviously tired after their resolute exertions against Ireland the previous week, are a poor team, were caned by the referee and not allowed to get into the game.

None of the above is true and most expected an even game, with England pulling away in the last quarter. Most were surprised that not only did England dissect the Italian defence regularly, they had support on hand on almost every occasion to finish. They may not be surprised in the future, should Martin Johnson's team continue building in such a satisfactory manner.

To characterise Chris Ashton's four-try contribution as that of a poacher is inaccurate, if by that you imply he just hangs about waiting to nab a score. His seeming omnipresence at the shoulder of breaking colleagues requires both intuition and hard running to be available for the scoring pass. It is *de rigueur* to slate the alleged lack of dimension in England's centre partnership, but Ashton's dazzle obscured much of the straight running and decoy angles cut by Shontayne Hape and Mike Tindall.

Last week England found a couple more players to add to the list of those who can handle Test rugby. This match enabled them to add Alex Corbisiero, which is particularly satisfying as he is a prop. There is still much work to do, but England are fashioning the tools with which to handle the task and with every such discovery do their prospects grow. However, Johnson knows that while England progress from walk, to jog, to run, the starting gun for the blue riband sprint is about to go across the other side of the world.

Of the other two potential championship and Grand Slam winners, it was the Irish who were responsible for all the rugby at the Aviva Stadium in Dublin yesterday; both good and bad. It is technically incorrect to state that Ireland were responsible for nearly all the points scored in the game, but as near as damn it that was the case. A succession of needless penalties, given away in kickable positions, and a simple one-on-one missed tackle by Gordon D'Arcy accounted for all but three of the French winning total.

Although the penalty count was only 9–8 against the Irish, the ones they gave away were in range of the posts and coach Declan Kidney has to lay down the law about this. In the end, it is pointless playing with as much passion and commitment as did the men in green if you continually undermine your effort by witless transgression.

Many neutrals and Irish supporters of a gentle persuasion expressed the view that they felt sorry for Brian O'Driscoll and his boys. Sorry, they do not deserve this munificent sympathy because all their misfortune was of their own making. Had the penalties been forced by French pressure and committed in extremis defending the goal-line, there would be a case for compassion; as they were not, there is not.

The French confidence about this game and beyond was expressed by their former scrum-half, Fabien Galthié, who said that the French have a clear goal in mind this year and are intent on achieving it. If becoming World Cup winners is truly that goal, the French will have to play substantially better than that to make it out of the group.

Against a side disciplined at the breakdown and one who refuse to flaunt unnecessarily with danger about the breakdowns, the French would have lost on Sunday. By the thinnest of margins and the thickest of benevolent gifts from Ireland, they remain on course for the title.

While Johnson's natural gloominess got an injection of levity and Marc Lièvremont's selection policy received undeserved succour, Andy Robinson, the Scotland coach, got only pain at Murrayfield.

When he sees the following statistic, he will feel even worse: Scotland made 199 passes and one line-break. In truth, it was miraculous that the Scots managed to hang on to that many passes because they were deficient in almost every other respect.

The lack of rigour was inexplicable from professional players and the problem for Robinson is that, without reasons for the shambles, he has nothing specific on which the team can focus to prevent its repetition.

In the end, Warren Gatland's selection of James Hook at No. 10 paid off, but the astute Kiwi must know that Wales's problems run deeper than which player occupies that shirt. Nevertheless, a long losing streak has been halted and things can only get better … can't they?

43

Six Nations 2011: Biased? Not me, but I do fancy England to overcome naturally talented French

February 2011

I am accused of bias while commentating, usually by one-eyed supporters of any team facing England who, despite being able to access alternative commentary, seem determined to sit through 80 minutes of alleged partiality, just so they can be offended fully. I am used to this and satisfied it is not so.

I go through every game and list the number of positive and negative comments I make about both teams and the balance invariably favours the team who make more attacks and have most possession.

Last week the detractors accused me of bias against the Irish. Given their opponents were the French, the ineluctable corollary must be that I was biased towards France. Many hurtful things are said and written about me, but this really is too much. I mean, what can you admire about the French, other than their health service, education system, refusal to kowtow to the United States and invade Iraq, preservation of independent retailers, cuisine and Chateau Figeac 1990?

Their rugby is the same: they offer little but a powerful front five, an industrious back row containing the athletic Imanol Harinordoquy, and instinctively talented backs who define how to successfully exploit opportunities from turnover ball and run effectively in confined spaces.

Therefore, it will be full trumpets for England at Twickenham next weekend, not for reasons of innate favouritism; rather that, thus far, England are the better team, marginally.

Although the French scrum is powerful, it did not repeat its demolition of the Scottish pack when faced with an only average Irish scrum. The English tight five can ensure parity in this phase of the game, provided they concentrate.

If France select Sébastien Chabal to add yet more muscle, the French line-out options are thereby lessened and in this crucial area England have been close to fault-free. This could see Martin Johnson's team gain a significant edge and would go a long way to deciding the match.

Although James Haskell cannot be faulted for his performances in the absence of Lewis Moody, the captain's reintroduction would be wise because a match-up of brute force is not in England's interests, given the way they are playing. Support for strike runners and getting to the resultant breakdowns first is more important than a straight bashing contest. Above all, the English have to match the number of players France commit to the breakdowns and get their forwards to arrive earlier; fractionally so will do.

Thereafter, they must drop any ball-carrier that sets to base a driving maul and make the French forwards carry the ball singularly into tackles, where they are vulnerable to turnovers and penalties for not releasing.

While teams like the French are renowned for tight driving play, the mistaken assumption is that they are not themselves susceptible to this tactic. France are as vulnerable to driving mauls as any other team and this tactic keeps their back row in or close to the action. The increased space out wide can then be used more profitably and when England do move the ball, they have to ensure the tackle area is outside the outside shoulder of French forwards on the fringe. This will test the mobility of the French front five which, although able to run and handle with aplomb going forward, is less than happy to cover ground in defence, as the Irish showed in Dublin in their last game.

Common wisdom is that the well-known French backs are, man for man, better than the English, but if you look closely at what they have achieved in this tournament you see a different picture. True, they ruthlessly exploited three turnovers handed to them by the Scots, but against the Irish, France repeatedly allowed themselves to be pulled out of shape defensively. Had Ireland's wingers taken a short or wide line off the looping runner, rather than running an ineffectual middle channel, they would have broken the line continually.

Players who have so successfully represented their clubs in the Heineken Cup and the international team in many tournaments have not been able to create much of note from first-phase ball nor in broken play, when not given turnover ball. The French backs made only one genuine break against Ireland, and whatever limitations mark England's centre pairing of Mike Tindall and Shontayne Hape, defensive frailty is not one of them. Aurélien Rougerie, Damien Traille and Yannick Jauzion are famous names, not playing famously, and even the French, if they are candid, cannot claim they have matched the performances of Ben Foden, Chris Ashton and Mark Cueto.

As a final observation, the shoot-out between the championship's best half-back pairings, Ben Youngs and Toby Flood for England and Morgan Parra and François Trinh-Duc for France, should be worth the £85 ticket price alone.

44

England *v.* France: After some displeasure, I will hail Steve Thompson for equalling my record

February 2011

Position	Player	No. Caps	Record held since
Prop	Jason Leonard	114	2004
Hooker	Brian Moore	64	1995
Second Row	Martin Johnson	84	2003
Flanker	Lawrence Dallaglio	85	200/
Scrum-half	Matt Dawson	77	2006
Fly-half	Jonny Wilkinson	82	Ongoing
Centre	Will Carling	72	1997
Wing	Rory Underwood	85	1996

As you can see from the above table, the records for the most appearances in a position for the England rugby team are held individually. That will change this coming Saturday when England meets France at Twickenham: the longest standing record will almost certainly be held jointly. It has stood for sixteen years. Why do I know this, other than by being an incredible bore when it comes to statistics? I know because it is my record, and I will no longer be able to claim to be the most capped hooker in English rugby history.

When I was at school and watched England play, I never thought I would get one cap. Any suggestion that I would one day hold a record number of caps would have been dismissed as quickly as an invitation to take Latin O level.

When a player embarks on an international career, the last thought is to achieve this sort of milestone. Indeed, the only aim is to ensure that you do not become an OCW (one-cap wonder). However, at least in my case, when you notch up a good number of caps your thoughts do drift to this point and to the player who holds the record. When you get near to the magic figure, it becomes a definite target.

In my case, the previous holder was John Pullin at 42 caps. Peter Wheeler won one less and he was more of a contemporary of mine, so I still went back and dug out old footage of Pullin and looked him up in the reference books.

What sort of a man did I replace and why did this matter? It matters because, as with Pullin, replacing a legend makes you look at yourself. Do you deserve to be in this rarefied company? Will people ever regard you in the same way? Can you stand tall, proud of your achievement?

Pullin achieved extraordinary deeds. In 1971, he was in Carwyn James's great Lions team who defeated New Zealand and he captained England to victories over South Africa, Australia and New Zealand. In 1973, his England team played in Dublin after the Welsh and Scots had refused because of the Troubles. His comment – after England had lost 18–9 – went down in rugby history: 'We're not much good but at least we turned up.'

I wish I had said that and no, I did not think I was his equal or that I would be held in equal esteem.

Why is the equalling, not the bettering, the focus of this matter? The answer is that although holding such a record outright is an accomplishment, once a player equals a record he has hit the top and 'most capped hooker' is accurate whether held singularly or jointly.

My equalling game, number 42, was against France at Twickenham in 1993. We won 16–15. Although I remember thinking about the statistic on the morning of the game, when I look back, it is another memory that dominates – it was Martin Johnson's first cap.

A quiet, gigantic edifice walked into the forwards' morning meeting, held in my hotel room. Johnson was early and, although calm, it was obvious that he was going through the mixed emotions that all first-cap players experience – a mixture of pride, doubt and expectation. Rather than play the old stager, I simply talked about what I felt when I first appeared in the white shirt. The point was to reassure him, indirectly, that it was acceptable to have elements of uncertainty about whether he would be able to play at this level and that he was not alone.

I wonder what Steve Thompson will be thinking on Saturday morning? Foremost, he must be thinking about whether manager Johnson will maintain his tactic of sending him on as a replacement towards the middle of the second half. I can reassure him; he will and with that, Thompson will hold, with me, a significant and satisfying honour.

What will I think when he runs on? Foremost will be one word (but this paper won't let me print it). Of course, I do not want to share my record. I want to take it to the grave and it will hurt when it goes. However, what is important is that Thompson will deserve his accolade. There is no disgrace in sharing and inevitably losing a record to such a servant of English rugby. A World Cup winner and a brave man, Thompson would have been forgiven for taking the insurance money and bowing out when he discovered he had potentially crippling damage to his neck. Instead, he recovered from surgery, paid back the cash and fought his way back into the England squad.

The inevitable comparisons as to which of us is/was the better player are otiose. You cannot compare eras, especially in rugby, where the game has changed markedly because of professionalism and changes in the laws. Thompson is bigger and more powerful in the scrum, but he would have had difficulty hooking in scrums refereed in my day, when often a hooker's head was a couple of inches off the ground. He is a better ball carrier at close quarters. I was faster around the field. And so you could go on and on and on.

Let us leave it with this: if, and when, Thompson takes the field on Saturday, after the briefest moments of displeasure, I will salute him. A great player.

45

A subtle touch would improve England's pack in quest for 2011 Six Nations Championship Grand Slam

February 2011

There used to be a saying in rugby: 'Don't talk, do.' To be fair to the French at Twickenham on Saturday, they laboured long to action their coach Marc Lièvremont's inflammatory pre-match talk. However, when it came to the crucial confrontations, England did the doing.

Martin Johnson's team remain on course for an improbable Grand Slam, aided by the strangest of selections, even accounting for Lièvremont's nationality. Dropping your scrum-half and No. 8 is justifiable only in extremis and when the replacement No. 8 is Sébastien Chabal, you have to consider more than his bulk.

Chabal's direct running unsettles some, but not a team willing to commit numbers to the tackle. Not only did Chabal fail to break England's first-up defence, he also marginalised Harinordoquy, a far more guileful runner, minimising the Basque's contribution.

Elsewhere, Aurélien Rougerie did the work of a flanker around the field but his efforts to fashion line-breaks went unsupported by illustrious colleagues like Vincent Clerc, Yannick Jauzion and Clément Poitrenaud. Apart from an incisive kick from François Trinh-Duc, which bounced over the shoulder of the diving Rougerie, France never looked likely to score a try.

An emphasis on power, rather than cunning, faltered from the first scrum, with the previously dominant French front row ignominiously driven back by a well-timed English drive.

Good counter-rucking sustained France to an even half-time score, but once England rectified their deficient numbers at the breakdown they gradually pulled away in the second half and won without much anxiety.

England's prospects as serious World Cup challengers underwent a thorough physical examination. Make no mistake, this mattered to the French. They flew into England in the early exchanges, where James Haskell, Tom Woods and Nick Easter proved they can probably scrap with any back row and make hard yards.

What remains uncertain is whether they can add dexterity and subtlety to their physical prowess. To become the complete back row they have to be able to link play without seeking contact and thereby keep themselves available in support of the ball.

Martin Johnson has discovered a hitherto unfamiliar robustness in Tom Palmer, the man of the match. In addition to another good line-out performance, Palmer toughed it out in the tackles and breakdowns. This game may be a turning point in his career, where he goes from journeyman to automatic choice.

When a front row has as little relative experience as England's, there is a danger of implosion once severe pressure is applied. A few bad scrums lead to capitulation, penalties and penalty tries. The England front row so far in this tournament has impressed with the way it has solved the difficulties posed without having to resort to diving to ground and praying the referee mistakenly comes to their aid.

You cannot teach this in scrummage practice. It is obtained only through players coming into direct contact with difficult opponents during live scrums and then only if the players have sufficient ability to solve the problem quickly. You can solve most problems once you sit down, analyse what went wrong and can practise the solutions, but that is no good in a game where the result depends on the issues being resolved before the final whistle.

England's half-backs were uneven and Ben Youngs needs to develop his service so that there is only an occasional bad pass, which any player can make. In the tightest games successively poor deliveries will sink his team.

The England centre partnership continues to draw criticism. However, while no fireworks have emerged from Mike Tindall and Shontayne Hape, their critics cannot point to replacement players that unequivocally show better credentials or come without similar flaws.

Of England's back three, what can be said other than 'more of the same'?

As a final note from elsewhere, the sometimes dismal standard of play at Murrayfield must have Scotland coach Andy Robinson tearing out what little hair he has left. At times, the performance of some of his players was not even of professional standard, never mind international.

46

Manu Tuilagi and Matt Stevens power their way into England's World Cup shake-up

March 2011

The way Saracens set about the Leicester forwards during their 15–14 win on Saturday was a heartening sight to fans desperately hoping for another title. Whether they will be rewarded will depend on whether their team can avoid choking at the last, something that has not been beyond them in a succession of title challenges.

What must stand in their favour is the few players they have absent for international duty, but if you are or have been a long-suffering Saracens fan, you could be forgiven for tempering your enthusiasm with a healthy amount of pessimism; after all, it is the hope that kills you.

An ethereal atmosphere gradually pervaded a sold-out Welford Road, contrasting markedly with the blood and thunder exhibited on the pitch.

At least part of the cause of this otherworldliness was the fact that for large chunks of the game the home side had no possession and visited their opponent's 22 only fleetingly. Moreover, for all the frenzied hitting of tackles and breakdowns and leaving aside a solo try from Leicester, neither side seriously threatened to get over the try line.

It is a strange yet indubitable truth of the modern game that it is possible for the ball to be in play for long periods of time, during which multiple phases of play occur, and at the same time for it to feel as though nothing is going on.

Thus it was for large periods of the second half, when Saracens put together passages of play that included one of 23 phases and yet which failed to gain more than 15 metres.

The ball swung left, right and back again, with the Leicester defence simply matching their number of defenders to Saracens attackers. For all the endeavour shown, the scoreboard was not altered and there descended an ambience that was essentially neutral; neither admiring nor admonishing.

Fortunately, there were two performances beyond the ordinary and which may yet have a wider significance than the Aviva Premiership.

Manu Tuilagi not only fashioned a most improbable try from 45 metres, he expertly robbed Saracens of three pieces of possession at the breakdown with swift hands redolent of Richie McCaw at his best. Although he is young, Tuilagi cannot be far from consideration by England coach Martin Johnson for a place on the plane to New Zealand this autumn. Some say that he does not have the hands of a creative centre, but on this evidence, his are no worse than those of the present incumbents and he is still learning. What must also be in his favour is that week in week out he will play with the England half-backs.

To add to this promise is the welcome return of the former Bath and England prop Matt Stevens after serving a two-year suspension for drug use. The front-row landscape has changed since Stevens played, and young props such as Alex Corbisiero have proved they will challenge Stevens's return to the England set-up. There can never be an accommodation for those who believe Stevens's crime should bar his return to international level. They are entitled to their opinion, but against this, you have to ask, what happened to the principle of doing your time?

If Stevens is not to be given the chance to rehabilitate himself at the highest level, this ought to have been made a part of his sentence, not the practical effect of a theoretical ban.

That his skills remain cannot be doubted after he coped with the potent threat of Martin Castrogiovanni while playing at the unfamiliar position of loose-head. Indeed, the Italian's limitations were demonstrated when he was made to bind legally on Stevens's shirt, as opposed to the illegal binding on the arm of opponents, which gives him an unfair advantage. Stevens also carried the ball well and his availability is a welcome problem for Martin Johnson, who could add an experienced player to a World Cup squad which is beginning to look stronger by the month.

In the other significant game of the weekend, Matt Banahan, the Bath centre and wing, showed that Johnson should take the risk of breaking up his successful Six Nations team with just one change in the centre partnership.

At some point Johnson needs to see what Banahan's inclusion would give/take from the centre partnership. It is far better for this to be done as a purposeful selection than one made towards the end of a game by way of a substitution or one forced by injury. With only five games left before the World Cup the Scotland game is the only practical opportunity for this step because it is not one to take when and if England go to Dublin in search of a valuable Grand Slam.

47

Brian O'Driscoll should be man enough to accept blame for Ireland's defeat against Wales

March 2011

Determined to live up to its maverick reputation, the Six Nations Championship delivered a football-style controversy in Cardiff, an epic of the unexpected in Rome and a close call in London.

The talk after Wales beat Ireland 19–13 was balls, specifically one ball, and whether it was the right one. It was not. The Scottish assistant referee should not have allowed a ball that was different from that punted into the crowd to be thrown to Mike Phillips, who then sprinted half the field to score in the corner.

However, the post-match comments of Irish captain O'Driscoll mirrored intellectual dishonesty and refusal to own a performance that pervades and demeans football. Ireland did not lose because of that decision. They lost because they kicked ball away, did it badly and in areas like the opponents' 22; because they were ill-disciplined at the breakdown and because, in the last minute, they butchered a cast-iron try-scoring chance.

Of the incident itself, the Irish had three forwards near the line-out, one of whom was a couple of yards from Phillips. All assumed the ball was dead – we all know what assumption makes of you and me. Blaming one incident and someone else is not a mark of winning sportsmen.

Perhaps it explains why, in World Cup year, Ireland find

themselves near the bottom. Had the Italians held their nerve against the Irish a few weeks ago, O'Driscoll's men would have been scrapping to avoid the wooden spoon. Given the talent in the Irish squad, this should cause consternation and introspection, if Ireland are not to repeat their dismal 2007 World Cup campaign.

The French being French did their blaming in a different and idiosyncratic manner. Coach Marc Lièvremont refused to take the easy way out and blame the referee. He lay the blame where it at least partially lay.

I would love Sir Alex Ferguson or Arsène Wenger to come out with the following words from Lièvremont: 'This match was an hallucination. I do not want to clear myself from the blame but they [the players] invented things on the pitch. There is a certain form of cowardice – when I speak with them, nothing happens, as usual, I feel like I'm responsible for this but the players are lacking courage. Some of the players maybe wore the France jersey for the last time.'

This unwise, but partially true, assessment of France's problems, have probably removed any vestige of French hope for the World Cup unless he or half his squad are changed.

There was nothing contrived about this Italian win, even accounting for a measure of 'surrenderitus' from the French. Using the ball in hand and multiple phases, including passing out of the tackle, were a measure of the progress made by the Italians under Nick Mallett. It also was a testament to the courage of the Italian kicker, Marco Bergamasco.

It is easiest to coach set drills, which is why the Italians have been a good set-piece team. What they have added is the general rugby awareness that comes from immersion into the game at an early age. Had the Italians coped better with the pressure against the Irish, they would have been mid to upper table.

England are still on for the Grand Slam and their laboured win against Scotland contained elements of the luck that all Grand Slam sides need. They were the recipients of having a

man advantage while Scottish flanker John Barclay was sent to
the sin bin at the start of the second half. While their scrummage
and line-out were ascendant, they have to learn the lesson of the
breakdown quickly and before it costs them a game.

Tom Croft's late try was important as it stretched England's
lead beyond one converted score and Croft did not display any
effects of his recent injury. Whatever you say though, this was
another confidence-building win and nobody will care about its
nature should they complete the job in Dublin next weekend.

48

England need not fear any team in one-off fixture

March 2011

Martin Johnson is a cautious man. This does not mean he is incapable of bold decisions; he does not lack courage. Rather, it means any choice labelled thus will be a calculated risk, not a flight of fancy. Throughout his tenure as England manager he has ignored the siren voices that insisted he jettison the old and install a raft of young players *en bloc*. Instead, his has been a steady programme of introduction and, at last, he has done something that was desperately needed, was blindingly obvious, but was not achieved by his two immediate predecessors – he has brought stability to selection.

As his team prepare for a Grand Slam finale in Dublin, the opinions on the quality have again polarised. This tendency to extremity is a relatively modern phenomenon, encouraged by the plethora of media sources that jostle for attention and try to attract it by hyperbole.

There may be a few supporters who acclaim this England team as world-beaters, but not many and none with any rugby nous. There are many who are keen to run down Johnson's men, describing them as merely average or alternatively attempting to diminish their results by claiming that this Six Nations Championship has been of poor quality.

Let us dispose of the quality argument first. You have to go back to the state of the teams as they entered the tournament. Scotland had a successful autumn campaign; France, on paper, had a wealth of talent; Ireland's players had performed well in the Heineken Cup; Italy had improved, save for the lack of a settled half-back pairing; only Wales had struggled coming into the first round.

All concerned knew this would be the last Six Nations before the World Cup. As such, whatever is now claimed, the six national team managers/coaches must have been planning to select pretty much their World Cup starting 22s. They would also expect their teams to perform well, given that they are nearing the apex of long-term performance programmes.

If England's four opponents thus far have all been poor then those responsible for their preparation should be fired. The fact is that much of the play has been typical of this competition, attritional and entirely result-driven, with quality suborned to the result. It is always thus.

To assess England's progress you have to start from what was known before the first kick-off, not from what is now apparent. Prior to the Wales game they lost their captain, Lewis Moody, two second rows, Courtney Lawes and Dave Attwood, and back-row forward Tom Croft. There were questions about whether the inexperienced replacements would cope with the pressure of playing at the Millennium Stadium. They coped and did not look like losing once they grabbed a ten-point lead in the first quarter.

England's 59–13 thrashing of Italy, though assisted by the Italians' ill-advised decision to play expansively from bad ball, nevertheless was a very good performance. Critics who dismissed Italy as a substandard side have to explain their other results – narrow losses to Ireland and Wales and a well-deserved win against France.

The win against France at Twickenham was a thorough physical examination, from a team chosen to pound England up front and seeking to maximise a perceived advantage in the scrum.

After initial problems caused by insufficient numbers being committed at the breakdown, England absorbed the pressure, emerged fresher, and closed out the game.

In each game a different problem has arisen and England have solved it, a trait of experienced sides, which they are not.

Some pundits stated that for England to have any pretensions to greatness, they had to trounce Scotland, but that was nonsense. Scotland were always going to rise to the English challenge and their performance was described by their former No. 8, John Beattie, as the finest he had seen at Twickenham. In the light of that, a win when not playing at the top of their game was again something that you expect of established teams.

If you want an accurate and insightful summary of how hard it is to achieve a Grand Slam, you should read the interview with Ireland's fly-half Ronan O'Gara that appeared in this paper yesterday.

'If you cut the hype and look at it objectively, England still have plenty to do. They have an away fixture – never easy in the championship – against opponents with a very handy record against them in recent years, six wins in the last seven matches. And England have only won once here this century. On the plus side they have momentum and confidence and a massive target.

'I always find Six Nations rugby incredibly tiring and intense – even if you are winning well you can be running on empty at the end. The improvement of Italy has made it even more of an achievement, with that extra match against hugely physical and draining opponents.'

There you have a handy précis of the difficult task facing England. If they do win in Dublin, their Grand Slam will be as much an achievement as the recent ones by Wales and Ireland, achieved with a relatively green team.

If you had the misfortune of sitting through the dross that was England's autumn campaign in 2009 you would not, in your wildest fantasies, have predicted they would be in this position.

The improvements are due to a bit of luck, but credit must go to Johnson and his coaches for guiding this young side. They are far from complete, but they have no reason to fear any team in a one-off fixture.

Those who say the Tri-Nations teams will not lose sleep at the thought of facing England seem to have forgotten that England have already beaten Australia. Further, whatever fans may say, you can be sure that the players and management of the Tri-Nations teams will not think likewise.

49

England defeat to Ireland in Six Nations Championship was a painful but necessary lesson

March 2011

Had you asked Martin Johnson and his England team before the start of the Six Nations if winning it without a Grand Slam would represent adequate progress from the autumn, they would undoubtedly have said yes.

That achievement will not console anyone involved in the England set-up, such was the nature of their loss in Dublin. The 24–8 Irish victory looks on paper to have been comfortable, but it was more than that. Had the Irish shown a little more precision, the scoreboard would have accurately reflected their dominance.

The match had elements that added to its significance – the state of the Irish economy, frustration at their previous performances and a potential English Grand Slam, which combined to spark a display of sustained Irish belligerence – it even contained two good old-fashioned foot-rushes from green-shirted forwards.

England knew, or should have known, that they had problems at the breakdown, given their first half against the French and the first 65 minutes of the Scotland game. Whether they appreciated the size of that problem before they ran on to the pitch in Dublin only they know. What is certain, and disappointing given the said forewarnings, is that they failed badly in this area and were beaten to the punch in almost every contact situation.

The balance between committing sufficient men to win quick ball and keeping enough of them to then carry it depends on your opponents' mood and the conditions. A Gordian problem, its knot can be cut if a side have powerful and experienced players from back to front. When, as with England, you lack experience and have a limited number of runners the problem is more difficult and can be insurmountable. It was on Saturday.

Several turnovers forced by good Irish counter-rucking and mauling and unforced errors halted any momentum England threatened. To add insult, the Irish often made huge territorial gains from England's mistakes. The pressure of the occasion and from their opponents caused uncharacteristic English ill-discipline. They gave up nine points early on from stupid penalties and added the brainless sin-binning of Ben Youngs for good measure.

This defeat will be a painful, possibly necessary lesson in the unforgiving nature of Test rugby for those lacking experience in the England camp, players and management.

Though James Haskell was one of England's best forwards in the tournament, a specialist openside is needed against quality back rows.

England's midfield is defensively sound but no more and Shontayne Hape has made no discernible impression in five games.

While you cannot fault the physical commitment of England's pack, the Irish game apart, there are technical aspects of their play that need to be addressed. Concentration at every set-piece is essential, particularly at scrums from which they intend to launch set moves.

Further, they have to learn how to set up properly and execute a driving maul, a skill at which England were once so successful the rest of the rugby world tried to change the laws to stop them. That weapon remains the only ploy that keeps opposition forwards honest and, if done correctly, produces tries and penalties as it is difficult to stop.

Leicester, during the tenure of Messrs Johnson, Wells and Rowntree, used to be masters of that art and surely between them they can teach their charges how to do it. The manner of England's loss does not invalidate claims that in a one-off game they can compete against any team in the world, but it does show that is the only situation in which they can pose a challenge at present.

Irish supporters' euphoria should be qualified with this question: why did it take a backs-to-the-wall situation against the English to produce this kind of performance, welcome though it was? That leads to a subsidiary question. At the World Cup, can Declan Kidney and his squad eradicate the ill-discipline and inertia that stalled their Six Nations challenge?

If Ireland can avoid self-inflicted wounds during their pool games, they might do themselves justice in the knockout stages, which more closely resemble the context of this win against England. The thorny issue for Kidney is whether the inconsistent performances of vital older players such as Paul O'Connell and Donncha O'Callaghan are caused by form or age. If the former, the variations can be minimised; if the latter, there is little that can be done. During a long tournament there is certain to be at least one game during which the body will not respond, however hard it is prompted by head and heart.

50

Manchester United manager Sir Alex Ferguson typical of a game that fails to respect officials

March 2011

The pulsating Premier League game at Stamford Bridge on Tuesday showed much of the best and worst of football.

The speed and control exhibited by Manchester United in the first half, especially by Patrice Evra and Paul Scholes, was sumptuous. It was English and United's football at its best. Chelsea's second-half comeback demonstrated character of the strongest kind and whatever is going on at their Cobham training ground, it did not affect their will to eventually take three points from the title favourites.

Having paid due accord to the combatants' athleticism and the rich entertainment, other matters must be addressed because they testify to the mess that football has allowed itself to slide into and which, at times, threatens to obscure all else. Further, the bad example set by those concerned appears not to register with them and there appears to be little will to recognise that and do something about it.

Discussion of David Luiz, Chelsea's recently signed Brazilian defender, concerned only whether he ought to have preceded Nemanja Vidic in taking an early bath for two bookable offences. That obscured Luiz's brilliantly taken volley that levelled the scores and showed the skill of a striker.

United's manager, once again, blamed the referee for his side's 2–1 defeat, claiming the decision not to penalise Luiz changed the whole game. Sir Alex Ferguson should have blamed his wingers and strikers for not scoring more than once from the six times United got behind the left side of the Chelsea defence in the first half. He should have blamed the poor defending that allowed Branislav Ivanovic to get in front of two defenders to head the ball on to an unmarked Luiz, whose volley rifled past an ineffectual challenge from Evra.

Does Ferguson not see the irony in his complaints over referee Martin Atkinson's decision not to book Luiz for a second time? Ferguson said, 'He does Rooney clear as day, [the referee is] six yards from it, he doesn't do anything.' Did he not, for a second, see the inconsistency in having the previous week said of Rooney elbowing James McCarthy, 'I have had a chance to see it. There is nothing in it.'

In a similar vein, Ferguson's assistant, Mike Phelan, must have been aware that making any comment at all would conflict with his words over the Rooney elbowing, of which he said, 'The referee saw what he saw and he kept the game rolling. We can't dispute a referee's decision. He is out there on the field to take charge of the situation.'

More insidious is the implication behind Ferguson's overall comments about Atkinson. The manager followed his claim that he 'feared the worst' when Atkinson was chosen to referee the match by adding, 'You want a fair referee – or a strong referee, anyway – and we didn't get that.'

That clearly implies that Atkinson is partial, whether through bias or weakness of character. That is probably the most serious accusation that can be levelled at an official. It goes beyond the accusation Ferguson made that Alan Wiley was physically unfit to referee Premier League games. Regardless of whether Atkinson was right not to give Luiz a second yellow card, that Ferguson will be allowed to publicly doubt that Atkinson is a fair referee will eat further into the Football Association's Respect campaign, for it shows no respect at all.

Phelan's comments after the Chelsea loss also show that his respect for officials and their right to make independent decisions, and their inevitable mistakes, exists only to the extent that it benefits his team. Such partial respect is no respect.

Two BBC radio commentators said that the Chelsea game was the fourth in a row they had covered recently that contained serious errors by referees. They may be right. However, when they went on to say that 'something surely must be done' they gave no firm proposals. Rather than suggest a remedy, they did little more than gripe. What do they want? Retrospective citing, video technology, what?

Unfortunately, football, from managers to players, from fans to commentators, refuses to see the inherent impossibility of creating and maintaining respect when they allow unbridled criticism of officials. Whether or not officials make mistakes – and they make far fewer than players or managers – once you allow everyone else to shift blame to them without sanction, you will have this response whenever a team loses.

Inevitably, the FA will come under renewed, though unspecific, pressure to 'do something'. Well, it should approach the Premier League and the Football League chief executives, who have two of three main board directorships of Professional Game Match Officials Ltd, the body that aims to maintain high standards of officiating, and publicly ask what action they will take against managers that publicly accuse referees of partiality. They should ask the same of the League Managers Association. When those individuals make plain what action they will recommend, the FA will be in a position to go forward, because it will have the assurance that these bodies really do want a change in the behaviour of those people at the top of the game who set the examples for the rest of football.

Until then, anything the FA does is undermined by the refusal of the professional game to take any meaningful steps to discipline their own. You could argue that this blame-shifting hypocrisy is no more than a reflection of the way society in general is heading. But that is no excuse and it all comes down to this point, yet again: if you will not look at yourself and reform, stop whingeing.

Self-interested parties prevent English football's big issues being tackled

March 2011

The Department for Culture, Media and Sport select committee is in the middle of a string of meetings and hearings, acquiring evidence from disparate football groups for its inquiry into the governance of professional football.

There is no conclusive agreement between the committee members or various interest groups involved as to why the private interests of football are a parliamentary matter and why government feels impelled to interfere, when it does not involve itself in other areas of business, ones involving infinitely larger amounts of money and which are far more important.

The prospects of anything tangible emerging from the committee's deliberations are poor at best. We have been here before. The report of Lord Burns was prepared for the Football Association as long ago as 2005 and is largely unimplemented.

Unless the committee is prepared to legislate, which involves already precious parliamentary time, there is nothing to stop the Football Association's conflicting interest groups treating any findings similarly. What has been interesting is the apparently naked bid for power made by certain specific interest groups, under the cloak of purported better governance.

In its written submission to the select committee, the League Managers Association made the following bold averment: 'The

LMA is firmly of the opinion that the current system is not fit for purpose and unable to provide the leadership that is necessary if English football is to regain its place at the top of the world game. There is an overwhelming need for increased accountability, transparency and communication within football and to make this happen, fundamental changes will be required.'

One of its solutions to these problems is for the LMA to have 'a role' in the decision-making process, i.e. a seat on the FA Board. This submission follows the LMA's demand for a seat on the board of the Professional Game Match Officials Limited, which oversees professional referees.

Let us get this right – the LMA is a union and, naturally, has the interests of its members as its primary focus. A cursory glance at its pronouncements on recent controversies shows its myopic support of its members.

Take chief executive Richard Bevan's recent defence of Sir Alex Ferguson, over the Scot's allegation of partiality against referee Martin Atkinson, when he said, 'If you're going to interview managers after a game when so much is riding on these games, particularly a game of such high profile, then unfortunately you will get emotions going over.'

Bevan clearly has no regard for any wider footballing interest.

If you examine the paucity of the LMA's contribution to solving the acute problem of referee abuse and the FA's Respect campaign in general, you have to ask, what will the LMA bring to football governance? If you go to the LMA website, you will not see many items covering football's general wellbeing.

The Professional Footballers' Association also wants to be at the party. The written submission of its chief executive, Gordon Taylor, to the committee stated: 'There is also a problem with the overall control and leadership at the top of football in this country.' Also that 'there is a need for strong leadership within the governing body and also a modernisation of the committees that make up the governing body.' Unsurprisingly, part of this modernisation should involve, in Taylor's view, the PFA being involved at the top decision-making table.

There are, frankly, too many comments to list which show the lengths to which Taylor will go to excuse the errant behaviour of his members and to ensure that they are treated favourably in relation to other sportsmen. One disgraceful example of this was his claim that making his members subject to the World Anti-Doping Agency drug testing code would involve the violation of a player's privacy at home.

Given Taylor's reluctance to condemn consistently and publicly his members' weekly demonstrations of a lack of respect for officials and even fellow professionals, you have to question whether he would be prepared to support any initiative that threatened the interests of his members.

In fact, if you look at many of the major issues in football – debt, governance, respect, technology, refereeing – you see relatively few definitive and constructive propositions from either the LMA or the PFA. Those that are apparent are recent and you cannot help feeling that the weighty matters being considered by Parliament are not ones that, hitherto, have exercised these pressure groups.

It is wryly amusing that both the LMA and PFA submissions to the select committee highlight the conflicts of interest that hamper the FA's governance of football, when their proposals will merely add to such conflicts. Before the select committee considers allowing these two bodies any vote about the future running of English football, which includes the majority, the millions that do not play professionally, it should ask for clear and sustained examples of both bodies acting altruistically.

The FA already suffers from the fact that its main board comprises equal numbers from the professional and amateur game. Any action that runs counter to the interests of either party, whether in the best interests of football as a whole or not, is bound to fail. Adding more power to the professional side of the game will marginalise the position of those who represent the majority yet further.

It is tempting to equate English football with the professional game, and the Premier League in particular, but that is not correct. Perhaps the only honest way to govern football is to divide professional and amateur games, but that is not going to get Fifa support.

The only way, like it or not, for football to progress in its widest sense, is for there to be more independent FA board members. Then again, we know what is said of, and what happens to, anyone who cannot show his medals.

52

PFA chief executive Gordon Taylor's argument for inclusion on FA main board just does not wash

March 2011

It seems that this column's comments on the suitability, or otherwise, of the Professional Footballers' Association and League Managers Association to sit on the main board of the Football Association has rattled a few cages.

In an extensive interview with my colleague on Tuesday, Gordon Taylor, chief executive of the PFA, went to great lengths to address points arising out of the above article. However, if he thinks his comments provide an irrefutable case for PFA inclusion, he badly misleads himself.

Taylor was at pains to list examples of charitable work done by the PFA and its members and all of that is welcome and was not criticised. Tens of thousands of less well-off people do likewise without claiming the largesse entitles them to anything and they do not demand credit for what they do.

While Taylor cited what must be an extreme case of a player being drug tested sixteen times last year, the fact remains that football, our national game, with the support of the PFA, is the only UK sport not to adopt the full World Anti-Doping Agency's rules. There is no legitimate reason for this and it is a disgrace. Why are Taylor's members more special than other UK athletes, many of whom are conspicuously more successful internationally?

Stressing the less-than-dignified process Taylor said, 'It's not exactly brilliant having to urinate with a stranger next to you but players put up with it.' Yes, it's drug-testing and every other athlete does similar, but without someone whingeing about it on their behalf.

Taylor says that 'It ill behoves me to spend all my time publicly condemning players,' which may be right but the occasional firm denouncement, especially in excessive cases, must also be right. It is no good reserving stronger private comment in highly public cases. One sign of a responsible body is that it is able and willing to unequivocally criticise that which is plainly wrong.

Referring to the Ashley Cole shooting incident, Taylor said, 'It doesn't help when you see what Ashley did having an airgun,' concluding his forthright admonishment by adding 'Excuse me! Accidents happen.' That told him then.

What was interesting about the approach of Taylor and the PFA to ill discipline was that they say they want tougher sanctions but their recommendations rely on other people forcing their members to behave. They do not wish to take the simple step of admonishing their own.

The recommendation that there be a five-yard exclusion zone around a referee that only the captain can enter would not be necessary if his members did not surround and bully officials regularly. Instead of going through the tortuous route of Fifa legislation, why not send each player a PFA code, the adherence to which is part of its membership requirements?

Above all, one point was not rebutted by anything said by Taylor and, irrespective of the points made above, it is the conclusive point against the PFA sitting at the main decision-making table of the FA. They will not sit as a body that has an unfettered discretion to vote in the best interests of English football as a whole. When an initiative is proposed that runs counter to the PFA mandate they will not, indeed probably cannot, vote against their members' interests.

If the capable individuals listed by Taylor, including the likes of Paul Elliott and Brendon Batson, have so much to offer the FA, they can only do so if they are independent of a union pressure group.

53

A victory for common sense – Rain Tax follow-up

March 2011

The following excerpts should bring cheer to the thousands of readers who signed *Telegraph Sport*'s online petition against the Rain Tax.

Penrith Rugby Union Football Club found out this week that their three-year battle against United Utilities over swingeing increases in surface water bills has finally paid off.

Instead of a potential £11,000 annual bill, United Utilities this week announced concessionary rates for 'Community Groups' whereby Penrith Rugby Club would be put into the lowest charge band of just £100.

In 2008, United Utilities introduced a move from rateable value to surface area in calculating the charge for removing rainwater from non-domestic properties. In Penrith Rugby Club's case, this meant an increase from £671 per year to almost £11,000, a 15-fold increase!

In the final weeks before last year's General Election, legislation was passed under the Flood and Water Management Act 2010 which allowed water companies to offer concessionary schemes for community groups, such as churches, scout groups and sports clubs.

The club's honorary treasurer, Chris Lilley, was delighted

with the news: 'This is significantly better than we dared hope for. A reduction would have been very welcome but a saving of £600 per year will help us to continue to promote community sport in the town, especially amongst our junior teams, which are the life blood of our club.'

Though slow and difficult, democracy worked here and, though coerced into the reduction, United Utilities deserves credit for its generous classification of sports clubs which now allows clubs to get on with serving their communities.

Clock is ticking on a wonderful Games

March 2011

When Omega unveiled their clock to mark 500 days to the 2012 London Olympics in Trafalgar Square, what was once abstract suddenly became much more tangible.

The excitement generated in the crowd was merely a taste of what will happen when the Games are imminent.

The sceptical will be converted, and although there will be some who remain determined not to join in this once in a lifetime event, it is safe to predict that Olympic fever will grip Britain.

Now that applications for tickets are open, let us hope those who said London could pay for the Games are not applying for tickets, because that would be hypocritical, wouldn't it?

India *v.* Pakistan match demonstrated the unique pressure of a semi-final

March 2011

In the immediate aftermath of the cricket spot-fixing scandal following the fourth Test at Lord's in August 2010, the following words appeared in this column, 'If this taint is not removed by rapid and firm action, which unfortunately will mean Pakistan and/or its players being banned, cricket could find the public has no faith in nearly half of its Test teams; that will be a tipping point.'

The investigation into the matter was conducted quietly and privately without the all-too common leaks of evidence that mar some investigations by governing bodies. Despite denials of wrongdoing by all three players, guilty verdicts were delivered against Pakistani trio Salman Butt, Mohammad Asif and Mohammad Amir and the International Cricket Board delivered hard but fair and proportionate sanctions. Butt was banned for ten years, with five of them suspended, after being found guilty of corruption by an ICC tribunal. Asif was handed a seven-year ban, with two of them suspended, while Amir was banned for five years.

Although appeals have been made to the Court of Arbitration for Sport in Switzerland, the severity of the sentences has gone a long way to restoring the reputation of the sport. Governing bodies are often the target for criticism but praise is due here and should be given to the ICC. The situation has also been helped in its rehabilitation by the excitement at last generated by the World Cup presently taking place.

Leaving aside the impossibly drawn-out qualification stages, the knockout games have been sport at its pressurised best.

Wednesday's titanic duel between India and Pakistan attracted huge publicity, some of which went wildly over the top in claiming that battles between these two protagonists had replaced the Ashes as cricket's premier rivalry. The Ashes has more than a century of sporting enmity behind it, sharpened by Australia's colonial relationship with England.

Pakistan, as a modern state, did not exist until 1947. It is true that they have a near 60-year history of mutual dislike and suspicion with India, which too often descends into violence, all with the horrific potential for nuclear warfare. There is no question that the populations of both countries project their nationalism into any cricket match between them. However, the ranking of sporting rivalries should not depend on how much hatred exists between rival fans and what form of disorder, even violence, might ensue if their team loses a game. Whether there is a possibility of players from the losing team being assaulted by their fellow citizens has nothing to do with sport. That the risk exists at all is barbaric and criminal, not something that merely spices up a cricket match. The difficulties created by the pressure of a local derby and a semi-final are sufficient without the addition of these non-sporting factors, but for both teams were, nevertheless, unavoidable. Such pressure consistently produces unusual results, even with the most reliable teams and players, and semi-final predictions are, at best, expressions of hope.

The side beaten in a final will at least be remembered for reaching it; nobody remembers losing semi-finalists. If there is a third and fourth place play-off, neither contestant wants to be there because once the big chance has gone, third or fourth makes no difference to a player.

The first requirement is that players think only about that game and their thoughts do not stray, even for a moment, to the final. This is not too difficult for a team starting as underdogs, but it is for a team expected to win. India were made marginal favourites and had to cope with the expectation of their home fans and while home support can inspire, it can also inhibit.

Pressure was undoubtedly a factor in the strange tentativeness of India's batting, Virender Sehwag being the exception, which suggested their batsmen had adopted a conservative approach that often seizes semi-finalists. This mood dictates that the aim is not making mistakes and not taking risks, but this can quickly slide into defensiveness and negativity.

Even the world's best batsman, Sachin Tendulkar, did not look fluent, despite receiving four lives from dropped Pakistani catches. However, one of the characteristics of great players is what they do when in trouble and without Tendulkar grafting 85 runs India would not have won.

India were also helped by the unexpected implosion of Umar Gul who, earlier in the tournament, had been Pakistan's best bowler. His eight overs returned no wickets for 69 runs, during which Gul visibly struggled to come to terms with the pressure of the occasion. He found, like many others in similar circumstances, that trying harder only made matters worse. Any neutral watcher could only have felt sympathy for Gul, whose torment was writ large, viewed by tens of millions, and was grotesquely fascinating.

Ultimately the more talented team did enough to win and India will almost certainly play better without the peculiar pressure of a semi-final.However, one thing they should shun is the deluge of congratulations and good wishes that will rain down between now and the first ball of Saturday's final.

Every message of support, every favourable review will be well meant but each is a potential distraction. They should also be specific about every playing aspect of the remaining game and not address the occasion and its significance.

Though Pakistan did not get close to winning they must be given credit for reaching the semi-final stage given the turmoil of recent times. In addition to the bans for Messrs Butt, Asif and Amir several players, including captain Shahid Afridi, were disciplined over various matters on their disastrous tour of Australia.

The last two years of Pakistani cricket have been a lesson in how not to prepare for this sort of competition, yet Afridi and his team accommodated the loss of significant players and other disruptions to mount a credible campaign.

56

Divided FA is disastrous for football

April 2011

Politicians must grasp the nettle over reforming national sport because the game will not act of its own volition

Richard Scudamore, the chief executive of the Premier League, gave a master class when he appeared before the Culture, Media and Sport select committee to give evidence to the inquiry into football governance. The contrast between Scudamore and Sir David Richards, the Premier League chairman, was stark. At times it was like watching a rerun of the Republicans' presidential campaign in 2008. Like John McCain with Sarah Palin, Scudamore visibly tightened each time it came to Richards' answers, waiting for the moment he would have to step in to prevent damage being done to their cause.

Scudamore would not have lost any sleep over the prospect of appearing before the committee because, as a form of interrogation, this was very much like, in the words of Denis Healey about Geoffrey Howe, being savaged by a dead sheep. Only the bluff Jim Sheridan displayed any relish for putting prickly questions to witnesses; the other members all but apologised for anything that might have been mildly uncomfortable. We must pray that, when it comes to its deliberations and recommendations, the committee is a good deal less timid or the process will have been a waste of time.

Perhaps the most startling statement from Richards (apart

from describing England's 2010 World Cup preparation as incredible) was a plaintive claim that he didn't understand how the committee reached the opinion that there was a possible conflict of interests in his role for the Premier League and the wider football interest of the FA.

When you consider the evidence given by various football people, such as Ian Watmore, Lord Triesman, Richard Bevan and Gordon Taylor, there cannot be any other conclusion than that there is a fault line a mile wide between the professional and non-professional games and there is no sign of it being filled voluntarily.

And therein lies the problem – the professional game cannot, or will not, acknowledge that it is inherently conflicted. The League Managers Association and the Professional Footballers' Association will not admit that they are constitutionally bound to act only in their members', and not football's, interests and that the two things are not the same. What is clear to anyone close to football must surely now be clear to the members of the select committee: the FA is hopelessly divided. It is no good for the very people who resist major structural changes to offer a few specific examples of co-operation, when the overall operation is now terminally sclerotic.

If the present constitutional mix is broadly satisfactory, why are we in this pitiful position? How will the addition of a couple of independent members, or even the introduction of more specific pressure groups like the LMA and PFA, change this?

It is impossible to reconcile the often incompatible goals and responsibilities of the factions that sit on the FA Board. It is similarly unfeasible to square the claims of Triesman and Watmore of obstruction and marginalisation at the FA with that of Scudamore and Richards, both of whom suggested only minor differences of opinion.

The committee is going to have to choose between the two visions and between the two bodies of testimony because it cannot back both without fudging the issue completely.

Watmore and Triesman are now disinterested parties, being no longer involved at the FA. Unless you dismiss their evidence as partial, what have they got to gain from the evidence they gave? They will not personally benefit if the changes they seek come about; can the same be said of other people who gave evidence to the committee?

The Minister for Sport, Hugh Robertson, chose to tackle this matter and now must see the hard choices to be made. Football will not make them. Indeed, because of these conflicts, it cannot make them. Does Robertson have the bottle to legislate and take the opportunity to make the necessary root and branch reform?

57

It's all in the mind as Tottenham implode in the Bernabeu

April 2011

It is impossible to be definitive about the immediate pre-game withdrawal of Aaron Lennon from the Tottenham side who faced Real Madrid on Tuesday. Straight after the game there were suggestions that Lennon's illness was psychosomatic, and that remains a possibility. However, Lennon stated yesterday that he reported feeling ill on Sunday morning, was put on antibiotics and felt worse just before the game. If Lennon is right, then either the medical staff or Harry Rednapp got it badly wrong because leaving the decision open until the last moment gave them no time to prepare for Lennon's absence.

Once the risk was taken to select Lennon, he should have been told to start and see what happened, because when he became involved in the game he may have found he could manage after all. Even if he had to come off it would have been essentially no worse for Tottenham, bar losing a substitution, and at least they would have found out whether it was all in Lennon's mind.

Pressure explains the different extremes displayed by players around big games; those who look unnaturally pumped and those whose focus appears distant. Both approaches work but have drawbacks.

Detach too far and you will not start with sufficient intensity, something that is very difficult to resolve in the maelstrom of battle.

If, like Peter Crouch, you go the other way and do not take account of the fact that you are unnaturally intense, what to you is non-malicious is clearly over the top to more balanced players and certainly the referee. When Crouch got his first yellow card someone had to recognise the challenge was atypical of him and what it said of his mental state. He could then have been made to recognise what he had done and why and the consequences of its repetition. As it was, Crouch probably thought he had been unlucky and that he was just 'getting stuck in' – hence he saw nothing wrong with the way he made his second challenge.

Pressure, it's all about pressure; and Crouch couldn't handle it.

58

Rory McIlroy's reaction to defeat was the most worrying part of his Masters meltdown

April 2011

Why is it called reality TV? The exposure of desperate fame-seekers, necessarily chosen for their propensity for the bizarre, may make what some think 'good TV', but however this recent genre of TV is classified, it is not real. The reactions of the participants in shows like *Big Brother* are automatically false because of the artificial context within which they take place.

The attraction for viewers is said to be the fascination of watching people under pressure and the various ways in which they respond. What many do not realise is that though they see responses to pressure, these are not ones that would occur in real life, only in an artificial environment akin to a prison.

There is no need for this artifice when you can see drama, pressure and human frailty played out on stages that are open to all and on which the contestants cannot hide or dissemble.

Nobody with a soul could have watched the implosion of Rory McIlroy in the final round of the Masters without some sympathy for the Northern Irishman. Every facet of his consciousness was laid out for all to see. Each shrug of his shoulders, the odd wry smile or grimace, all of it was morbidly compelling.

McIlroy drew praise from all quarters for what was described as his magnanimity in defeat and his determination to see this as only a minor setback from which he will return stronger.

There can be no doubt that his behaviour was dignified but the applause for McIlroy's post-traumatic behaviour and the implicit assertion that this is how sportsmen and women should behave comes straight from the British notion of keeping a stiff upper lip. That expectation is, in itself, unnatural and to laud it and hold it up as being proper is to misunderstand the context of sporting contests. What commentators do, when they tacitly impose these values, is take sport out of its natural setting and put it in a social setting. There are different mores in sport and the criteria by which its participants should be judged should not be those of the ordinary person.

This does not mean that abusive behaviour should be condoned but it should mean that reactions which might be deemed impolite are not automatically decried. The widespread condemnation of Tiger Woods after the Masters for being 'grumpy' was ludicrous. Where are the accepted rules for post-match reactions? Why should a disappointed player not be bad-tempered after losing? We should not demand that players suppress their natural emotions and behave with abnormal equanimity or else we will denounce them as bad sports, whatever that means.

Would you prefer to see the natural response of a sportsman, which comes from his competitive nature, or an aberrantly calm acceptance of fate?

In some ways McIlroy's calmness could be seen as worrying. Vince Lombardi, the legendary coach of the Green Bay Packers, would certainly have thought so, as his was the famous quote, 'Show me a good loser and I'll show you a loser.'

It is said that McIlroy is young, but this was said of Andy Murray, and that excuse sits uneasily with the claim made in support of young players that 'if you're good enough, you're old enough'. There is no certainty that McIlroy's near miss ensures future triumph. His talent suggests this, but the effects of such a devastating experience will run deeper than McIlroy thinks.

It is right that he can learn valuable lessons from the defeat, but it is not as straightforward as avoiding the mistakes he made in the final round. McIlroy will have to find a way to quell the dread that will inevitably appear when he remembers how badly he unravelled. We should hope that McIlroy can find the necessary mental toughness to return and win because of all the disappointments in sport, unfulfilled promise is one of the saddest.

With every contest comes a reminder that players treat success and failure in extremely varied, sometimes unpredictable and uncharacteristic ways and we should not seek to alter this. It is just one of the facets of sport that makes it so compelling. Casey Stoner's tempestuous reaction to, and his outburst against, Valentino Rossi for unseating him on the ninth lap of the MotoGP race at Estoril last week; Michael Schumacher's pit-lane stomp to confront David Coulthard in Spa in 1998; the painful saga of Fernando Torres's quest to score his first goal for Chelsea – all provide real human interest and of the type that can never be created by any reality TV format. So what if Andy Murray is cantankerous after another Grand Slam final defeat? At least that reaction has behind it a modicum of passion and is that not one of the things we admire, nay demand, that our sportsmen display?

When we do so demand, we must accept that the passion when thwarted is likely to provoke behaviour that would not do around the dinner table.

We in the sporting media must also accept some responsibility for framing this issue in the wrong context and for not understanding why you cannot legitimately inflict extraneous values on sport. We should also accept that when a sportsman refuses to assist with our need for a story it is not automatically bad behaviour.

Co-operating and answering questions posed by the media has now developed into what many claim to be part of sport. It is not, it is part of broadcasting and entertainment; sport is about what goes on between the start and finish of the contest.

It would assist the media's case if interviewers displayed the civility demanded of proposed interviewees. They would also get more if they asked proper questions and they should be chided for giving their own opinion and holding out the microphone, without asking a question at all.

59

Sky has raised standards in sports coverage – but at a price for the viewer

April 2011

No one can deny Sky TV's influence on sport and sports coverage over the past 20 years. It has raised the expectations of viewers and forced competitors to innovate and alter their broadcasts to remain relevant.

It is not just about money, although that allows more technology and cameras. It is a willingness to push boundaries and to overcome the conservatism of some sports rights holders. Even those of us who work for the BBC acknowledge that Sky can rarely be faulted over what appears on screen, and its commentators and pundits are uniformly good.

However, Sky is at least partially responsible for developments in some sports that are questionable at best and harmful at worst.

Football is the sport on which Sky Sport was built and by which it is still underpinned; it is also the sport most altered by Sky's presence. The huge sums obtained by the Premier League for its live TV rights has enabled its chief executive, Richard Scudamore, to export the Premier League to the point where its popularity exceeds that of any other top division in the world.

Sky's money has rebuilt clubs' grounds, but much more has gone straight into the pockets of players. These preternatural rewards have led to a separation between players and fans that is unlikely to be reversed and which is indirectly responsible for the poor attitude of some players, on and off the pitch.

Premier League live TV rights money is passed down to lower leagues and assists the running of the amateur game through the FA, but the disparity between the top and all else has widened enormously. The gulf in turnover between clubs in the Premier League and the lower divisions means that any side trying to get to, and stay at, the top table has to borrow hugely or find a wealthy benefactor. This situation is more acute in the top third of the Premier League where most clubs are financed by billionaires, national states or wealthy foreign investors.

It cannot seriously be denied that the professional game, and the Premier League in particular, dictates to the rest of English football. However, Sky's money has so disproportionately enriched the professional minority that although the professional and non-professional games have equal votes on the FA's main board, the reality is different and will remain so without government intervention.

You may say that as Sky has no control over the administration of football, it is innocent. Strictly speaking that is true, but the effects flow from Sky's actions and they have to shoulder some responsibility, however indirectly. You cannot claim to have saved football and deny the inconvenient consequences.

Minority sports' problems are different, but no less important. Sky's money increases the amount that can be spent on developing the sport, but the number of viewers decreases dramatically. Minority sports need more money and exposure to grow but they cannot have both.

Rugby demonstrates this point fully. When Sky won exclusive rights to show England's Five, now Six Nations Championship matches, the viewing figures were a fraction of the BBC numbers. The Home Unions Committee – France and Italy have separate deals – were alarmed by the decrease in exposure. They were also aware of numerous complaints about rugby not being free-to-air and the contract returned to the BBC. The viewers on Sky for the last round of games in the Heineken Cup, a top quality European club tournament, varied between 100,000 and 185,000. This year's England *v.* France game had a peak audience of over 9 million on the BBC.

Cricket also faces this dilemma. Sky's money has led to better salaries for professional cricketers and money for the amateur game. Without it, cricket would struggle to maintain its present development initiatives, but far fewer people see cricket and as such its public profile has been lost.

Another unintended side effect is that Sky's money has allowed the ECB to duck the decision about how many counties should play professionally. Privately, practically everyone thinks the present number should be halved, allowing the distilled talent to compete more intensively.

It is no secret that News Corp, Sky's majority shareholder, is vehemently against the protected list of sporting events in the UK which mandates that certain events must be shown on terrestrial television, free to air. The retention of the list means that events that go beyond sport and have a wider social relevance can be seen by everybody.

This would not be the case if Sky owned the rights because there are millions of people who cannot afford Sky. The basic sports package for the 15 million people still to get Sky is £39.75 per month, or £477 annually, from which Sky's profit margin is about £17 per month. In contrast, the amount spent on sport, including sports rights and production, out of each annual licence fee of £145.50, is around £15. Whatever your view of terrestrial and satellite sports coverage, you cannot honestly ignore the fact that the latter is far more expensive.

Furthermore, if Sky succeeds in its quest to deregulate sports broadcasting it will effectively become a monopoly broadcaster because of its financial position. The BBC cannot increase its bidding power, and the failure of ITV Digital and Setanta shows that any other broadcaster would need billions of pounds to challenge Sky. Even so, it would be naive in the extreme to believe that Sky would not increase the cost of sports viewing further.

Ultimately, British viewers can have whatever sports broadcasting they want, but if it turns out to be much more expensive they cannot say they were not warned. Furthermore, there will be no way back.

60

Wales need Gavin Henson and Andy Powell – but they should grow up or go away

April 2011

After one England *v.* Scotland game at Twickenham I went out to the Alma in Wandsworth with some of my England colleagues and a Scottish friend. As we drank quietly, a Scot walked past our group on his way to the bar and out of the corner of his mouth said, 'Moore, you're a ****.' He did the same on his return.

I thought about it, looked at him and then turned away. My Scottish mate, a former Glaswegian doorman, wanted to rip his head off. I tried to calm him down by pointing out that the guy had nothing to lose whereas we, I, would make the papers for getting into a pub brawl. We left the pub because that was the only way to avoid trouble.

I was also aware that a few years earlier I had got into serious trouble in a Nottingham pub when, after the third time a drunk had had a go at me, I, wrongly, punched him and ended up with a conviction for assault. I know how trouble that you do not start can happen; I also know the starkly different outcomes that flow from how it is handled.

It may sound hypocritical in the light of this, and against the old-school background of rugby drinking, to address any words to Messrs Henson and Powell, now called by the Welsh Rugby

Union to account for their latest misdemeanours. It is not, because there are important distinctions.

We are not talking about then, we are talking about now and, as many are keen to remind us, rugby has moved on. It was played by us as a pastime; a serious one to be sure, but nevertheless, it was not our job. We didn't accept large sums of cash for being professional athletes. Every bystander did not then have the means to capture any incident on camera or, which is even more incriminating, on video. There was no 24-hour news and the internet, YouTube, Twitter and Facebook did not exist; it was not possible for a story to become national, possibly global, within a few hours.

Standards are different today, but then so are the rewards. When you are paid approximately half the national average annual wage for one international, we can demand different standards and if players don't like it, they don't have to play.

I have not, hitherto, been in the anti-Henson camp. The fripperies like the fake tan, shaved legs and hair gel are tolerable, provided Henson backs it up where it matters – on the field. That caveat has a further stipulation: he does it right on the training field and at his club in general, because these areas affect what happens during games.

Rugby has now got to the point with Henson where it is entitled to ask – why should we bother with you any more, when there are hundreds of youngsters who will crawl over broken glass to play for us and accept all that it entails? What, in your flawed and largely failed rugby career, makes it worth taking another chance, possibly upsetting other players, in order for you to be given another lifeline?

The answer to these questions is one word: talent. Henson has the answer, but has rarely shown it and talent, with each tick of time, fades, less likely to reappear. At 29, he is no longer young, and backs do not get quicker with age. They can get better with experience, but then, not understanding their relative merits, Henson absented himself from rugby to chase celebrity for nearly two seasons. He started only one game this season for Saracens before moving to Toulon.

A contract with the best-paying club in Europe and another, undeserved, chance to resurrect his international career should have found Henson on his knees to the patron saint of final chances. Instead it found him allegedly worse for wear, and accused of abusing his captain Joe Van Niekerk and Saint Jonny.

Instead of denigrating Wilkinson, Henson should have been taking lessons in making the most of what God grants. With less natural talent, Wilkinson has achieved far more and been the best he could have been. Though Henson can include Wales and the British and Irish Lions on his CV, he was not convincing for more than a fleeting tackle and kick in either jersey, though he flattered more often.

Henson should examine his relationship with alcohol in general, because of his reactions to it. Many of his reported incidents are drink-related and some of his actions are not normal, even accounting for alcohol.

In 2007 an ordinary train journey from London to Cardiff, not a football special with rival fans in confrontation, led to allegations of abusive behaviour. Charges of disorderly conduct were later dropped.

The Toulon incident was with his team-mates, again, not normal; and most worryingly, Henson is said not to be able to remember the incident.

Yes, I, and many other readers, I suspect, have occasionally been the worse for wear and the previous night's details have been less than clear – but we're not the ones begging for another chance.

As for Powell, you would have thought that being caught having driven a golf buggy with a traffic cone on top, in the inside lane of the M4, was sufficient notice that you are not always at your sharpest after a few sherbets. It should have been enough to understand that going into a lairy Aussie bar in London and entering into drunken banter with a crowd of QPR fans had the potential to get out of hand.

The fact is that Wales do not have enough depth of talent to have two of their better players banned, especially if it is because they cannot take their drink. It is no longer, if it ever was, just about these two individuals. Their reselection will irk other less talented players, who suspect, probably rightly, that they would not get one second chance.

It is simple – Henson and Powell should grow up or go away.

Return of Sir Clive Woodward is a gamble worth taking for the RFU

April 2011

Within rugby there are a number of camps when it comes to the question of Sir Clive Woodward. They range from the enraptured acolytes – and this includes a good number of journalists – to those who will not give him an ounce of credit, apart from acknowledging his ability to spend phenomenal amounts of other people's money.

It is an open secret that some in the Rugby Football Union have wanted Woodward to return for some time, and wanted him ahead of Martin Johnson for the role of England manager and certainly as a replacement for Rob Andrew, had the organisation of elite rugby stayed as it was.

The schism between former chief executive Francis Baron and Woodward was toxic, which is often the case when intimates fall out of love. Not until Baron departed and John Steele took over was there any chance of Woodward returning, and there are still a number of people who do not want him. With some of Woodward's detractors it is simple: they don't like him and don't think he could accept not being in total charge of the national team.

Whatever you think of Woodward, you cannot deny that his mind springs numerous ideas: inspired, bold, odd and downright daft. The key to dealing with his challenging demeanour is sorting out which is which and understanding that behind the theory and science are fervour, emotion and a well-disguised temper that occasionally bursts forth in fits of pique.

If you can put aside these infrequent flounces you will see that from this cornucopia of complementary, sometimes conflicting, characteristics, comes the extra 2 per cent of brilliance that is not found in the average person. This has been supplemented by more than a decade of experience of working around elite performance and Woodward's overview of the elite plans of numerous sports makes him the outstanding candidate by some margin.

Woodward's return would have to be managed carefully because two other people's idiosyncrasies have to be considered. Johnson is a transparently strong character and so is Andrew, in a less demonstrative manner. For it to work the three of them would have to work together and have the same objectives. Unless their roles are specific and lines of responsibility strictly demarcated, there is potential for all-out civil war, as each undermines the others.

Johnson is said to feel his position would be compromised by Woodward's return but the longer-term organisation of England's elite rugby goes beyond his tenure and, frankly, it is not for him to decide the management structure of the RFU. All three men would need to be mature about this and, if they can put aside personal insecurities, they could form a powerful alliance.

Woodward cannot be given any day-to-day control of the England team because you cannot have two chiefs, but it would be silly for Johnson not to consult Woodward and draw on his maverick perspective. The one area that has caused England to underperform for the past eight seasons is selection. Woodward was an unconventional but shrewd selector and Johnson's own appointment as captain was an eloquent demonstration of this. Johnson should seek and give due weight to Woodward's views on selection, while retaining the ultimate power to choose.

Even if this collaborative approach comes about, there is one player who it seems would irrevocably divide Woodward and Johnson – Danny Cipriani.

Woodward believes Cipriani is potentially one of England's greats and sees his periodic brushes with the media and celebrity as the product of youth which can be managed. Johnson simply does not like Cipriani or his celebrity associations.

Of the two views, Johnson's should change. He has to be a bigger person about this and accept Cipriani's inclusion as a challenge for his managerial skills, rather than as a potential source of discord.

For his part Woodward would have to accept he should not be the focus of media attention and turn away the numerous requests that would come from journalists for his views on every conceivable subject. The RFU would have to help by making clear he would not speak about things for which Johnson was responsible.

Their personal differences have to be set aside in favour of the national interest and the RFU has to talk bluntly to each individual and, if necessary, tell them to grow up.

If the whole thing is managed properly England could have a powerful triumvirate leading up to the 2015 World Cup on home soil. The prize of England reclaiming the world crown makes Woodward's return worth the gamble.

62

What price another northern hemisphere team in the rugby World Cup Final?

So what, following the Six Nations Championships, did the form of the participants tell us about their likely chances in the World Cup later this year in New Zealand? Not much.

There are a number of reasons for there being only a very limited amount of useful information that can be used predictively. Chief among these is the nature of the Championship itself. What many, especially those from the southern hemisphere, fail to appreciate is that although the Six Nations purports to be a tournament akin to a mini World Cup, it is in reality a series of one-off games which stand in isolation and which have minimal relevance to those that go before and after.

Recognise it or not, believe it or not, agree with it or not, the fact is that a fixture like England versus France – in fact, England versus any of the other participants, save perhaps Italy – is unique and is one which also alters subtly, but importantly, depending on whether it is played home or away.

While the Celtic and Gallic supporters admit this, there is a special motivation to playing and beating England and most of it stems from the historic and political relationship between each individual country and England. One point that can be made in support of this assertion is that it does not matter at what point in the Championship the game is played nor in what position the countries find themselves, although naturally if a Championship title or Grand Slam is involved for either team the tension is heightened in line with the occasion.

The pundits' view of England's prospects took a sharp dive because of the manner of their defeat by Ireland in the Grand Slam decider. The frankly lazy phrase that was most parroted was that 'nobody in Tri-Nations will worry about England'. This comment reveals that the pundits do not have very good memories. Since its inception, there have been six World Cups, and a northern hemisphere side has reached the final in five of them. As only the 1991 tournament had an all northern hemisphere semi-final, this shows that historically there is an 83 per cent chance of a northern hemisphere side beating one from the southern hemisphere and making it to the World Cup final – and 2011 will be no different.

England have appeared in half of all the finals held thus far, winning once; in the other competitions they were knocked out in the semi and quarter-finals. They have never failed to get out of their pool in a tournament.

You cannot say that at the time of writing (April 2011) England have a strong case for becoming world champions in New Zealand, but they do not go with only a theoretical chance. Unfortunately, the squad is roughly one year away from being in with a serious shout as winners.

Martin Johnson has now got decent competition in about two-thirds of the positions, and if he had another year to find the players to fill the problem positions, he could be approaching the tournament with more than what they call in boxing 'a puncher's chance'.

This vital year is, not coincidentally, the same amount of time that was wasted by the RFU prevaricating over the decision to appoint Johnson as replacement for Brian Ashton and by Johnson's unavailability before the autumn internationals in 2008. Had that decision been taken immediately post the 2007 World Cup, it is highly likely that England would be going into the 2011

World Cup as one of the favourites, rather than with an outside chance.

Statistically a World Cup-winning side has an average of over 40 caps per player in its starting XV. Its squad all have to be fit, on form and sufficiently talented, and these factors have to combine for the seven-week period over which the tournament takes place. It is no good getting it right for the three previous years; only that short period matters.

If you look at previous winning sides you see that in every position on the field they had at least two players who were genuinely capable of playing well in the international arena. The incidence of injuries and the length of the competition make squad cover essential, not a luxury.

Taking each position in turn, England at present have the following players contending for inclusion in the World Cup squad.

At full-back, Ben Foden and Delon Armitage, when he is fit and confident, are both capable, and present attacking options because of their pace. Neither is suspect under the high ball, but both need more experience.

On the wings, Chris Ashton has been a real discovery, and his support play and finishing mean he is an outstanding prospect. Mark Cueto has significant experience and although he no longer has blistering pace, he is an intelligent attacker. Dave Strettle has the class to play at the highest level and, but for injury, would probably have been an outright choice for the past two seasons. Injuries have robbed him of the chance to accumulate important game time but as a squad member he merits inclusion. Ugo Monye, if he recovers properly from injury, has international and British Lions experience but needs to show the right form for Johnson to pick him.

It is at centre that England really do have problems. Mike Tindall is vastly experienced but no longer has a turn of speed and, while very solid defensively, is not the best distributor. Shontayne Hape, for all his promise, has shown very little in any of his eleven appearances for England. Matt Banahan has converted from wing to centre but does not yet have the overall tactical appreciation to make him an automatic choice and outside this Martin Johnson has nobody who can legitimately claim a Test place.

Toby Flood's increasing authority provides an alternative to the known talents of Jonny Wilkinson, and inside them at scrum-half, Ben Youngs and Danny Care are international class but neither is sufficiently good enough to direct games in the way that Matt Dawson did for the 2003 England side. Both scrum-halves have pace and can make breaks but both need more experience.

Though Alex Corbisiero only started his international career this season, he coped well in the scrum and can carry the ball. His appearance now gives England cover for Andrew Sheridan, who is a proven Test player although he has not shown anything like the form of three years past and he needs to have a prolonged run of games free from injury to recover his form.

Although young and inexperienced, Dan Cole will be a top class tight-head, and the return of Matt Stevens, following a two-year drugs ban, means there is competition for a position that is crucial because of its importance in anchoring the scrum.

Hookers are not a problem. Dylan Hartley continues to improve and Steve Thompson is a World Cup winner. Johnson also knows that Lee Mears is available and has Test and Lions experience.

Second row should not be a problem either. From a position where two seasons ago everyone was lamenting the dearth of talent in this position, there are now five players who contend properly for inclusion: Courtney Lawes, Dave Attwood, Tom Palmer, Louis Deacon and Simon Shaw. The likelihood is that, of the five, Louis Deacon will be the unlucky player to miss out.

England's back row is a problem because it is unbalanced at present. There is no shortage of players who can fulfil utility roles but against the best back rows England will not compete with three generic back-rowers. Specialist blindside flankers Tom Croft and Tom Woods mean that the No. 6 slot is covered but it is the No. 8 and openside positions that are short of specialists and decent cover.

At present Nick Easter holds the No. 8 shirt but he needs to increase his work rate and, although he does a lot of work that goes unappreciated, he can disappear in games and is not a top-class line-out option. He does not have anyone pushing hard for his position; while James Haskell can play No. 8, Johnson has to make up his mind where he wants to play Haskell and only consider him for that position. In the Six Nations, Haskell did a good job filling in for the injured Lewis Moody at openside, and, although he was powerful and works hard, he is not a specialist openside and against Scotland and Ireland it showed.

When Moody returns he is likely to be first choice at No. 7, but his injury record means that there is at least an even chance he will miss games during the World Cup and therefore it is vital that another dedicated No. 7 is found and given sufficient game time to familiarise himself with his back-row colleagues and with the intensity and pace of international rugby. If Moody stays fit he is ferociously competitive but is still a converted openside and does not link play in the manner of most No. 7s. He has to add this facet to his destructive capabilities or else he risks being exposed by more experienced specialists.

Hendre Fourie has had a few cameo performances but this is insufficient for Johnson to make a definitive judgement about his candidacy. As a specialist openside, he should at least start in one of the three warm-up games before the start of the World Cup.

As a final point concerning England's chances, it can be seen from the positional and player analysis above that England are not too far from having a very good squad. The 2011 Six Nations uncovered three players, Tom Wood, Alex Corbisiero and Chris Ashton, who might not have figured in Johnson's World Cup starting squad but all have proved they now demand consideration.

How much better a position would England have been in had they had another series of autumn internationals, another Six Nations and a summer tour to play with? Even if just one player emerged from each set of games, see how much nearer to the ideal it could have been. On top of that, consider what an extra 15 caps would have given the rest of the squad.

As for France, not even the Delphic Oracle would willingly take on the task of predicting how they will fare in the forthcoming World Cup. They could be hyper-disciplined and shut out a team of the calibre of the All Blacks, as they did in the quarter-final of the 2007 RWC; or they may decide not to get out of bed, metaphorically, and ship over 50 points as they did last autumn against the Aussies.

The cliché that the French are unpredictable is so because it is true. Those who say that it is merely lazy stereotyping should have a chat to the former French captain Olivier Magne who, when asked to explain this contrariness, shrugged his shoulders and said, 'I don't know, I'm not a psychiatrist.' The idiosyncratic nature of French performance has to be a factor because it is capable of inspiring and, just as easily, inhibiting any challenge in New Zealand.

As if this was not enough to contend with, the French have always had their own approach to selection and even when playing well have regularly changed personnel – and not just in ones and twos. Marc Lièvremont, their coach, did nothing to reverse this trend in his early years in charge, and the only reason the bewildering number of experiments with players and combinations did not cause a revolt was because French players have long had to live with this insecurity. A total of 81 players, used in 36 matches, tells you all you need to know about the French approach to picking players.

It did look as though Lièvremont's madness had method when, last season, he started to stabilise selection and, most importantly, appeared to settle on a pair of half-backs in Trinh-Duc and Parra. However, the sheer awfulness of some of the French play during the Six Nations and the widespread reports of infighting within the French camp led to Lièvremont exploding with rage after the Italy game and issuing one of the most candid post-match comments ever recorded when he said that his team 'betrayed us, they have betrayed me and they have betrayed the French national team shirt'. And it did not stop there, as he added, 'In terms of the tactics deployed it defied belief. I did not recognise anything in their performance that we had worked on. Do you really think that I told them to play as they did against Italy? I was ashamed. I do not have the impression we asked them to walk on the moon. I do not ask for complicated things. This match was an hallucination. I do not want to clear myself from the blame but they invented things on the pitch.' He finished with this savage denouncement, 'They are lacking in courage. They are good guys but cursed with what is obviously cowardice.'

After these claims he dropped six players. Yet France soundly beat Wales the following week, which shows that, however contrary things appear with the French, you are never on safe ground making bold assertions.

The power of the French pack is undoubted, and depending on what page of the elite referees' guide to mishandling scrums a particular referee is using, they can decimate opponents. Their line-out is functional but throwing can be a problem at times. In the loose, if they feel like it, they represent a tough physical challenge and their counter-rucking has improved markedly. They have forwards who can all handle, but more importantly who know how to use narrow spaces by drawing men and attacking the inside shoulder so that their passes leave runners in space, not crowded towards the touchline. Defensively they are now as good as anybody when they concentrate and it will not be up front that France are found wanting.

Unusually, given the amount of tinkering done by Lièvremont, there is still no agreement as to what will be his first-choice back-line – in fact, there isn't much agreement about any single position. Not only has Lièvremont played players in unfamiliar positions – Rougerie in the centre being just one example – he has dropped and reintroduced a number of experienced backs.

When you look at the French domestic league and the way their teams perform in the European cups, you can see they have talent in every spot; but what should worry them is that seasoned inter-nationals like Jauzion and Traille look tired and uninspired. Médard and Clerc must be looking around and wondering which of their team-mates will make it on to the plane in September.

It is frankly scandalous that France will go to the World Cup not knowing their starting squad and not having given those play-ers the maximum opportunity to play together. Lièvremont has not been short of time and has had his head screwed on when it comes to World Cup preparation. If his players do not respond, the fault lies only partially with them, and it is clear that there is discord akin to that experienced by the French football squad in South Africa 2010.

The one caveat – and it is a big one – is that from seemingly hopeless positions we have seen France conjure up remarkable feats and it is for this reason that even though the situation looks desperate, France cannot be dismissed as likely World Cup fail-ures. Their grouping means that whether they qualify behind or in front of favourites New Zealand they will not face them again until the final. Their likely draw pits them against England and Australia, and all bets are off when it comes to an isolated game. Can they take the lot? Very unlikely. Will they scare anyone? Only every team they face.

Ireland's thrashing of England in the final round of the Six Nations left many wondering where this performance had been hiding. On paper, Ireland have a squad that is capable of reach-ing the World Cup semi-finals and, as has been repeatedly stated, when you get to the pressured stage of 'win or you are out', strange things can and do happen.

For some of their best players, this World Cup will be the last in which they can seriously expect to take part and, given their previous poor showings, there should be sufficient motivation for players like Brian O'Driscoll, Paul O'Connell and Donncha O'Callaghan to lead their younger team-mates to achieving results that match their talent.

The true story about what went wrong in 2007 in France has still to surface and will not do so until the senior players retire and write their autobiographies. Suffice to say that Ireland's terrible form can only be explained by deep dissention in their camp, and whatever happens they have to avoid this in New Zealand.

If you look closely at Ireland's potential starting XV there are question marks in key areas and how far they progress will depend on how successfully they deal with each of the possible problem areas.

Their front row is young and struggled at times against the French and Italians. They will not get any quarter from the Springboks or Kiwis, and stability in the scrum is vital because refereeing at elite level has made the scrum something of a lottery. Once a side is seen to have a couple of bad scrums, the flow of penalties will invariably go against them and the loss of the art of striking quick channel one ball means that a pressured scrum has no way of avoiding opposition pressure. Once scrums start taking place near the goal-line, any scrum that is in trouble is highly likely to concede penalty tries and have members of the front row yellow-carded to boot. There is reason to think that Ireland's front row will improve but experience is everything in the front row and you cannot create stability on the training field. Players have to experience awkward opponents and learn how to handle them.

In the second-row pairing of O'Connell and O'Callaghan Ireland can claim to have the equal of any other second row in the tournament if, and only if, both players are at the top of their game. In the Six Nations they performed only sporadically, and the difficult, but vital, question is whether this unevenness is due to age or form. If the latter, the coaches and players can work hard and try and ensure they peak at the right times. If the former, there are going to be occasions when they simply do not play that well, and if that occurred in a sudden-death game, that is something Ireland would almost certainly not be able to overcome.

Up front, the Irish have a strong back row and equally good replacement players and whatever combination is picked it will compete with the best back rows. Importantly, they have genuine openside flankers to choose from, and the balance that gives the selectors means Ireland must be looking to their back row to lead any challenge.

The scrum-half selection is settled and Ireland have the good fortune to have the very experienced Peter Stringer on the bench. It is at No. 10 that the debate still rumbles. Jonathan Sexton dispatched England with aplomb but did not perform at anything like that tempo during the other Six Nations games. Ronan O'Gara gives you a measured control of the game from his kicking but Ireland will have to play wider if they are to make a serious impression in the World Cup because O'Driscoll and D'Arcy are too good to end up chasing kicks for most of the game.

When you add the options that Ireland have in their back three, they amount to a set of backs who are the equal of anything else in the northern hemisphere, and are effective in both attack and defence.

In the end, the possible vulnerability of the front row and doubts about the second row to produce six outstanding games in a row must cast doubt on whether the Irish pack can supply sufficient and sufficiently good ball for their backs.

What must also be considered is what happens if Ireland slip off the pace in their pool games. Australia, Italy, Russia and the USA will all pose a physical challenge up front. The Russians especially must not be dismissed in this regard. Ireland are quite capable of topping this group but it is not impossible to see how they might not get out of the group if their minds are not fully on the task in hand. If they win their group they will probably face Wales in the quarter-final and should be confident of reaching at least the semi-final.

Wales will approach the World Cup confident that they have talented backs and, when all their forwards are fit, a pack that is capable of scrapping for parity with nearly anyone. Unfortunately, they have problems that cannot easily be solved and some are likely to be exposed by the nature of the tournament.

Anyone who dismisses the following as prejudice bordering on racism should pause to ask themselves whether they have better knowledge than I when they contest the claim. Wales, historically, do not tour well and their players, of all the home countries, are prone to homesickness when a tour goes beyond a few weeks.

If you ask the tourists with the recent British and Irish Lions teams, this has been so on nearly every tour. If you ask the Welsh players themselves and they are honest they will admit that it can be a problem. There is nothing unmanly about getting homesick but for the Welsh management to brush over this possible problem would be unwise because there are ways of coping with it, but only if its existence is acknowledged.

During the Six Nations their backs only sparked occasionally and, given the players they have, they gave only an average account of themselves. The debate over whether James Hook or Stephen Jones plays at No. 10 appeared to be going the way of Hook, but as Wales have only three warm-up games they have to play Hook at fly-half from the outset and for all the games to give him any chance of forming the necessary familiarity with the talented centre pairing of Jamie Roberts and Jonathan Davies.

The find of 2011 for Wales was Sam Warburton, who managed to fill the hole left by the international retirement of Martyn Williams at openside. His form and fitness gives Wales balance in the back row and it is crucial that he remains uninjured for Wales to compete at the breakdowns, especially when they face South Africa, whose back row is capable of physically dominating this phase of play if they are not challenged and matched for physical commitment.

While Wales coped relatively well with their second-choice props, the fitness of Adam Jones and Gethin Jenkins gives them a front row that will not be pressured by many opponents, and without these two players Wales will find, as they did at times in the Six Nations, that they are hanging on in the scrums and that is not a platform from which their backs can work successfully.

The recent weakness in the line-out did not feature in the Six Nations and as this is an area that can be improved by simple hard work the fortunes of their line-out is in their own hands.

Wales finished the Six Nations with an outside chance of being champions, but they finished fourth, and while they won three out of five games, they were not convincing in any of the wins, though they did reverse an eight-match losing streak.

When you look at what Wales can produce and the players they have available, if fit, it is impossible not to conclude that their recent poor results must be due to something other than lack of talent. Although this is a contentious matter with the Welsh management, the pattern of play whereby Wales continue to attack the blind side and play the same way until they reach the far touchline once produced results because of the width available to their backs when the ball finally came back the other way. This has been a recognised tactic for at least the last three seasons and yet its diminishing returns have not persuaded the Welsh management that it has become predictable and, as a result, easy to defend. If this tactic is maintained, we will see which of the two points of view is correct, but Welsh supporters had better pray that their managers have got it right because World Cup campaigns are sufficiently difficult without your style of play being an impediment.

★

Scotland's chances and their limitations have not changed much since 2007. They work hard and in Andy Robinson have a coach who has tasted World Cup glory with England in 2003. For that reason they should be properly prepared for the New Zealand odyssey, but that necessarily means they will have to take with them a long-term problem in scoring tries and capitalising on the often heroic deeds of their forwards.

Richie Gray and the Scottish back row stood out for Scotland in the Six Nations but their scrum and Ross Ford's throwing were weaknesses that cost them on every occasion they surfaced.

The question of who to play at fly-half is still outstanding – do they go with the reliable but limited Dan Parks or throw caution away and back Ruaridh Jackson, who is more creative but more erratic. Chris Patterson and Max Evans can trouble defences but they cannot do so regularly if they are not serviced properly by their centres. Although Sean Lamont came into the centre in the Six Nations and put himself about a bit, he is not the ball player to release outside backs.

Scotland have a difficult pool because Argentina and England are better sides if they play to their full potential. Scotland did well when they toured Argentina last year but the World Cup will be a different proposition. Georgia and Romania should not prove difficult but both those teams possess abrasive packs, and if Scotland cannot shore up their scrum they could have a nasty surprise. At the very least they can expect a thorough physical examination during both those games, and whether they have the depth in the forward squad to then peak against the stronger two teams remains to be seen.

A short note on the Italian challenge. Italy have improved every year they have competed in the Six Nations Championship. Though 2011 will go down in Italian rugby history as the first time they beat France, and deservedly so, they could have added Wales and Ireland to their scalps had they shown a bit more nous near the final whistle. The experience necessary to close down games which are tight comes only with regularly finding yourself in that situation, and for Italy it is a new experience.

Their pack can match most teams and their No. 8 Sergio Parisse would get into nearly any team in the world. This year they looked far more comfortable keeping the ball to hand, and the passages of play they put together when beating France were of the highest order.

They have Ireland and Australia as major nations in their group and, as stated above, much depends on the form of Ireland's key players. If the Italians are on the top of their game they will beat any pool opponents, bar Australia, that are not similarly playing at full throttle.

63

Sporting red tape and how to remove it

In March 2011 the Sport and Recreation Alliance (SRA) published an important paper on the numerous red-tape barriers that unnecessarily thwart or diminish the efforts of thousands of volunteers who provide sport for millions of people in Britain.

The report did not receive much publicity from the mainstream sports media because it wasn't about highly paid celebrity sportspeople. That fact is, in itself, a scandal; it betrays a lack of understanding about the reality of everyday sport and from whence come the stars of tomorrow. In what is set out below, I make no apology for having plagiarised large parts of the SRA paper. I did so because I believe in the points they made and in the solutions suggested. In some cases I have gone further in making my own observations on what can and should be done by the government. The essential point is that both I and the SRA think that a great deal more can be done. Some measures will have a small cost; others could actually save money.

A couple of years ago, I asked readers, through my *Daily Telegraph* column, to send me details of national and local government red-tape problems that were preventing sports organisations from getting on with their affairs. The examples poured forth. Among the many letters about things such as the Rain Tax, there was a letter from a reader who highlighted the statutory and administrative requirements that faced anyone wanting to set up a small sports club from scratch. It ran to three pages and that just covered the headlines of the various points that had to be addressed.

Why have the bureaucrats been allowed to put us in this position, and what can be done about it? As it happens, quite a lot and, as you will see below, without too much expense or bother. When you read of the sort of obstacles that exist you must concur that such illogical and pointless requirements cannot be justified and if you care at all about sport's future you are urged to add your comments and support to the SRA campaign. The battle to overthrow the Rain Tax shows that your voice can be heard, but without it nothing will change.

In addition to the specific points argued later in this article, what is needed for sport to flourish in Britain is a change in the government's and particularly the Treasury's attitude to sport. It is a scandal that both the position sport occupies in millions of people's lives and its many benefits for society are not reflected by having a seat at the Cabinet table. Sport's inclusion in a department which is also responsible for culture and media means that it does not get the warranted attention. The day a government creates a separate Department of Sport will be the day it proves its commitment to sport, as opposed to just talking about it.

The Treasury is notorious for not wanting to spend money, but it should be made to accept a fact that it already knows but does not want to admit to, namely that investment in sport at all levels saves money in other areas. The millions spent treating obesity would be cut by greater participation in sport. Similar sums would be saved from the enormous cost of dealing with anti-social behaviour and crime. There are countless examples of sport diverting young people from unproductive or destructive lives. When the total cost of wasted lives of crime is calculated, it dwarfs some of the funding requests from sport.

Another of sport's benefits is the general feel-good factor that encourages pride and achievement in Britain when our athletes succeed on the world stage. You should take into account the fact that sport is the only aspect of British society that is properly egalitarian. When you play, your background, religion, family, class and wealth are of no import. Relationships formed through sport cross the boundaries of ethnicity, and sport can be, and has proved to be, an agent for changing attitudes and for promoting social cohesion.

For all these reasons, sport demands to be treated as a separate case and distinct from other organisations that represent single interests and causes or that are open only to people who share a particular belief or background. The government can reflect sport's uniquely inclusive nature not only by making the changes listed below but by giving sport the benefit of the doubt whenever a decision has to be made about aiding sport.

Specific problems exist in many areas but they can be split into those which are administrative and those which apply to funding. As a general point, regarding administrative issues, the language in many documents is opaque, bordering on incomprehensible, and the processes are too complex, with clubs sometimes having to spend money getting advice on how to comply with numerous stipulations. A one-off, comprehensive exercise should be done to simplify as many of these issues as possible, and any future paper-work or process should have to be easily understood before it is introduced.

The Clubmark accreditation scheme was introduced in 2002 by Sport England to encourage young people to take up sport. To achieve Clubmark status a club must meet minimum requirements in four areas: coaching, training and competition; safeguarding and protection of children and young people; accessibility for the community; club management.

However, what began as a useful way of ensuring good practice and encouraging longer-term development in clubs has recently become burdened by extra requirements imposed by some sports' National Governing Bodies (NGBs). Many of their clubs believe the additional stipulations are too onerous and that they receive no practical benefit from having to meet these extra requirements, other than having ticked boxes they feel are unnecessary anyway. Often the extra evidence required for Clubmark status relates to things that the NGB wants to measure and from which it produces an increasing number of statistics of dubious relevance. The checklist alone provided by NGBs to ensure all the necessary supporting documents are present when applying for Clubmark accreditation is over ten pages long. The Department of Culture, Media and Sport (DCMS) should require a governing body to demonstrate the practical benefit created by any extension to the Clubmark scheme and this should not include the vague and generalised benefits that NGBs claim come from statistical analysis. A measure which does not so demonstrate should not be allowed, even if the NGB thinks it would be useful for its own purposes.

While on the subject of form-filling, the Data Protection Act 1998 is a provision that would be a good candidate for Most Unintelligible Statute. Its application to even small clubs, with a handful of members, causes confusion, and when applied to larger clubs prevents them from communicating with members effectively. It should not apply to clubs with fewer than 50 members, and for larger clubs there should be no restriction on a club's officers, such as fixture secretaries, using gathered information internally. Issues such as data being passed to a club's sponsors for marketing purposes are important and need to be addressed properly, but there are thousands of clubs which do not have sponsors and for them there is no need for such protection.

The increasing obsession with health and safety issues is, in part, driven by the rise in conditional fee litigation where costs often exceed damages. However, the situation is not helped by the heavy-handed approach of local authorities who make further stipulations when sports clubs use council land.

While sports clubs should not be exempt from their legal obligations, legally the government can take steps to ensure that as non-profit, volunteer-run organisations these clubs are not held to the same standards as professional counterparts and profit-making businesses.

By far the most onerous and confusing task facing volunteers, when it comes to health and safety, are risk assessments. While a minority of clubs reported a benefit from having to make assessments, twice as many said they were not beneficial, and if you have ever had to complete one you will know why they cause problems.

Assessing any activity is necessarily a subjective exercise and one which is reliant on the level of experience possessed by the person making it. In small clubs there may not be anyone who is suitably qualified to make a comprehensive assessment. What then is the club to do? Pay for an expert, which most cannot afford, or not carry out the activity?

NGBs should be made to employ an expert to write risk assessments for every normal activity that a member club normally undertakes. This would provide the basis for a club's assessments, which could then be amended to account for any specific matters that apply to its environment. This would also have the additional benefit of making any risk assessment more robust should it later become the focus of legal scrutiny.

Another unwelcome effect of health and safety paranoia is the way it has influenced local authorities over the question of insurance. Mandatory public and occupier's liability insurance cover of anything between £2 million and £10 million is demanded by most authorities, failing which a club will not be allowed to use its land. These sums are not mandated after a careful assessment of the realistic potential liability of the club; they are simply blanket requirements and ones which are expensive.

The government could and should make local authorities carry out a proper analysis of the club's possible liability before it orders a minimum insured sum. In fact, if the authority was required to take on the liability as part of its other insurance responsibilities and charge the club the relevant premium, the sum would be lower for the club than taking out its own insurance because the authority, as a large premium payer, could demand discounted rates.

When you consider the next issue, you will probably, like me, be left in a state of stupefied incredulity. Did you know that grants to clubs from Sport England for facility funding, which originate from the Treasury, carry a requirement for the club receiving funding to pay VAT back to the Treasury?

What this means is that either the club has its grant cut by 20 per cent or must find that figure from elsewhere, which in turn means that 20 per cent of the grant figure that could be used to run the club is paid to the Treasury. This ludicrous clawback should be stopped immediately, and if the extra sum reclaimed is not to be made up, at least if there was a 20 per cent cut in the grant from the outset, this would avoid the time-consuming and expensive paperwork required to hand the money back. What was it they said about joined-up government?

Additionally, Sport England requires NGBs to pay a legal charge to secure ownership of the land should the club fold, even though for an NGB to recover land from a club in this manner is rare. Clubs must be able to demonstrate that they have the right to continue to occupy the site, by either owning the land or having a lease which runs for a minimum of 7 up to a maximum of 21 years. The DCMS should relax the legal processes on securing the land for facility funding given that NGBs do not tend to need to reclaim the land. Further, to protect the land's use from non-sporting purposes, the award of Sport England facility funding should protect the lease of the site for at least 25 years.

What is needed when it comes to finance and sports clubs is a change in the mindset of government and, in particular, of the Treasury. They need to understand that clubs are not businesses. Most clubs barely break even and if they do produce a surplus it is very small and does not attract tax, even under the present unfriendly tax regime.

Even large clubs which may have a few employees are not businesses in the normal sense. Essentially a club is a closed entity, and the objective is to provide for its members and to make sufficient money to do so. To the extent that clubs make a profit, it is re-invested for their people who, through their subscriptions and purchases from club shops, the bar and so on, have created the income in the first place. There is no monetary shareholders dividend and as such you can make out a case for clubs not having to pay corporation tax at all, provided that any cash surplus is not distributed but is retained for contingencies or saved towards a capital-based project such as building new changing rooms.

What makes this matter yet more senseless is that, counted within a club's income is money given through NGBs. Thus clubs are forced to pay tax on income that comes from the Treasury; and that tax, like the VAT referred to above, is returned to the place from whence it came. I'm going to lie down for a minute.

Furthermore, club treasurers can be personally liable for corporation tax on income from non-members, including bar income or sponsorship, where the club is not incorporated, even where the levels of income are relatively small. The job of club treasurer is a thankless one. Most treasurers are volunteers and do not charge for their services. Thus they are in the doubly disadvantageous position of being personally liable as above, which they would not be if they did the books at arm's length, and they do not get paid.

A nil-rate band for Community Amateur Sports Clubs' corporation tax should be introduced to ease this burden for clubs with taxable profits of less than £15,000. The requirement for clubs to make an annual self-assessment return, unless its tax liability is less than £100, is time-consuming and expensive. If you have filled in a personal tax form you will know that it is not straightforward and a club's return is even more complex.

This is in effect what happens: we pay tax so that civil servants are paid to distribute bits of that tax to NGBs and sports clubs as grants. Different civil servants then have to be paid to analyse returns from clubs to confirm that they do not have to give us back the part of the tax given to them in the first place. Alternatively, they are due to pay back a proportion of the same money we gave them, via the civil service, in the first place. Only the civil service, in full Sir Humphrey Appleby mode, is happy about this situation because, thereby, they gain jobs for their members.

Clubs should be able to apply for exemption from filing returns and this could be suspended if they made a profit of more than £15,000, though unspent, undistributed surpluses should not count as profit. In fact, it would be better if NGBs and sports clubs were exempt from corporation tax completely, with the caveat that no dividend or distribution from retained surpluses is made to members.

What should happen is that someone should calculate which would be less expensive for us as taxpayers: the total amount of lost tax by exempting NGBs and sports clubs completely, or the cost of paying numerous civil servants to decide how much, if any, of the money we gave them was due to be returned to us and then for them to collect and process it. Remember also, that the civil servants whom we pay to do this circular, money-chasing exercise also pay tax; and other civil servants have to be paid to assess how much of our money they have to pay back. Further, we pay the pension contributions of both these sets of civil servants.

If the former scenario is cheaper, create the exemption from tax; if the latter, then we should still make the partial exemptions discussed and lessen the administrative burden as far as possible. Perhaps the following fact might give you a clue as to the likely answer to this question: the UK is the only country in Europe which does not offer exemptions on corporation tax for its National Olympic Committee or sports bodies.

As you can see, the issues are ones that with the right attitude can be sorted out without major upheaval or the spending of much more money, if any. Sport deserves to be placed in a separate category for what it gives to the country.

64

British tennis – where does it go from here?

There are few sports played in Britain that enjoy unbroken coverage of a home tournament for a full two weeks each year, from which the sport then receives an annual dividend of around £30 million. Few sports have year-round coverage of most of their major tournaments on satellite TV. Even fewer sports have supreme athletes contesting those tournaments time and again and yet fewer have had a player or players from Britain that generate home interest.

British tennis has all these, and yet its world ranking has gradually fallen over the past 25 years. Whatever measures it promises will finally reverse this trend fail dismally, leaving the sport a sad joke when compared to other sports which enjoy a fraction of its advantages in terms of profile and funding. The decline is all the more alarming when you consider that in modern sport the precedents are there for successful administration, coaching and all-round development. There are other tennis federations, both traditional and relative newcomers, which show what can be achieved and how it is done.

To understand why a revolution is needed and why things cannot evolve you have to understand the history of British tennis and how it came to be the upper/middle-class-dominated sport of today.

The game now called 'real tennis' was popularly played during the Middle Ages across much of western and central Europe. In Britain it was played by royalty and the aristocracy; indeed, the court built at England's Hampton Court, in 1625, is still used today.

Lawn tennis began to be played after Charles Goodyear invented a vulcanisation process for rubber, and during the 1850s players began to experiment with using the bouncier rubber balls outdoors on grass. Then, in 1874, Major Walter C. Wingfield patented in London the equipment and rules for a game fairly similar to modern tennis.

In 1875 lawn tennis was first played at the All England Croquet Club at their Worple Road ground in Wimbledon. When, in 1877, the inaugural Lawn Tennis Championship was held, the title of the club was amended to the All England Lawn Tennis and Croquet Club (AELTC).

In the first ten years or so of lawn tennis, almost all players were players of real tennis who played the new game in the summer months. It was J.M. Heathcote, called the 'outstanding real tennis player of his generation', who took charge of the first AELTC sub-committee to decide on the first set of rules for lawn tennis. The close affiliation of real to lawn tennis meant that the latter had almost instant acceptance as a prestige sport. In only a few years, the Wimbledon tournament established itself in the social calendar of the upper classes, ranking equal to Lord's, Henley and Ascot as a sporting event at which it was essential to be seen. Advertisements to promote lawn tennis stressed the importance of playing the game on grass in private gardens, something that only the landed class possessed.

Lawn tennis at this time was run, played and watched by the upper class and, because of this, their rules of etiquette, both written and unwritten, became part of tennis. The framework of rules provided for 'fairness', for equal chances to win for all contestants; so on the court it was the cult of the amateur: it was more important to take part than to win. Before and afterwards the expectation was self-restraint and civilised behaviour.

Tennis became a sport to which the affluent, professional middle class aspired and the expansion of this class between the First and Second World Wars created a similar growth in the number of private tennis clubs throughout Britain. Joining the sporting upper class meant adopting the same values and rules; codes of dress and conduct were rigidly enforced and adhered to. From that time to this, little has changed.

One reason for this inertia, possibly the main one, is the example set by Britain's oldest and highest tennis institution – the All England Lawn Tennis and Croquet Club. It is the British sporting club that is most difficult to join, and when you look at its membership regulations and joining policy you see clearly why it remains elitist, exclusive and snobbish; by comparison, getting full membership of the MCC is a doddle.

The club has a maximum limit of 500 members from its full, life and honorary sections. The honorary members are invited and include past Wimbledon singles champions and people who have rendered distinguished service to the game. In order to become a full or temporary member, an applicant must obtain letters of support from four existing full members, two of whom must have known the applicant for at least three years. The applicant's name is then added to the Candidates' List. It is then, as AELTC admits, a case of waiting, for a long time. There is no timetable against which an application will be considered, and the granting of full membership is entirely discretionary. Honorary members are elected from time to time by the club's committee. Membership carries with it the right to purchase two tickets for each day of the Wimbledon Championships. Some temporary members are elected year on year, but such membership is also limited.

Members become part of a club that has nineteen grass courts (including the Centre Court and No. 1 Court), eight American Clay courts, and five indoor courts, two being Greenset Velvelux and three Greenset Trophy. In Aorangi Park, the area north of the Centre Court, there are 22 grass courts for practice before and during the Championships and two green acrylic courts. The total area, including the club's car parks, covers over 42 acres.

The chances of an ordinary person being able to comply with the nominations stipulation are practically nonexistent. This means that existing club members can ensure that only their sort of people become full members; well, they don't want any riffraff now, do they? On previous versions of its website (the section has been removed from the current site), the LTA tried to justify this elitism by claiming it was in the general public interest. Risibly, it reasoned that because membership came with an entitlement to two Championship tickets for the entire fortnight, allowing more members would mean fewer tickets for the general public. Breathtaking bollocks, you might retort: why can't they simply create different types of membership that do not have the ticket entitlement, yet allow ordinary people to play on their numerous courts? They do not do this because they do not want to and do not need to. The phenomenal success of the Wimbledon fortnight means they have no funding problems and can afford to ignore the divisive lead they give to the rest of Britain's tennis clubs.

A sport's image is framed by the lead given by its highest institutions and organisations. Until the AELTC abandons its restrictive approach, British tennis is doomed to remain irredeemably middle class and thought of, by everyone else, as unfriendly and snobbish.

The contrast with other countries is stark. To give the reader some idea of how differently tennis is organised and played elsewhere, various comparisons are made at appropriate points below with our nearest neighbour, France. This is not just because of its geographical proximity to us. Both countries have roughly similar populations and socio-economic levels. Neither has a disadvantaged class that sees tennis as a way out of poverty, like those in Eastern Europe and the Far East. One thing is different, though, and it is highly significant given the history of British tennis: France does not have a monarchy, and while there are ancient French families which were once part of their aristocracy, they do not still sit at the top of a defined class system, as is the case in Britain.

The French are obviously doing something right because they have been churning out Top 100 players for years. In the last thirty years, they have produced Grand Slam winners in Noah, Amélie Mauresmo, and Mary Pierce (who was raised in North America so to be fair did not come through the French system); Grand Slam finalists in Leconte, Pioline, Clément, Tsonga and Marion Bartoli; and have been recent Davis Cup winners on more than one occasion. They have more top-level coaches and courts per capita than in the UK, and a totally different, welcoming approach to encouraging youngsters to play. French tennis clubs are open to all, most are family-based and many courts in France are municipally owned, even if they are used by members' clubs. Furthermore, the courts at Roland Garros, where the Fédération Française de Tennis (FFT) is based and the French Open takes place, are open to any FFT member (the equivalent of an LTA member), and can be booked on-line.

If you doubt that class is an issue in British tennis or that the AELTC does nothing but maintain the rigid demarcation between the right and wrong sort of people and that it engenders similarly elitist tennis clubs, all you need do is pay a visit to a few of Britain's private tennis clubs. I have witnessed this first-hand. My experience of trying to join one of these places was a salutary lesson, confirming to me the reasons why the social mix in tennis clubs has only widened marginally over the past 70 years and why tennis remains a staunchly middle/upper-class game in Britain.

I am a knockabout player, with reasonable hand-eye co-ordination. If I played regularly I would probably be a decent club player. Only half a mile from where I live in Wimbledon is a private members club, to which a friend of mine belongs. At his suggestion, I went down to enquire about joining and was eventually put in touch with the Membership Secretary, a late-middle-aged man, who seemed to regard my desire to join the club as an inconvenience. After handing me several forms to complete, he went through the annual fees which, as I was a middle-class lawyer at the time, were not a problem. He then added that before I could apply I would have to be proposed and seconded by two existing members and attend a number of 'social sessions'. During these, I would be watched by members of the Membership Committee to see the standard of my play. As I could actually play, this would not have been too much of a problem, but what about someone who wanted to take up the sport and who had not played before? These sessions, I was told, would also allow the assessors to 'see what sort of person you are'. It was at that point that I tersely declined to go any further. What sort of person did I have to be to make myself acceptable? What right did they have to make such subjective judgements anyway? What does that sort of stipulation say about the club? How would a stranger be able to get the required nomination and seconding?

I am white; middle class; a former international sportsman; am used to being in the public eye; and had a university education. They might, or might not, have deemed me suitable, but how daunting would that sort of scrutiny be to a relatively uneducated, less assertive person? Given that my friend told me he had never seen a black person in all his time at the club, anyone from an ethnic minority would undoubtedly be extremely uncomfortable being judged in this manner.

In addition to this list of entry inhibitors, the rules of the club strictly prescribe its dress and behavioural codes, both on court and in the clubhouse. Playing times for children are limited and the booking system gives longer-standing members priority over newcomers. It is well known that in this and similar clubs, the older elite dominate club affairs. With their knowledge of every rule, they hog court bookings. By insisting on compliance with every rule and code, they effectively freeze out less established and less confident people. The antipathy of elderly members to children is well documented, as is the unfriendliness to anyone who, for whatever reason, does not quite fit in with a club's in-crowd.

Contrast this with the vast majority of clubs in France where, provided they have room, there is no need to be 'played in', nor indeed to know if you can play. You pay the fees, you're in. Juniors can play when they want, as well. All-comers are wel-come. You can often, if you're visiting the area, just pay a temporary members' fee for a small amount and thereby join the club. I played at a beautiful private club in an exclusive wooded area near Chamonix towards the end of a ski season. No prob-lems; one form to give the address of where I was staying; book; play; use the changing rooms, bar, restaurant and a wish for a '*Bonne journée*'.

The AELTC does not acknowledge that it is part of the prob-lem nor that there is a problem at all. It is unassailable because of its commercial success and its exclusive connections with the great and the good. Much is made by the AELTC of initiatives with local schools and the fact that many youngsters are given the chance to visit and, in limited circumstances, to play at the club. It is true that AELTC coaches visit schools and provide free coaching and the AELTC runs educational initiatives that bene-fit local children – all this cannot be disparaged. However, though this is good work, readers will note that it does not allow anyone who is not known to existing members to join the club. They will use the huge profits made from their Championships to aid at a distance, but they will not let you in.

In addition to the above initiatives, the AELTC is able to salve its conscience at not having ordinary people as members because the annual surplus produced by the Wimbledon Championships is given to the LTA. In turn, the LTA is in hock to the AELTC and cannot demand that it opens up its membership and starts the process of changing the British public's perception of tennis.

These problems have thwarted attempts by the LTA to make British tennis more accessible and egalitarian. Initiatives that prioritise the importance of junior players, encourage ethnic diversity and professionalise coaching with a view to creating the winners of tomorrow, can, and are, simply ignored. Private members clubs are just that – private. Why do they have to care about what anyone else thinks? After all, if it's good enough for the AELTC, why can't they do likewise?

Only when the LTA provides funding for a club can it hope to have an influence in changing attitudes and even then it has difficulties. While it can attach caveats to any grant, it cannot adequately monitor compliance and even if it becomes aware that the caveats are being ignored, it cannot effectively discipline offending clubs. It is not that the LTA has not tried to improve British tennis; it has not been radical enough and has tried to work within the present system.

In 2006, the current chief executive of the LTA, Roger Draper, implemented his plan for improving the game's world standing. His 'Blueprint for British Tennis' has cost around £250 million and has, from its inception, proved to be controversial, with criticism of its aims, methods and implementation. That year, Stuart Smith, Draper's predecessor, predicted that Britain could have five players in the Top 100 ATP rankings by the end of 2008. At that time Britain had two such players and its Davis Cup ranking was 25. The two Top 100 male players were Tim Henman and Andy Murray, though it should be noted that Murray was coached firstly by his mother in Scotland, and then as a teenager at the Sanchez-Casal Academy in Spain; thus he did not come through the LTA system.

In 2007, Paul Annacone, then the head coach of the men's game for the LTA, claimed that Britain could have at least four male singles players in or around the Top 20 by 2012.

In June 2008, Draper claimed that Smith's prediction of Britain having five players in the Top 100 by 2008 had been 'the wrong target in the first place' and he extended the time-frame for hitting this target to 2010.

By the end of 2010, Britain had one male and one female singles player in the Top 100, Murray and Elena Baltacha. In 2011, Britain's Davis Cup ranking had dropped to 43. In fact at the end of 2010 the LTA had missed all five of whichever targets it was aiming at:

- Average ranking of the top five male singles players – Target: 160 Actual: 204
- Average ranking of the top five female singles players – Target: 113 Actual: 151
- Number of singles players of both sexes in the top 100 – Target: 3 Actual: 2
- Number of players of both sexes in the top 500 – Target: 30 Actual: 25
- Number of doubles players of both sexes in the top 100 – Target: 5 Actual: 4

At the time of writing (April 2011), the comparative figures for British and French-ranked tennis players are as follows:

Men, France
Top 10: 1 (Monfils)
Top 20: 3
Top 30: 5
Top 100: 9
Ranked 101–200: 13 (in addition to 9 in top 100)

Men, UK
Top 10: 1 (Murray)
Next players ranked 221 and 280

Women, France
Top 100: 4
101–200: 7

Women, UK:
Top 100: 2 (Baltacha and Anne Keothavong) both ranked below
   the French top 4
101–200: 1 (Heather Watson)

There is another point that comes out of the Anglo-French comparisons. France has, and has had, several black players within its top ranks: currently, they have two gifted and athletic players, French No. 1 Gael Monfils, and Jo-Wilfried Tsonga, ranked 18 in the ATP world rankings; and let us not forget the brilliant Yannick Noah. There are other black French players in the Top 200, but can you name me a single black male British tennis player? We have the young Heather Watson among the British women, but she was raised in Guernsey and has been based in the US at the high-performing Nick Bollettieri Academy for a number of years, so, as with Andy Murray, you cannot claim she is an LTA success story.

How can it be that black athletes have made their mark in British football, rugby, cricket, athletics and many other sports, but not in tennis? It is inconceivable that there is not the potential talent within Britain's black and other ethnic communities to at least equal the current crop of white British tennis players. So why are they not there? Those who run tennis will not like this, nor will they admit it, but remember the 'what sort of person you are' test I highlighted above? Why would any black, ethnic or working-class family want to go anywhere near clubs that make that sort of subjective judgement over people who want to take up the sport?

In all the visits I have made to a dozen or more British tennis clubs I have never seen a black face. Sorry, that is a lie: I did see one fixing the showers in one club in southwest London. There are undoubtedly some black club members whom the LTA could identify, but I would wager a small fortune that the proportion of black and ethnic minority members of British tennis clubs is nowhere close to equalling the proportion of black and ethnic minorities as a percentage of the total British population.

Britain's record of producing coaches has also worsened during Draper's tenure. From a historic average of about 550 new coaches a year, in 2009 fewer than 100 coaches qualified through the LTA's grading system. The LTA claims it is meeting its participation targets but Sport England's 2009 figures showed no significant increase in adult participation in the previous two years. Furthermore, British Tennis Membership (as the LTA now call their membership scheme) currently stands at 320,000; contrast this with France where there are over 1.13 million FFT members, not to mention participants. That same year, 2009, a further £26.8 million in lottery funding went to British tennis for the sole purpose of growing the game. That, plus all the measures promoted by the LTA, has not produced the promised benefits.

It is blindingly obvious that the failure is not one of investment, and because of this the LTA has to look beyond the issue of money to reverse the decline. It cannot just be about money because the LTA has had stacks of cash. Other minority sports would kill for a fraction of the LTA's guaranteed annual income. The problems stem from the game's elitist reputation, its insular private clubs and the fact that the LTA cannot compel those who run tennis, at the highest and club level, to make the changes needed.

Many commentators and others involved in British tennis have produced ideas for its rescue. *The Times*' respected tennis correspondent, Neil Harman, has made several sensible suggestions in a number of articles in which he has addressed the failures of the LTA. However, his and others' suggestions demonstrate that within the sport there is nobody prepared to be sufficiently radical, no one who will advocate the revolution necessary to reverse the decline and ensure that in future British tennis draws its talent from all sections of British society.

The National Tennis Centre at Roehampton cost £40 million and from its inception it has been a source of controversy. Some say it is elitist, too opulent and, further, that there is not the talent to justify an elite training centre anyway. There is nothing wrong with establishing a centre for excellence and a sport must have a programme for its elite athletes. However, the players at Roehampton are not elite by any objective international standard, and the facility is therefore underused. As it has been built at great cost, there is no point in abandoning it, but the way it is used can be altered.

One part could be retained as a high-performance centre, and if a point comes when Britain has sufficient numbers of truly elite players, the whole centre could be used as first intended. However, until that point is reached, the facilities should be made available to ordinary players and people. The chance to use top-class facilities and to train and play alongside Britain's best can only inspire others to achieve. Giving people a glimpse of what they need to do to succeed, and of what they will get if they do, would be a powerful recruiting tool. Whatever the state of British national tennis, the centre should be open for the public to view and to watch the preparation of Britain's elite tennis players. Not only would this be inclusive, it might also rid some of Britain's underachieving, but cosseted, players of the notion that they are somehow God's gift and better than everyone else. The centre should aim to create the same standing and function as has Roland Garros, which is open all year round, has an enormous shop for clothes, merchandise and equipment, has a great museum, fantastic restaurant, and most importantly has courts which can be booked and used. That sort of access would contrast hugely with the attitude of Britain's private tennis clubs and the AELTC, where you can look around the museum and go on tours of the facilities, but you will never be allowed to play or be a member. It would be a practical demonstration that would convince people that the LTA, if not the AELTC, was a body that practised, rather than talked about, tennis for everyone.

In this way the LTA could break the public perception that the AELTC was the pinnacle of British tennis. Neil Harman had a powerful and knowledgeable ally in Judy Murray, who had stated that rather than building one £40 million centre, the LTA should have funded forty £1 million centres across the country. They may be right, but it is now too late to use that money, and if it is used in the way I suggest, the National Tennis Centre could become a symbolic and practical focus for a new approach to British tennis. The LTA needs to sever its relationship with the AELTC because it can then order its own affairs.

Throughout the country there are municipal facilities that are underused and dilapidated. Partnerships with local authorities could renew existing courts and build new ones. Long-term leases could be negotiated so that the LTA or possibly jointly owned clubhouses and changing rooms could be built and made available to everyone, with the focus on family participation and youth development. These sorts of clubs would have a totally different atmosphere from their private counterparts and would attract a diverse membership, including people from poorer backgrounds. There would be no requirement to be the right sort of person and the family focus would necessarily make the clubs friendlier and more down to earth.

The LTA should stop giving money to private clubs and invest in British coaches and in its own performance initiatives. The status of LTA club coaches would be raised and this, in turn, would attract better-qualified applicants for coaching positions. The private clubs won't like it, but so what? They are part of the problem anyway. Fairly quickly the message would come across that to get quality coaching and to progress the best talent had to use LTA clubs. Finally, local authority partnerships would mean easier access to school kids who want, or could be encouraged, to play tennis.

The seismic changes that are needed to reposition British tennis depend on the breaking of the relationship between the LTA on the one hand and the AELTC and its private club clones on the other. What are the chances of this happening? Unfortunately, they are slim to nonexistent. To shun the British tennis establishment would be an unpopular move, and the social and political connections of tennis's elite go right to the top of society and government. For some people involved with the LTA there is a chance for them to join the AELTC's super-elite as a reward for their services to tennis. Rather like being mentioned in the official honours list, an AELTC membership is a reward for which some people work their entire life and they are not prepared to rock the boat and jeopardise that. The chance to rub shoulders with royalty and the great and the good is an irresistible opportunity for some people. What would they do if the AELTC decided not to allow them to use the private members' areas during Wimbledon fortnight? They might not get tickets and – shock, horror – they might not get the chance to sit next to the Royal Box.

What would the LTA do without its annual bounty from the Wimbledon Championships? Could it subsist on government money alone? Well, if the details recorded in *The Times* of 12 January 2009 are accurate, they would not have to face this unpalatable penury any time soon. That is because in 1922 the LTA signed a document with the All England Club and Ground Company guaranteeing the LTA received the annual surplus from the Wimbledon Championships. In 1998 this was £33 million and the figure is usually between £20 and £30 million. This payment was guaranteed under a new contract that stipulates that from 2011 the LTA receives 90 per cent of the surplus until 2053, in return for which the LTA sold back its 50 per cent share of the Ground Company by which it owned half of the grounds of the All England Club.

So, there is seemingly nothing the AELTC can do to stop this funding without breaching contract. The LTA can therefore use a substantial guaranteed income to finance multiple community tennis centres and do all the things it cannot compel private tennis clubs to do. It has 42 years before the automatic cash runs out and surely it will then be on its own anyway. In the long-term interest of the LTA and British tennis in general, the LTA has to be totally independent and be in charge of its and tennis's destiny. Forget hobnobbing with the alleged cream of society, many of whom are rich and thick; if you really love tennis and not the social trappings that go with Wimbledon, you know that what it takes to succeed does not lie in the British amateurish approach to winning.

The LTA has four decades in which to secure the future of British tennis. Will it tackle the difficult decisions? Will it get it right by the middle of this century? On past performance you wouldn't bet your life on it.

65

'You are the worst, most biased commentator in the world'

Of all the allegations that can be and are made against commentators, and particularly those who, like me, are co-commentators or pundits, one of the most frequent is that they are biased. It is also the criticism that is the hardest to shake off and the one that is most disliked by those it is made against.

Some broadcasters are less sensitive to the allegation and will only consider the question at all if it is so extreme that it effectively compromises their coverage by opening the opinions of their pundit to ridicule. If the alleged bias is not so extreme and chimes with the likely views of the majority of fans then, again, some broadcasters will not interfere.

When it comes to the BBC it is a wholly different matter. As a result of the way the BBC is funded, via public subscription and the restrictions in its Charter, it takes allegations of bias extremely seriously, whatever disappointed complainants who routinely call for sackings may think. The BBC also has to deal with the spectre of governmental and party political scrutiny, and while this usually relates to political coverage, it heightens the tension around the subject of bias, and ensures that programme-makers, in whatever genre, are aware that the issue has to be kept firmly in mind.

In order to view this subject in its correct context, it is necessary to take account of the relative contributions to BBC funding made by the viewers it serves.

According to UK National Statistics the projected figure for the number of UK households in 2011 is 26.2 million. This is broken down by country as: England – 22.52 million, or 84 per cent; Wales – 1.28 million, or 5 per cent; Scotland – 2.41 million, or 9 per cent; Northern Ireland – 0.65 million, or 2 per cent. As nearly every household has a TV and is therefore liable to pay for a TV licence, the same proportions are taken as being applicable to BBC licence payers. To put these figures into further perspective, there are approximately the same numbers of licence payers in Lancashire and Yorkshire as in Wales, Scotland and Northern Ireland combined.

One way in which the BBC could divide its income, which would be proportionate to contribution, would be to establish separate corporations for each country, funded by the amount of money paid by their licence payers annually, to spend as it saw fit within the confines of the overall public broadcasting charter.

It does not do this for a number of reasons, chief among these is that there would be hugely wasteful duplication of basic administrative functions, but also because to do so would leave the non-English corporations with insufficient money to bid for TV rights, provide credible outside broadcasts and so on. It is to the advantage of Scottish, Welsh and Northern Irish viewers that they are not left on their own because if they were, the range of programmes made and genres covered would be severely diminished, even if they had the compensating satisfaction of being able to control exclusively what output was possible.

As it is, they are provided with regional stations titled BBC Scotland/Wales/Northern Ireland, which focus on their national issues and news, and employ a high percentage of people from their country. In addition, they can show, without paying for them, programmes made by the BBC in England, and can also screen material bought from overseas producers which they could never afford if they had to use a budget set strictly according to the amount of money annually collected from the licence payers in their country alone.

Sport, particularly rugby, is a good example of how this system benefits the three countries other than England, although the way in which the BBC is criticised for its coverage, you would not know it. The TV rights to the Six Nations, as broadcast outside France and Italy, are periodically put out to open tender, and the BBC competes against ITV and the satellite broadcasters to show the live coverage. If the BBC was funded along the demarcated lines set out above, the four BBC corporations could still combine their bids; but if they were asked to contribute to the cost in line with their number of licence payers, the amounts payable from their total annual income would be disproportionately high because of the amount committed to establishing and maintaining the necessary infrastructure to run their corporations. Furthermore, once their called-for contributions reached a certain level, each of their corporation's managers would be forced to conclude that buying their share of the Six Nations TV rights could not be justified because it left insufficient money with which to make or buy programmes for viewers not interested in rugby. The single bid made by the BBC has allowed the BBC to win the live broadcast rights for the Six Nations and it has shown most of the matches since the game turned openly professional in 1995.

The frequent allegations of bias towards England extend not only to the commentaries but also to the composition of the studio panels, pundits and interviewers. Criticism is invariably made of any supporting features recorded to accompany the games and even the order in which the teams are discussed.

To see what, if any, evidence there is to support such claims, let us look at the 2011 Six Nations coverage which attracted the same criticism that has been levelled at the BBC in every previous year. The main studio anchors were John Inverdale (English) and Jill Douglas (Scottish). The permanent studio analysts were Jeremy Guscott (English), Jonathan Davies (Welsh), Keith Wood (Irish) and Andrew Nicol (Scottish). The three match commentators were Eddie Butler (Welsh), Andrew Cotter (Scottish) and Alistair Eykyn (English) and the co-commentators, used in all five rounds of matches, were me (half Malaysian/half English), the said Messrs Davies, Nicol and Wood, plus Lawrence Dallaglio (English) who was used on one game. The touchline interviewer was Sonja McLaughlan (half Scottish/half English) and the touch-line analysts were Phil Matthews (Irish), Colin Charvis (Welsh), Chris Cusiter (Scottish) and Lawrence Dallaglio.

So the BBC Six Nations 2011 output featured, by nationality and relative to the percentage contributed by that country's licence payers to the total BBC budget, as follows: England, four and two halves for 84 per cent; Scotland, four and one half for 9 per cent; Wales, three for 5 per cent; and Northern Ireland, two for 2 per cent. Which of the said four countries does not have a proportionate number of people working on this coverage?

In fact, that is not the whole story when it comes to coverage because in previous years BBC Scotland has provided alternative coverage, using the main BBC broadcast footage but presented, commentated and commented upon by an exclusively Scottish team.

For the Welsh, this year's championship was also shown by S4C, with exclusively Welsh presenters and commentators, and was broadcast in Welsh. S4C's primary source of funding is the UK Government's Department for Culture, Media and Sport (DCMS) i.e. general taxation, the vast majority of which is paid by the residents of England and especially of London.

Even when given their own channel and coverage, the Welsh still complained loudly about unbalanced representation, though some of this carping may be due to the fact that only 20 per cent of them can speak their native language.

Given the above facts, it is impossible to conclude in all honesty that the English are disproportionately represented. There is even more trouble when it comes to the issues of commentary and opinion. To illustrate my point, I am going to use a practical example and look at the final game of the Six Nations when England travelled to Dublin in search of a Grand Slam.

Before focusing on the reactions to my comments during the game, it is worth noting how the BBC covered the game in respect of the nationalities of the people involved on camera or behind the microphone: if anything, the English licence payers and viewers were substantially under-represented proportionately. The studio, commentary and pitchside teams for the game were as follows: studio anchor, John Inverdale; studio pundits, Jeremy Guscott and Keith Wood; commentator, Eddie Butler; co-commentator, Brian Moore; interviewer, Sonja McLaughlan; pitchside pundit, Phillip Matthews. Given the stated nationalities set out above, English licence payers got three and a half English people for 84 per cent; the Northern Irish people got two people for 2 per cent; the Welsh got one person for 5 per cent and the Scots, half a person for 9 per cent. I should also point out that Northern Irish viewers had the alternative of watching the coverage of the Irish national broadcaster, RTE.

By the way, I am in favour of balancing the coverage in this way, even though it is disproportionate to the majority; I just don't expect to get abused having made the concession to the minority.

Research shows that it is possible for two people to see the same event and yet to interpret it in a completely different way. With no hint of dishonesty, both will stress different parts of the event to bolster their opinion and minimise, ignore or even not see things that might cast doubt on their point of view. There are a number of factors that influence and distort perception. These factors can be present in the perceiver, in the object or target being perceived, or in the context of the situation in which perception occurs.

Later on in this piece I set out some of the Twitter reactions to my commentary, which give real-time reactions to my opinions given during the game and which illustrate the points I make about bias, but there are general points to make before those comments are considered.

First and most important is that the very nature of my job as a co-commentator is to make comment and give opinions. With comment on factual matters there is right and wrong; but the opinion that flows from facts is necessarily subjective and there is no definitive right or wrong. An opinion can be given that is strongly supported, but the fact that another person or even a majority of people do not agree does not make that comment objectively incorrect.

The average viewer for that game would have been a supporter of one or other team, even if they were not Irish or English. If they were, then their motivation, interest and expectation – or at least hope – would be that their team should win. Their attitude to the game, how extreme their reaction was to events and my comments would depend on how passionately they followed rugby and how vociferously they identified with their nationality. The more involved, the stronger their emotion and the less objective their perception. The major mistake most fans make is that they wrongly assume that they approach my comments as neutrals and are always open and fair-minded. They are not, and the fact that they have a strong, sometimes overwhelming desire for their team to win means they can never be so. This does not mean they are all rabidly one-eyed and incapable of fairness but it does mean that in situations that are open to interpretation they will usually interpret things in favour of their team or their opinion.

Another factor is what theorists call 'the target', and when it is me who is the target, this appears to be singularly apt. Targets are not heard in isolation. The relationship of a target to its background and the target's own supposed characteristics influence how it is perceived by others. My background in sport is framed in an English context, with all that that implies for non-English viewers.

This is coupled with what is called the 'attribution theory'. Our perception and judgement of someone's actions or opinions is significantly influenced by assumptions we make about that person.

Attribution theory was developed to explain how we judge people differently depending on the meaning we attribute to a given behaviour or comment.

Shortcuts are also frequently used when judging others. Individuals engage in selectivity. They take in bits and pieces of information and these are not chosen randomly; they are selectively chosen depending on the attitudes of the viewer. Selective perception allows us to 'speed read' others but not without the risk of being inaccurate. Assumed similarity has the 'like me' effect. A viewer's perception of others is influenced more by the viewer's own characteristics than by those of the person observed. We sometimes form a general impression about someone on the basis of a single characteristic.

Even before I open my mouth almost every rugby fan and a good number of occasional rugby watchers will be aware that I played for England many times. When I played I was unapologetically and rabidly for the England cause, to the exclusion of all else. As a player there is surely no other way to be. I was not a popular figure, never courted sympathy, and the way I played and carried myself was aggressive and confrontational.

What was apparent from the TV screen is the only information on which all but a tiny fraction of viewers can base their perception of me as a person because they have not and will not meet me in a normal environment where they have a chance to see my off-field persona. As such, they are left with the playing image – aggressive, confrontational, unlikeable and anti-anything not English – and it is against that persona that they hear my opinions.

If I was Irish and had been and done all that I did and was in a green jersey, I would have been well received by Irish fans and not so by the English. People assume that because I played for England, I am an England fan; and while deep down I want my country to win, I am not present at their games as a fan, I am there to work as a co-commentator. I am well aware not only of the BBC requirement that I do not approach the game as a fan but also of their sensitivity to the issue of bias. Before every tournament the BBC holds a full day's meeting which stresses this and other issues.

The final factor to take into account is the situation in which viewers watch games. Those who are in the stadium do not have the benefit of the images seen by TV viewers. Those watching TV do not get the overall impression that only spectators at the game can appreciate. I get both and also have the benefit of sometimes seeing replays which are not shown to the general public.

Additionally, I sit in an advantageous viewing position: on the halfway line on the front row of whatever tier the broadcasting gantry is on, and with an unobstructed view. Nobody can jump up in front of me at the wrong moment. Also, I am working so I do not have my mind anywhere but on the game. I don't have a friend or friends around me to distract me. I am not in a pub heaving with people jumping about and having the distraction of getting to the bar, nor am I watching in a crowded front room where discussions and arguments take place which can mean that I miss some action or only partially hear a comment.

I also watch and comment with the benefit of numerous international appearances and of knowing exactly what happens on an international field and in particular in the front row of the scrum, a notoriously opaque area for analysis. I am a qualified referee, and although not formally trained, have coached a number of teams. Though this may seem the self-serving list of a braggart, all that is stated is fact and highly relevant when you consider whether it is me or a viewer who is more likely to have an accurate grasp of the facts and whose opinions should carry more weight.

What invariably happens – and did so again, as will be seen later – is that many people who do not like me do not listen to what I actually say; they listen only to comments that reinforce their already set prejudice against me or England. When I go through comments with people I find that they have completely forgotten positive comments I made about their team, remembering only criticism.

In fact, the biggest influence on my comments is which team plays better and which team has more possession in attack. There are many more things to say about attacking options and moves, as against the obvious comment that a defending side is defending well or badly. If you went through the transcripts of my co-commentary, the team that attacks more invariably has more positive comments made about it and is mentioned more frequently. It is as simple as that.

What often flows from preconception is that if I make a mistake, which I do, and it is a comment over something relating to a non-English team, it is immediately attributed to bias, when in fact it is a mistake pure and simple.

The assumption of bias also encourages the mistaken conclusion, made by some critics, that because they do not agree with me I am poor at my job. Given the subjectivity involved, this is illogical and yet it is the foundation of much of the abusive comments and the calls to the BBC for my dismissal.

I set out below a small number of the tweets made during my co-commentary of the Ireland v. England game. They are reproduced verbatim, exactly as they were tweeted. If you are offended by foul language then stop reading this piece here. If not, read on and you will see the irrational level of hatred behind some of the comments, and how points I make are supported by fact. I think it is also worth giving a brief description of the game as it helps to frame the context of the comments.

The England team faced an Irish team that had played in fits and starts in their previous four games, and although with better discipline the Irish team could themselves have been in the same position as England, had their opponents in the Italian and Welsh games had a bit of luck, Ireland could have finished next to bottom of the table. The game was a huge occasion because the Irish fans and players knew that their team were capable of playing far better rugby than they had up to that point. They were facing an inexperienced England team and had beaten England in six out of seven previous encounters. Furthermore, the prospect of an historical enemy taking a Grand Slam at their newly opened Aviva Stadium at Lansdowne Road was a prospect that was sufficiently motivating on its own for most Irishmen. England won the first kick-off and pretty much nothing else. They were spanked by an Irish side that played with immense physical commitment and no little skill. As such, Ireland had the vast majority of the attacking plays, and throughout I recognised their superiority and praised what was praiseworthy.

Here are a few examples of preconception in these tweets (please note that they are reproduced verbatim):

KildareGunner Kildare Gunner
@noelwade Brian Moore is a prick of the highest order. Always was and always will be. He's on a pedestal with Gary Neville

Not much chance of this man approaching my comments with an open mind. Mind you, he was not alone:

gardsmeister IAN GARDINER
why do the bbc continue to employ Brian Moore? such a sad bitter & twisted man

Willalmond Will
I fucking hate you brian moore

And as an example of someone who has no idea what I am employed to do:

edsbrother Eds Brother.
Brian Moore, please fuck off. Just call the game, we don't need to hear your shit views you cunt.

The next tweet came after my comments about problems with the scrum. Bearing in mind I probably took part in close to

100,000 scrums during my career, games and training included, I think I have a reasonable idea about this facet of play. Despite this, and without giving any reason, the following tweet came in response:

jonnyxf jonny f
@bighaty brian moore in one ear. My former high level
amateur prop father in law in the other . Stereo bull shit

Mind you, this know-all-know-nothing doesn't only dismiss my views but those of his near relation who he admits also played at high level.

As England were outplayed, even some of the Irish fans realised that I had recognised this:

MrMulcahy Patrick Mulcahy
17–3 to Ireland at HT. What has happened to Brian Moore? He
is particularly unbiased this evening – only explanation . . .
pod person

Patriccus01 Patrick Cusworth
Typically insightful commentary by the always erudite Brian
Moore #sixnations

However, when I gave Ireland the praise they deserved, English viewers, presumably expecting me to be commenting as one of theirs, started criticising my objectivity:

dixon10 James Dixon
Does Brian Moore know he used to play for #England not
EVERYBODY ELSE! Tosser #sixnations

englandrugbyrwc Paul Clark
watching south african cunts cheat with irish cunts and brian
moore the cunt making excuses for the cheating cunts

At half-time, Ireland went in with a 17–3 lead and were unlucky not to have been further ahead; I said as much in my short half-time summary and this tweet from a Welsh viewer, and thereby a neutral, followed:

> *OwenRogers Owen Rogers*
> *Brian Moore has spent the whole half slagging England.*
> *Deservedly. Bet some celtic tossers will still call him one-eyed.*
> *#6nations*

And right on cue came this:

> *HenrySheehan Henry Sheehan*
> *Is Brian Moore the most biased commentator in world sport.*
> *He is no @ghook that's for sure #sixnations*

Shortly after the start of the second half, the Irish captain, Brian O'Driscoll, scored a try which put Ireland out of sight, and even though there was half an hour of the game left, I commented that it was game over. This led to gloating tweets addressing me as if I was a fan:

> *anitajaneharris Anita Harris*
> *RT @balletjanet Brian Moore, not as gobby now are you. /// LOL!!*

> *philippabowen Philippa Bowen*
> *@Joel_Hughes and hasn't brian moore gone quiet!!! #6nations*

> *ATaylor Ade Taylor*
> *Brian Moore just said game over. Hows that for supporting your team? England quitters*

> *JAMIE_BELFAST JAMIE H. SMITH*
> *Brian Moore whats the score ??*

Some people agreed with me:

tonykear1 Tony Kear
@IanThomas1979 @sjamesjourno Brian O'Driscoll over .....
Game over. Best Brian Moore quote ever!

But this upset some English fans who seemed to expect me to be cheerfully optimistic and therefore to deny the evidence seen with my own eyes:

jongaunt Jon gaunt
England are playing poorly but does Brian Moore have to be so bloody pessimistic and defeatist

At the end of every Six Nations Championship, as well as the autumn internationals if the BBC have the highlight rights, the Head of Sport and the senior producer thoroughly review the coverage. This extends to all aspects, including commentary, co-commentary and punditry.

There have been occasions where my blunt style and willingness to go against convention in terms of political correctness have led me to be spoken to and warned, but never in respect of my partiality. As seasoned BBC people, the management also know that people are far more motivated to complain than they are to praise, by a factor of 20 to 1. They are also sensitive to the demographic differences, and will not and cannot publicly make the sort of points I have made earlier in this piece, though they know that the BBC audience has a huge English majority. If there was any serious evidence that I was biased, the BBC management would not hesitate to address this because their public funding and public service charter mandate that they must. Anyone who thinks the Corporation is a cosy cabal where a blind eye is turned to matters such as this is entirely wrong, at least when it comes to sport.

There is some comfort to be had from knowing that most of the other commentators and co-commentators get similar allegations of bias, all similarly unjustified; but they do not get comments that are as vicious and personal as those thrown at me. I have had to get used to this treatment, though the very fact that I have chosen to write this proves that I have not been able to brush away the barbs. While I could be less bothered, to me that would indicate a lack of passion and pride in what I try to do when I work, and as I said before, it is easy to 'just ignore it' when you have not been in the same position. I don't ask the reader to feel sorry for me, but I would ask for the chance to be heard and to have my work examined from an open-minded aspect.

Out of all this, the only thing that is certain is that whatever I say, in whatever manner, somebody will criticise me and be abusive. It may come with the job, but if so I want a pay rise!

66

Twitter: freedom of speech or freedom to abuse?

In twenty years' time, someone will undertake a sociological study on the influence of social media and in particular of Twitter. They may even undertake a study of its implications with regard to English law, given the recent Ryan Giggs case. For those not familiar with this medium of communication it is necessary to set out a brief explanation of its origin, workings and attractions before getting into its effects.

Twitter is a website based in San Bruno, California, through which an estimated 200 million users send and receive messages, called tweets, of 140 characters or less. It can be accessed via the internet or mobile phone or any personal digital assistant that has web connectivity.

To join Twitter is simple. You create a profile on the website and can start tweeting, with your tweets appearing on your profile page. Tweets can usually be read by anyone, but you can also keep tweets private and these only go to your list of friends. You can subscribe to tweets from other people – this is called 'following' – by logging on to that person's profile page and simply clicking the 'follow' button on the page. Subscribers are known as 'followers'.

Initially you find out which of your friends or colleagues are listed on Twitter and you follow them; but you can also use a search facility through which you can find people you do not know but might wish to follow, usually those well known/famous. Once you create a list of those you follow, the site sends a list of people you might wish to follow based on the characteristics of the people you have already chosen.

This all sounds a bit antiseptic and as much fun as reading an IKEA instruction booklet, but this depends on what you want out of Twitter and how you interact with it.

You can use tweets in the same way as you would text messages, provided you are happy with all your followers seeing the contents. Though some limit their tweets to people they know personally, most follow other tweeters who might be recommended by their followers. These are often well-known people but not necessarily, as 'ordinary' people whose tweets are entertaining or interesting will also attract followers.

Although Twitter is essentially a simple communication medium, its success is due to the fact that it is used in various ways and for a variety of reasons; also because its users relate to it and to other users in a multitude of ways, some of them unexpected.

For a number of years, since I stopped practising as a lawyer, I have worked from home, as do many other self-employed people. There are advantages and drawbacks in working in this way. Chief among the latter is the fact that it can be a lonely existence, and though I did not realise it, I miss the interaction that everyone who works in an office or factory takes for granted. The office chatter and the contact with colleagues bring some variety to a day and it is not until they are gone that they are missed. I imagine that many others in a similar position have similar feelings of isolation from time to time, and some of them will be on Twitter for company, albeit at arm's length.

Twitter cannot replicate the human interaction of an office, but it is a form of interaction, and as such can help to break up a working day and allow you to get different opinions on whatever matters are being discussed. In any one day, there will be a huge range of subjects raised, from the news-breaking to the mundane and the downright strange. Anywhere you find office banter, you find gossip, and Twitter is particularly effective at spreading it, justified or not. The fact that some people have millions of followers means that a tweet or retweet (where a tweet is forwarded to all of a person's followers) by several of them can almost instantly reach more people than can conventional news outlets.

The potential for a topic to become widespread news is aided by top tweets and trending. The Twitter website has algorithms which spot how many times a tweet has been referenced or retweeted and can label it a top tweet. This means that it appears at the top of any search done against the topic by name. Similarly, trending is identified by the website when it spots that a subject is attracting an unusually high number of tweets. On your profile you can choose to be notified of the trending topics in a particular country or region. Any topic that comes in the trending list will get many times more viewers than otherwise because by clicking on the topic you can see all the recent tweets about it. It is safe to say that once a topic trends, it is news, whether worthy or not.

An increasing number of people now rely on Twitter as their main source of news. Indeed, there are now sufficiently large numbers of journalists and organisations using Twitter as a medium for disseminating both news and the very latest information that Twitter has become a credible source for both these elements. While there are dangers in relying on a limited information source such as this, if you follow recognised and respected journalists and you know they are at a game, place or event, you can get contemporaneous news and opinions faster than those delivered on the internet – and without having to be near a TV or radio.

Scanning the tweets of well-known people is now established practice in all kinds of media, and celebrities' tweets are now the basis of many of their stories. Further, and probably one of the most addictive reasons for digesting news this way, you can immediately deliver your 140-character opinion back to the author and pose your own questions about the subject. Thus, people whose views would never normally be aired or brought to the attention of well-known people or organisations now have a direct line to them. Even if they do not get a response, they know that if they follow the tweeter their comment will be received and will register.

The extent and immediacy of Twitter means that it can be a valuable aid for campaigning, whether in the conventional political sense or for things such as fund-raising. Publicity can be gained which is out of all proportion to one person's contacts, and when used in conjunction with another form of social networking such as Facebook, the results can be startling if a matter happens to catch the prevailing public mood. A practical example of Twitter's usefulness was the way in which survivors of the terrible Japanese earthquake and tsunami in March 2011 contacted their followers, many of whom included family and colleagues, to say that they were safe and uninjured. It was also used to promote the charities that collected funds for earthquake relief.

It was inevitable that this form of social medium would be used as a marketing vehicle for companies to sell products and services. The particular attraction of Twitter as a marketing tool is that the communication between tweeter and follower is personal, at least notionally. Once a few tweets have passed between two people, even if they do not know each other in any meaningful sense, some form of relationship has been established.

Most people agree that personal recommendation is one of the most powerful, reliable and relied-upon forms of marketing. The nearest a seller can get to this with conventional advertising is to use a popular figure to endorse their product in the advert. If the person used has the right image and reputation, such marketing unarguably increases sales. Even so, there is invariably a degree of risk in using personalities in this way and a seller can never know in advance how successful this form of marketing will be. With more conventional advertising, a product is simply put before a potential consumer and the seller has to work hard to ensure the advertisement comes to the attention of the target market and that the advert is sufficiently good to engage the target consumer's attention. With Twitter, the brevity of the message usually ensures that it is at least read before it is forgotten. Moreover, the fact that it has come from someone you have chosen to follow means that you value, to some degree, that person's views.

If you want to organise something like a night out and most of your intended guests are followers, one tweet will relay all the information in the same way as a text, but without the need to scroll through and enter individual numbers. If you have tried to do this by text with a large number of people, you will appreciate how much easier and quicker it is to use Twitter.

As alluded to earlier, perhaps the single biggest factor that separates Twitter from all other forms of social networking is the ability for an 'ordinary' person to follow people who are well known, whom they admire or in whom they are interested, but will never ordinarily meet.

Followers know that receiving tweets from such people does not mean they have a real relationship with them, but because tweets appear much like text messages, there is the pretence that this is so, and that is enough. In some cases, the followed do exchange tweets, and again, although this cannot be said to create an intimate relationship, similar to the one between friends, there has at least been interaction which otherwise would not have occurred. In these instances the pretence of a relationship is stronger, and again, it is enough.

Some social commentators have labelled the relationship between the followed and the follower as one between exhibitionist and voyeur. Undoubtedly there is an element of truth in that claim, but it is more complex than that. Followers will only see that which a followed wants to reveal and this can range from a little to a lot. Additionally, the usual definitions of the said two depictions imply passivity with no interaction likely between the parties; clearly this is not intended or actual with Twitter.

I reluctantly joined Twitter because I was told that it was a good way to disseminate things like my *Daily Telegraph* columns directly to people who might not subscribe to the paper; plus, I was assured, Twitter could actually be fun. I also cannot deny that as a fledgling author it was another way in which to publicise current books and to build a following of people who might consider buying any future publications.

As well as tweeting links to anything I penned for the *Daily Telegraph*, I also tweeted weekly wine recommendations, as I had done for a number of years in my weekly wine column for the *Sun* newspaper. Recently there have been a number of highlighted cases of more famous people tweeting about products, without disclosing to their followers that they have been paid to do so. My tips were unpaid and they were popular with followers, a number sending feedback and making their own recommendations. This made me understand how powerful Twitter can be as a tool for marketing products and services and why an increasing number of companies and brands are using well-known figures to increase sales. Given that my comments were able to persuade a number of people to buy a particular wine, there can be no doubt that favourable comments from better-known figures will sell whatever they recommend.

I was on Twitter for about four months and initially the promises of fun were fulfilled. I followed a number of other sportspeople, journalists, broadcasters and friends and I started to attract followers. Like many in my position, I found the attention of followers flattering, and anyone who has any sort of public profile, if they are honest, must admit likewise.

With me there was a further issue: validation. Though I try hard not to crave it, given the sort of person I am, formed by well-publicised issues from my childhood, I simultaneously try to pretend that affirmation does not bother me and yet seek it for comfort. Twitter gives you the chance to attract followers of a similar ilk and naturally they are more likely to be favourably dis-posed to your musings. This courting of acolytes may, viewed from a certain perspective, seem sad and rather pathetic. However, I didn't want followers who automatically agreed with anything that I tweeted or wrote. I wanted and got many follow-ers who were prepared to qualify points or to disagree with me. I never minded a counterpoint, provided it was argued intelligently and with some civility. That did not mean without colourful language, it meant without abuse.

After the first few days on Twitter, I got some appreciation of how it was used by other people, and what I did and did not find entertaining. In truth, there are people who are very engaging and others who are dull, as well as many degrees in between. I set out to try and make any tweet that I posted either informative or what I considered to be interesting. I made a conscious decision not to post anything that I thought trivial and/or boring, accepting that this is entirely subjective.

For the first three or so months my tweets and responses delved into the worlds of film, music, wine, cooking, sport and a host of other things. Many times I laughed out loud at a tweet that was particularly witty or enjoyed an observation which was acute and caused me to ponder. Sometimes I saved the tweets for future ref-erence, as they expressed a view that I endorsed but had not formed; or they expressed something in a way that was better than anything I could concoct.

Just for entertainment, I ran weekly competitions asking for things like the best cameo performance in a movie, the best soundtrack, the best sporting film and so on. I gave a free signed copy of one of my books to the person I thought made the best suggestion. During big sporting events I would tweet my views on what was happening. As I cover sport in general for the *Daily Telegraph*, in my weekly comment column, I have an interest in and a reasonably good all-round knowledge of many sports beyond rugby, with which I am most widely associated.

One particularly enjoyable tweeting session was when I tweeted by way of a commentary on the England *v.* Ireland game from the 1992 Five Nations, a game in which I played. Another memorable night involved tweeting simultaneously on three different sports, which I was able to do by watching one game on TV, another on the internet and listening to a third on Radio 5 Live.

Gradually my number of followers grew from a few score to a few hundred and then to a few thousand. Just before my Twitter career ended – I will come to how and why later – I had nearly 8,000 followers. This is not many by some people's standards, but a large proportion of them were active tweeters, and my timeline, which shows how much interaction is going on, was always busy.

As the number of followers grew, it was, I suppose, inevitable that one or two nutters would follow me. At first, when I got abusive comments or ones which I thought were biased, prejudiced or simply plain wrong, I would spend a lot of time trying to disprove or out-argue someone. I am not good at letting things wash over me and the advice to ignore the idiots did not help because I wanted to set the record straight, as far as I saw it.

I was always careful to distinguish between people's views on matters which were subjective, where I knew that I could not with any validity prove that my opinions were correct, and those views which were based on factual inaccuracies or which were illogical. God knows how many hours I wasted trying to prove the fallacy behind some tweets or that they were non sequiturs.

The real trouble started as a result of a retweet I made. One of my followers penned the following harmless joke and I retweeted it to my followers: 'Apparently Gary Glitter is the new Aston Villa manager ... He heard the strikers are Young, Bent and possibly Keane, boom boom.'

From that point on, it was retweeted by hundreds of other people, including four other well-known people. Though they chose not to make similar accusations against anyone else, my retweet was seized upon by the Justin Campaign, an organisation formed to combat homophobia in football and named after the sadly departed Justin Fashanu, one of the first footballers to reveal his homosexuality. They called it a vile homophobic joke and demanded an apology from me on Twitter. They linked the joke to an article by Lindsay England that not only made tangential reference to stigmatism of homosexuals but also alluded to them being linked with paedophilia.

Below, I set out one of the subsidiary articles based on Ms England's piece, so that you can see how the allegations spread over the internet and Twitter. I have included a cross-section of comments left by readers of the article and they are reprinted verbatim, including the spelling and grammatical errors (indeed, this is the case for all tweets in this piece). The article is one of dozens spawned by the England piece, all of which are now permanently available on the internet when you search under the parameters 'Brian Moore vile homophobia'. These ridiculous and defamatory allegations are something that will come up any time those words are searched. They originated from Twitter activity and, though they are wrong and hurtful, there is practically nothing I can do about them.

Before considering the article, there are a few points that I think need to be made. The joke is not really about homosexuality at its core; if anything, it is about paedophilia, hence the reference to Gary Glitter. There is no derogatory slant against homosexuals at all. At worst, the joke is about predatory paedophiles and, as I was a victim of one, I know they exist. Even so, I believe that it is possible to find humour in a subject without holding derogatory views about the subject matter. It is possible to have sympathy or in this case empathy for anyone who has suffered from an act of violence or abuse and my retweet of this joke is proof that I am able to make this distinction. This differentiation is a subtle point and requires the ability to separate the two factors without getting lost in the knee-jerk and often feigned offence on behalf of others that is now a feature of modern life.

The article appeared in the news section of the pinkpaper.com. Jeni Quirke wrote a piece in response to the article, reproduced below along with the comments left on the website by readers:

Ex-England rugby player refuses to apologise after Tweet

Jeni Quirke

24 January 2011

Ex-England rugby player Brian Moore is being accused of homophobia after publishing a Gary Glitter joke on social networking site Twitter. The 49-year-old, who is currently a rugby presenter and pundit on the BBC, has received much criticism after he retweeted the post.

Almost immediately, the post sparked questions. The Justin Campaign, which works against homophobia in football, asked Moore to publicly apologise for what they described as 'a vile homophobic joke'.

But Moore refused, saying, 'I will not apologise for your misinterpretation and disgusting insinuation.'

Lindsay England, freelance activist, campaigner and author of the Just a Ball Game blog, said the message was inappropriate.

'Words which once again stigmatise an LGBT community with the links to homosexuality and paedophilia.

'Many young LGBT's who struggle at an early stage with personal understanding and acceptance of who they are in the world themselves, will only too likely then shy away from "coming out" and being at least active if not fully engaged in participating in sport because of the fear of ridicule and isolation and abuse that goes with the above mentioned so called "banter, bit of a laugh, leg pulling, name calling, casual homophobia".

29/01/2011 23:05:42
I'm not quite sure what some people are reading but 'Bent' is a reference to homosexuality – sadly still used as a term for someone being gay. It's a little sad when gay people are so wrapped up in their desire to make fun of other people that they do not realise they are also one of the subjects

26/01/2011 13:56:48
This is one of those cases of people being over-sensitive. It's a Gary Glitter joke for heaven's sake

26/01/2011 12:17:09
Brian Moore should know better. Surely he must have been aware of Gareth Thomas' words when he was interviewed after coming out. Gareth spoke about how jokes and jibes were like tiny cuts all adding up to create the hurt. Brian Moore should think about what he has just done.

24/01/2011 22:12:05
Word play with subtleties.

24/01/2011 22:10:10
Er? Reference to the strikers being young and bent? . . . Oh of course it's not homophobic if they aren't homosexual . . . oh of course, how could the strikers for Arsenal be gay? Gays don't play football. Context missing from how this scenario panned out – Mr Moore claimed his joke was about A homosexual, when in fact it was not, it was about a paedophile. Hence suggested linkage by Lindsay England

24/01/2011 21:56:12
Yes. Let's not lose our sense of humour. It's just a word play joke. I don't get Lindsay England's reference to stigmatising the 'LGBT community with links to homosexuality'. Er? . . .

24/01/2011 20:41:33

I am sorry but the justin campaign need to stop being so silly and learn how to laugh! I am also a gay man and that made me giggle!

24/01/2011 15:30:35

Gary Glitter was a paedophile not a homosexual. As a gay guy I'm amused by his joke and not offended

24/01/2011 13:26:49

I agree with the previous poster. As far as I can see, mr Moore made no real reference to homosexuality. I actually thought the joke was pretty funny. If we do want to be taken seriously as part of the wider sporting community, we need to learn not to jump on these kind of remarks claiming homophobic abuse! Otherwise we're just going to come across as being over-sensitive.

24/01/2011 12:28:51

Why such a big reaction to a trashy joke. Where is our sense of humour? This is not the sort of joke that is likely to incite violence or bullying. What kind of journalism makes this an issue. Grow up!

As you can see, the comments made are wide-ranging. Some support the allegations, while many more agree with me that the joke is not homophobic and others support my assertion that the joke is not really about homosexuality at all. There are a few comments that are so incomprehensible it is difficult to make out which side of the debate the poster is on.

These comments probably echo the range of opinions of many other readers of the article who did not comment and they conclusively prove that it is at least arguable that the joke is not homophobic and that at least some of the gay community took no offence at all to it, some even finding it funny.

The allegation of homophobia is not a trivial matter and should not be made without unequivocal evidence. In circumstances such as this, Ms England should at least have made it plain that there was an alternative view of the issue in the gay community so that readers could gauge the reaction of the gay community properly. Her unqualified condemnation gives the misleading impression that there is no room for argument and that she speaks for the entire gay community, which thinks as she does.

None of the posters who agreed with my point of view about the joke is condemned and, as stated earlier, none of the other publicly known figures was subjected to this allegation and comment. Why should it be different for me?

A couple of weeks after this furore I was due to start my co-commentaries for the BBC on the 2011 Six Nations Championship. I suppose the above spat should have signalled to me that things would not be straightforward, as it had demonstrated the way in which Twitter can almost instantaneously create difficult problems for someone in the public eye.

The audiences for the 2011 tournament set new viewing records. In fact, they were higher than the figures for any other sporting event shown on the BBC, bar the FA Cup Final, the Olympics, the Fifa World Cup and the Wimbledon Tennis Final. The first game, Wales v. England, was played on 4 February, a Friday night, and was screened during the BBC's evening prime-time period. It had an audience peak of 8.2 million viewers.

Before I used Twitter I did not appreciate how many people tweet while they watch live events. For those of us who started watching sport on TV without the possibility of exchanging messages instantly, it is difficult to comprehend how many people now do this, or alternatively watch with their PCs in front of them and do the same thing on Facebook. Suffice to say that, out of the 8.2 million viewers, there must have been hundreds of thousands of people tweeting during the match.

Given the high number of viewers and their partisan allegiance to one or other country (or more accurately the fact they support either England or The Rest), I knew that there would be a greater than average reaction on Twitter, but I was totally unprepared for how extreme the comments would be and for the sheer spite that poured forth.

The comments to which I refer were reactions to opinions I offered as part of a job in which I am employed to comment on and explain, as far as I can, what has happened. I am not there to stick to the pictures and effectively describe what has been seen, nor to summarise what has happened by way of verbal précis. I am there to give an opinion, and I do so. I am also there to give my opinion on the technical issues that arise on the field, including refereeing decisions.

Whatever is claimed by viewers, it is a fact that I have far more experience than 99.99 per cent of them. I have played at every level of the game, from schoolboy and junior level, right through to the highest level of the British and Irish Lions. I have played in the Five Nations and in three World Cups and was part of an England team that won three Grand Slams, including the rare achievement of back-to-back Grand Slams in 1991 and 1992. I am a qualified referee, have coached at junior level and I played in the front row, an area of rugby which is notoriously difficult to understand and interpret. I watch matches, I write weekly articles on rugby and I discuss the latest technical advances with Premiership coaches, players and elite referees. Whatever I say, I do so against a background of considerable knowledge.

My comments and opinions are necessarily subjective; they cannot be otherwise and there is no definitive right or wrong. Whether anyone agrees with my interpretations is a different matter and they are free not to do so. However, viewers cannot legitimately claim that I have no idea about the game, past or present.

An additional point that should be noted is that for this game, viewers had the option to press the red button and listen to alternative Radio 5 Live commentary, and Welsh viewers had their own language commentary on S4C. If my words distressed them, even slightly, they had easily available alternatives through which they did not have to hear anything I said.

Moreover, while the game was important to rugby fans, it was not and never could nor will be an issue of true national importance. It wasn't a war in which men would die or an issue that would affect the lives of viewers, beyond the 80 minutes during which it occurred. It was a game of rugby.

The sort of abuse and the campaigns to deprive me of my job continued into the other games on which I worked, as is shown by the small sample of tweets shown later in this piece. What is interesting is that the vast majority of abusive tweets and those alleging error or bias contain no specific examples from which anyone seeing the tweets can form an opinion.

I have dealt with the issue of bias in an earlier chapter, and particularly the way in which I am perceived by viewers, some of whom are already irredeemably biased before they even consider what I say. I think those points are demonstrated amply by what follows in the rest of this chapter. The tweets below, again reproduced verbatim, represent a small selection of the sort of comments that were made about me during this match and the rest of the Six Nations Championship. I apologise if the words offend anyone, but they were not authored by me and if they do offend, think how much more offensive they are when directed specifically at you. If you do not like foul language, it is probably better if you skip the tweets and pick things up further down.

TSW_Stu Stu Davies
Please RT @Tir_na_nOgO: @garemsjames @TSW_Stu
#sackbrianmoore Retweet now. Get BBC to notice Brian
Moore – 4 Feb

RLPullen Robert Pullen
#BrianMoore Needs a good slap. – 4 Feb

Cottsy Andrew Cotton
"@Big_Gee: @brianmoorerugby fuck off you bald biased cunt"
#sackbrianmoore – 5 Feb

6reeno Greeno
"@ArtsUnknown: @IamAustinHealey can you please help us
bully @brianmoore out of a job? You want to see this (cont)
http://tl.gd/8mgcn2 – 7 Feb

Cottsy Andrew Cotton
So Brian Moore's wife is a BBC sport producer, I wonder how
@brianmoorerugby got his job commentating on BBC?
#sackbrianmoore – 8 Feb

VinlayFALENTINE Finlay Valentine
Brian Moore shut the fuck up. You are probably the biggest
cunt in the world. #englishtwat – 13 Feb

matthewjones22 Matt Jones
mental note to self: if ever in the company of brian moore,
punch him as hard as possible, preferrably in face. – 13 Feb

mohbhoy71 Moh Bhoy
I would seriously love to plant a #GlasgowKiss on Brian
Moore – TOSSER! #6Nations #Scotland – 13 Feb

dancafs Dan Mccaffrey
Love the #sixnations but wish they would #sackbrianmoore.
The impartial prick – 13 Feb

s16nyg Tits M'Gee
@6reeno Brian Moore looks like a retarded midget – 13 Feb

h4yls Hayley Wilson
any one else want to stab #brianmoore in the eye! #6nations
#england #france – 26 Feb

Manny_Moo Gavin Roberts
@Sparkyrite #eddiebutler rhymes with botal stunt.
#brianmoore rhymes with arrogant little cunt who knows fuck
all about law or rugby – 26 Feb

Jinks67 Hairscareclairebear
@jonesyaj good man, I would never tire of punching his wee
scrunched up face in! #BrianMoore #6Nations – 26 Feb

As you can see, the assorted unpleasantness includes graphic threats of violence. The language is base and excessive, including the disgusting wish from a woman to stab me in the eye. In other tweets I had death wishes and, most distressingly, one hoping my children got cancer, though this was withdrawn before I could copy it.

There is the defamatory allusion in one tweet that I owed my position to the fact that my wife is a BBC sports producer, rather than to my wide experience in rugby. In fact, I worked as a pundit and co-commentator years before we got together and she does not work on rugby anyway.

One tweet, from Mr Dan Mccaffrey, calls for me to be sacked for being impartial. Stupidity and ignorance abound in many other tweets, which I have not bothered to include, but idiocy such as Mr Mccaffrey's at least allows a brief smile.

While this abuse is bad enough, you will note that there are other disturbing features to the tweets. Many amount to cyber-bullying and the word bullying is specifically used in the tweet from the person with the moniker 'greeno' who is asking for support to bully me out of my job.

I was upset and angry about this treatment and I do not think unjustifiably so. Some people said it came with the job, but since when did offering my views on a game of rugby mean that I am fair game for abuse towards me and my family? I also reiterate the point that I have many people who take the opposite view of my work and enjoy it immensely. That my detractors cannot see how anyone could hold a positive view of what I do does not invalidate those views.

Some of my followers advised me to ignore the idiots, but that is easy advice when you are not the target. If the same thing happened to you, I am sure that you would not be able to brush off the abuse without reaction. Furthermore, when people publicly campaign for you to be deprived of your living, you have to take this seriously. Fortunately, this experience is not one that will be visited on 99.9 per cent of those on Twitter, which is no comfort if you find yourself in the remaining 0.1 per cent.

After hours of abuse and insults, a tweet came from a person named Sam Downes. It was not as vile as others but again alleged I was biased and incompetent. One of my followers, after a prolonged exchange with this man, tweeted a question asking whether Downes was his surname or his medical condition. While edgy, I thought this had an element of humour and it was a question/put down, not a straight joke. I retweeted it, adding, 'I wish I'd said that' and this caused no offence among my thousands of followers and no comment was made by them.

Note that the comment is specific to Mr Downes. It makes no reference to those with Down's syndrome in general, and I do not believe it mocks them in any way. Furthermore, for what it is worth, I was for three years the president of a national charity that worked for handicapped children, enabling them to take part in sport; a number of those helped had Down's syndrome.

However, via a circuitous route, that retweet came to the attention of one Ms Kate Sanderson who, it turned out, was not a follower of mine, but was more akin to a cyber-stalker and one who had made it her business to be offended by previous tweets of mine. As she was not a follower, my tweets can only have come to her attention if they were retweeted; if they were not marked as such, the only way for her to see them was to purposely search for them.

The following is a long tweet I posted – spelling mistakes, typos and all – using TwitLonger, a facility that enables people to make longer tweets than the 140-character norm. It sets out what became known as the @TheKGP problem (KGP was the author of the original tweet to Mr Downes) and includes things that I found out as a result of digging into the history of Ms Sanderson's long-standing antipathy towards me. It was purposely written formally, as by the time it was drafted there was a real possibility that the issue would get out of hand, as will become clear below. Also, as Ms Sanderson advertised in her profile that she had legal knowledge, I wanted her to be in no doubt as to the seriousness I attached to this matter, even if she had not thought through her actions. It also became apparent that I would have to consider expensive and unwanted legal proceedings to defend myself and my job as a result of a clear campaign to defame and vilify me.

To help you understand the way the exchanges took place and the claims I made about Ms Sanderson's tweets, I reiterate how the Twitter timeline works. If you follow someone, their tweets come directly to you. If you follow someone and use their twitter name in your tweet, that tweet will come to their attention. If you mention that person's name (not to be confused with his or her twitter name) in a tweet but you are not a follower, that person will only see your tweet if it is retweeted by one of their followers or if they search for it or it appears as a trend on Twitter. Ms Sanderson – @K8KGS was her Twitter name – was not a follower of mine and so my tweets could not have come to her directly.

@K8KGS,
Without prejudice to whatever may appear in subsequent
legal proceedings,

Dear Ms Sanderson,
Given that you state on your Twitter profile that you are
employed as a Global HR Director, Law, I write the following
assuming that you are aware of the legal consequences of
any words between us. Furthermore, that you were aware
such consequences when you made the statements to which I
refer later in this missive.

On 4.2.11 I re-tweeted to my followers a tweet that one of
them had sent to a man who had posted the following tweet
from samdownes1 sam downes-

*@brianmoorerugby is literally the worst, most biased
commentator in the history of rugby, sport and the universe.*

This was only one of many tweets to me on that date,
following my commentary on the Wales v England rugby
match that night, containing defamatory and personally
abusive comments, including one with a death wish and one
hoping my children were harmed.

As you know, the tweet from my followers posed the
question as to whether that man's surname was descriptive of
his medical condition.

I retweeted this because it has an element of humour and I
believe it refers to Mr Downes maintenance of his views; the
allusion is to mental capacity, which is unfortunately
diminished in many Downes sufferers. It is a question and not
an allegation and mentions no other person than Mr Downes.

When I retweeted that tweet I did so knowing it would go
only to people that had chosen to follow me and who knew
from my biography on Twitter that I was not a person who

had bland or necessarily mainstream opinions. I also assumed as my followers had volunteered to follow me that they had similar outlooks on life and in particular a similar sense of humour. As you are aware, humour is a subjective matter.

I did not ask and had no control over whether any of my followers retweeted my re-tweet. Moreover, the recipients of any subsequent re-tweet cannot have been said to have received it with my agreement.

You stated that 'Asking if surname Downes is their med condition – poor' and later that 'To retweet such an inappropriate comment let's you down badly.'

Whilst you make clear you do not approve of the original words, which you assume can be attributed to me by virtue of my Retweet, you did not specify whether any particular offence had been caused and nor did you claim offence to any named person.

The following was my response to your complaint direct to me –

@K8KGS I won't explain comedic devices as you've made up your mind and they weren't my words. I don't want vicariously offended followers

You replied admitting that you were not a follower of mine and indeed your timeline has tweets naming me which did not appear on my timelineWitness –

K8KGS Kate Sanderson
@brianmoorerugby I am not a follower and you retweeted . . .

It is thus clear that you became aware of the fact of my re-tweet following at least one and possibly many re-tweets of the original tweet. You have not specified how you became so aware.

Whilst the above quoted comments are not especially condemnatory they must be read in conjunction with other comments and facts that I did not know at that time but of which I am now very fully aware.

Prior to my re-tweet you posted at least the following re-tweet and tweets; there may be others yet to be discovered –

peterdash Peter Dash by K8KGS
Brian Moore: every year I forget how bad a commentator he is. Man thinks he's a walking rugby bible. – 4 Feb

K8KGS Kate Sanderson
Please BBC find another, better commentator than Brian Moore. He ruins it for me every single year. Strong feeling on twitter – please sort – 4 Feb

As proved by the above you believe that unfit to carry out my job as a commentator and before my re-tweet had publicly called for the BBC to replace me, i.e. sack me, which would deprive me of some of my income from which I support my wife and two young daughters. As a person who openly states a legal connection you cannot have been unaware of the consequences to me had the BBC followed your demand, which you claimed was supported widely on Twitter.

You failed to mention, or did not bother to find out, before demanding my removal that there are hundreds and probably thousands of tweets which take a diametrically opposite view of my work.

Further, your antipathy to my work and by direct inference myself is, as you clearly state above, long standing, going back a number of years.

I believe that when read with together all the above evidence feigned or at least motivated offence as claimed by

you. In further support of this I set out tweets made by you
to the author of the original tweet

K8KGS Kate Sanderson
@TheKGProblem thank you. Of course accepted. Sadly BM did
not see the wisdom of doing likewise and I am afraid it will be
escalated. – 6 hours ago

K8KGS Kate Sanderson
@TheKGProblem whilst I appreciate your sentiments I am
afraid it can't end there. It was an offensive comment which
crosses the line. – 6 hours ago

I draw your attention to the following parts of the above two
tweets –

'I am afraid this will be escalated' and 'I am afraid it can't
end there. It was an offensive remark which crosses the
line'

You claim the remark was offensive – I do not agree and I am
aware that had the author known of your previous personal
dislike of me and you calling for my dismissal, he would not
have apologised to you for its making. Not one of over 7,000
of my followers claimed offence at the re-tweet and given
that that re-tweet was itself re-tweeted by at least one and
possibly many others it seems there are thousands of people
who do not agree with your construction of the original
tweet.
    You have not stated that you have taken similar action or
made similar threats to any other person who made re-tweets
subsequent to me and it is my belief that I have been singled
out for causing your feigned and/or motivated offence
because of your long-standing dislike of me/my work.

When this is added to your public calls to deprive me of part of my livelihood over a subjective issue, one that is incapable of definitive resolution and by reference to partial evidence, I consider this a personal vendetta to harm my employment and wider standing, however, high or low.

This purposeful and long-standing antipathy is attaching itself to a deliberately emotive construction of a remark, which I did not author.

There is no line which governs what I or anyone else can and cannot find amusing. You have no authority to be the instrument of its enforcement even if it did exist. Your self-appointed arbitrator role is tantamount to saying that you decide what others and I should find amusing and that if we dare to differ you will escalate matters – i.e. cause harm.

As a legally connected person, you cannot be unaware that in matters of reputation the publicity surrounding an issue like this is in itself sufficient to cause damage. Further, that bodies like the BBC to which you referred may well be influenced by such publicity; indeed, I believe this to be something on which you intended to rely in your admitted vow to escalate this matter.

You have stated that I have not seen the wisdom of apologising to you but given what I now know I expect the reverse.

Finally, please not that I take threats to me and my families livelihood very seriously; the disgusting personal abuse I have had to suffer from others who, like you, simply disagree with my commentary is as naught to the outrage I feel that you have attempted to mount a damaging campaign against me.

If I do not receive an apology my rights to sue you for any and all; loss and damage, direct and indirect, that may arise from your action, are expressly reserved – as is my right to seek injunctive receive to prevent any further repetition of

previous damaging comments or any that you may, unwisely,
choose to subsequently make.

Following this tweet I received an apology from Ms Sanderson
and she closed her Twitter account. Unfortunately, by this time
the tweet had come to the attention of the BBC, which routinely
monitors Twitter for potential problems and comments made
about the corporation.

One of the senior managers called me and made known their
displeasure at my retweet and though I pointed out that it was a
comment from a follower and went through the arguments about
what constituted humour they were adamant and made it plain
that my continued involvement in Twitter was unwise.

I had to agree an apology that would be used if the issue was
taken further but at no point did they offer to add a comment that
they abhorred the personal abuse that I had suffered, though they
were keen to tell me they supported all their people in the face of
this type of thing.

There was no official complaint. In fact there were many tweets
supporting me and urging me not to leave Twitter. There are still
people who contact me via my website urging me to return to
Twitter, saying that they miss my tweets. This is flattering, but I
knew from the BBC reaction that I had to leave Twitter.

One aspect that the abusers did not consider or did, but did not
care about, is that their abuse can be seen by the children of those
they abuse. My nine-year-old daughter lives with her mother, but
stays with me for roughly half the week. She is computer literate
and like all kids of that age she knows her way round social networking sites. While I was looking through some abusive tweets
she came into the room without me noticing. She looked over my
shoulder to see what I was looking at and I could not prevent her
reading some of the abusive tweets. She was very upset, not only
by the language in the tweets but also by the judgements made of
me as a person. In the morning, I found a note she made that

night. It said, 'My Daddy is Brian Moore. Some people don't like him because he says what he thinks but he is a good Daddy and I love him.' That nearly broke my heart.

Twitter has been an advance in freedom of expression for most people. They are free to say whatever they want and do so. But I am now aware that I am only one tweet or retweet, made in a moment of frustration or inattentiveness, from possibly losing my job.

The usual balances, such as the libel laws, are expensive and open only to those who have a spare £500,000 lying around – that is what the average libel trial costs when both sides' costs are considered. Further, even if successful, a libel win does not automatically remove articles from the internet, nor posts on blogs, nor tweets that are defamatory. This can only be done by notifying every web-host, every carrier of web information and every offending author or publisher – which is virtually impossible.

It is true that anyone on Twitter can be the subject of hateful tweets or fall foul of today's thought police. The difference is that well-known people run a greater risk of the thought police attacking them and in a more public way than a normal person, a way which can really harm them financially and personally.

One reason why Twitter will make a fascinating sociological study is because it has blurred and in some cases broken traditional boundaries of communication. A letter is private between sender and recipient and, unless it is widely shown or copied, it remains so. The development of the fax simply speeded up delivery of letters and documents but again, unless disseminated, its contents remained private. Emails are also private, subject to hacking and the inadvertent pressing of a key, as in the Claire Swire affair. However, emails, along with text messages which are also private unless forwarded, have a feature that makes widespread distribution of their contents far easier. Friends lists or groups on a computer or phone memory make delivery to a few or to many simply a matter of pressing a few keys. All the above means that whether the contents of the missives are banal, bountiful or bestially abusive, they do not get a public airing without at least some effort being made by someone to remove their privacy. Moreover, the recipients are usually, or at least should be, known to the sender.

Twitter breaks these boundaries. Tweets are not private unless steps are taken to make them so, which in part defeats one of the main purposes of the medium. On top of this, the direct recipients are followers which the tweeter may or may not know personally. In the case of well-known people they may have millions of followers, and obviously nobody who uses Twitter can know how many times a tweet may be retweeted and to whom it is so sent.

What this creates is an unusual and some would say unholy alliance of a medium that is concurrently anonymous and distant – i.e. one tweeter and thousands/millions of followers and people receiving their tweets via retweet – yet it is also intimate because the comments are received in the same manner as might be a text or post on Facebook from a close friend, family member or a loved one.

It is simultaneously the equivalent of the shouting rant at the TV, at home or in the pub, except that the rant goes straight to the attention of the person to whom it is addressed, rather than dying in the ether of a front room or saloon bar.

Freedom of expression is taken for granted in many countries but it must be remembered that users can receive and send tweets via the US-hosted website from countries that do not allow public dissention and where information is strictly controlled. Twitter's assistance in making comment and information widely available in such countries is transparently beneficial.

Quite a number of people see Twitter not only as another backward step in maintaining any sense of privacy of exchange but also a step further down the line towards pointless, time-wasting inanity.

It can also be seen as an advance in people's growing narcissism and their overblown sense of importance or 'uniqueness', which makes them believe that what they have to say is of the slightest interest and value to a wider audience. This is often said of 'celebrity' tweeters but logically it is no different for 'ordinary' tweeters, the difference being only a matter of how many people share in the delusion as followers. Both well-known and unknown tweeters pour forth in the same manner on whatever topic they wish and are free to do so.

The reality is that 90 per cent of tweets are banal and would barely merit dissemination further than the proverbial garden fence, where most of our exchanges used to take place. However, the fact is that few garden fence conversations now take place. People are more isolated, even if they are closer than ever geographically. Twitter can fill the emptiness of people's lives and whether they gorge on trivia is surely nobody's business but theirs.

You can decry the dwindling face-to-face social interaction but that is happening anyway. If anything, Twitter and other social networking sites have created communications and relationships which would not otherwise have been made, even if they are a poor substitute for intimate meetings.

The advances in technology and speeds of communication have not, as predicted, given more leisure time; they have heightened the stress of work because we expect people to deal with our concerns by return and to be available at all times. Twitter at least responds to the increasing lack of time by allowing short communications with many, and at times (such as when we are in transit) which cannot normally be used to communicate, other than by making the odd phone call.

Naturally there are downsides to Twitter. Some are specific, others relate to all the recent developments in social media and information transmission in general. With regard to the generalities, Twitter is another driver of the instant response, snap judgement and often poorly thought-through reaction. It adds to the pressure to see issues in only a short-term manner. Restrictions in the length of comment polarise opinions and can create tabloid-speak from tabloid-thought.

As I think my experience shows, the herd mentality can easily be encouraged concerning a topic or a person, and that frame of mind is rarely even-handed and well reasoned. Going along with the crowd, without thinking, encourages cyber-bullies and people who become very brave from the safety of cyberspace. Most are well aware of what they are doing and do not care about the effects. They are examples of the worst sort of cowards who use Twitter to gang up on somebody they dislike, even though they have not and never will meet him or her. They say things that they would never dare repeat face-to-face, and even when challenged their mocking is at a safe distance. This sort of bullying is not reserved for the well known, though they are disproportionately targeted. Any examination of the calls to the Samaritans and Childline will see how Twitter and other social networking sites can be misused in this way. For every victim it is a searing experience, made worse by its public nature.

Some of the people who tweet abuse do so without thinking. They do not understand the potential hurt they cause nor the potentially serious consequences of their abuse, and although they are less culpable, they are no less dangerous. Many times when I or one of my followers responded to abusers we would find similar responses being given by the unintentionally thoughtless. 'I didn't think anyone read this stuff', 'No one takes any notice of it', 'Sorry, I didn't realise you would get to see it', 'It was said in the heat of the moment', 'I didn't really mean it'. Though these are explanations, they do not take away the damage that is done.

The potential to create gang-like pressure also encourages the aforementioned thought police. It is a sad fact that there are an increasing number of people who insist stridently on exercising the freedom to convey their own thoughts, yet seek to deny others the same largesse. You must not think differently, you certainly must not say so; and this extends to things about which there can only ever be subjective opinions.

These people have no authority or mandate to stop anyone from expressing their own views. They do not appreciate how incredibly arrogant they are in believing that theirs is the only legitimate point of view. Such people form a large part of another growing group, those who delight in becoming vicariously offended on behalf of some section of society, usually without asking the alleged victims if they are actually offended.

Both the way in which Twitter allows almost instantaneous censure and the polarised way in which denouncements are made have loosened restraint and fed extremist opinions. With less time for balanced reflection, those found on the wrong side of these thought-Nazis are condemned directly and are without recourse to civilised debate about the things said and the judgements passed.

I miss being on Twitter because during my time on the platform I formed a good relationship with many of my followers. At times we had fun, made each other laugh, exchanged interesting views on a wide variety of topics and, as I stated earlier, for me it took the place of the office gossip that I no longer experience because I work at home on my own.

I cannot deny an element of flattery was gained from adding numbers to my followers' list, but in that regard I was no more or less guilty of seeking attention than anyone else who tweets and has followers. You could say that as a public figure I knew what I was doing and that, in the end, it was my choice to be on Twitter. If I didn't want to run the risk of abuse or worse, then I simply should not have taken part. These points are pertinent, but I would counter them with the following thoughts. Why should I not be able to take part in a global phenomenon without me, my job or my family being abused and threatened? What does it say about some people that they act in the way shown when they have never met me and know me only from comments I make as part of my job and over a game of rugby? What does my experience say about a growing section of society that is intolerant and aggressive, even violent, if only in thought?

Twitter, like other forms of communication, has significant attractions and problems, depending on how it is used. It would be a great pity if it became unusable for some people because of its misuse by others. At present, that is how it is for me. However much I got from Twitter, the potentially disastrous consequences made it not worth the risk; a great shame.

67

Beware of the aftermath: the repercussions of writing an autobiography

It took me nine months to write the second version of my auto-biography, *Beware of the Dog*, but at least its title was an improvement on the title of the first book: *An Autobiography*. The book was better too, not because I am a better writer than Stephen Jones, the journalist who ghosted the first book, but because it came with a certain detachment from events that were contemporaneous with the release of the first book, such as my retirement from rugby, and also because my story was not told via a third party.

I thought long and hard about what to include and what to leave out of the book, not least whether I should include the fact that as a nine-year-old schoolboy I was sexually abused by a teacher, who was also a family friend. Its inclusion became inevitable once I had settled on the style of the book. I tried hard to make it a book, first, and about sport, second. Although it ended up with a lot of sport in it, I wanted it to stand on its own as a piece of literature – and if that sounds pretentious, so be it.

I was also keen to avoid the pitfall which damns many sporting autobiographies, which is to focus on matches and their results, many of which are familiar to readers anyway. I wanted to make the book more about the themes I had been able to define in my life and the reasons why I had made certain decisions, acted in certain ways, and become the sort of person I am. Once I decided to concentrate on the *whys* in my life, as opposed to the *whats*, I knew that the details of the abuse had to be included, otherwise much of what followed would not make sense. The extremity of my emotions and my illogical choices could not be accounted for without this piece of knowledge.

I was aware, and I was right, that some people would accuse me of including this detail to sensationalise the book and to increase its sales. The whole serialisation and what followed was in itself an ordeal that was shaped as much by what had happened in my early life as by the actual release of the book.

I don't know what I expected to happen when the book was released. As someone who works in the media and the written press, I should have had a good insight into how things would be portrayed and what would come with it. Suffice to say, either I had not thought sufficiently about what might happen, or I was naive. When something exists inside your head as an idea or memory, in a strange way it does not seem as real as when it appears in print or on film. The day the *Daily Telegraph* ran the first extract of its serialisation, the book featured prominently on the front page of the main paper, not just the sport section. It was inevitable that the revelations about the sexual abuse would be prominent, but although I knew what was coming – well, sort of – it left me numb.

As online columns and features now invariably have attached Comments sections, I was able to see the instant reactions of readers of the *Telegraph* and of the other papers which ran stories. A number of comments were along the line of 'Why is he telling us this now?' Others said that the abuse story had been released to create a media frenzy to sell the book. One or two actually accused me of making the whole thing up.

Some of these comments came because their authors do not understand how books are published and how newspaper serialisations work. The final copy for the book which was to be published in January 2010 had to be with the publishers at the beginning of August 2009. The details relating to the abuse were not written separately; they were delivered at the same time as the rest of the manuscript and were therefore public, at least to a limited extent, several months before publication. Further, the revelations were not separate from the book; they were taken from it and were the ones that appeared first as part of the *Daily Telegraph*'s serialisation. They were not released *alongside* my book, they were released *as part of* it. The way a serialisation is positioned, which photographs from the book, which passages are featured and in what order, is entirely up to the newspaper that buys the rights to serialise. Provided extracts from the book are not reordered so as to alter their meaning within the context of the book as published, the newspaper is free to do what it likes by way of presentation and promotion. Their aim is solely to sell more newspapers in order to recoup the money they paid for the right to serialise the book in the first place. I had no input into and no notice of the way the *Daily Telegraph* treated the serialisation. The prominence afforded the book was one of the things that jolted me when I first saw it. In fact, so large was the headline that first day that I did not look at the extract for about an hour, and only after my wife had reassured me that it was not bad.

As for the scurrilous allegations of fabrication, eventually they were disproven by a comment left by a reader of the *Independent* newspaper following a feature on the book. He, sadly, had his own story to tell about the same teacher and had suffered at his hands. In any event, the *Daily Mail* were tenacious in their search for the identity of the abuser, and it did not take long for him to be named by them, nor for several other similar stories to feature concerning pupils who were his victims. It was speculated – and was probably not far from the truth – that the number of his victims could well run into treble figures.

One unfortunate consequence of today's readers being able to instantly comment on stories is that a few intellectually challenged or malicious comments are made among the normal range of favourable and unfavourable comments. I don't like unfavourable comments – nobody does – but I do recognise when they are at least sincerely held and are not the product of what must be a disturbed mind. A few, however, went beyond the usual and acceptable.

One man claimed to be a contemporary of mine at my junior school, Whitehill Infant and Junior School, which was where the abuser worked. He also claimed to know one of my brothers-in-law. He said later that he included this detail to give him more credibility. At first he alleged the story was made up. Then he switched tack and took to mocking my reaction to it, saying that I was making something out of nothing and that, irrespective of his claims about authenticity, the details had only been published in an attempt to create publicity to sell the book. At first I made the mistake of answering this man's comments but, as I should have known, this only served to encourage him and to give him some form of misguided authority to comment. In the end, I left the deconstruction of what he posted to other people, some of whom were victims of other paedophiles, and who had read his comments and felt compelled to answer. However, this was not the end. He started to follow me on Twitter; when I blocked him, he started leaving abusive messages on my Facebook page under a pseudonym. It was only after doing some digging that I equated his abusive comments with those made earlier and was able to block him again. Only he can account for his behaviour, but as more than one person said in reply to his comments: he needs help.

The detracting comments that strayed into the abusive revealed a lack of tolerance and pity that is another unfortunate and growing trait of life today. Not only do people hold opinions which are unpleasant, they take delight in ensuring that these opinions are widely read, and take some perverse satisfaction in trying to ensure they come to the attention of the people over whom, unappointed, they sit in judgement.

The truth is that this sort of revelation is not one that is tossed out into the public arena by a victim without serious thought, and it is almost never done for the cheap purpose of publicity. Not only is the revelation highly personal, it is one that can stick in the mind of the reader, as the act is so abhorrent that it subtly taints the victim by association. If you think this is fanciful, I can only offer the following as proof of the way my revelation led to one piece of banter. On the Army Rumours website, used by serving soldiers, the following comment was made amid some banter relating to my commentary during the 2010 Six Nations Championship: 'I always thought Brian Moore was a cocksucker; now after reading his book it turns out I was right.'

During the six weeks or so following publication I did a number of interviews about the book on TV, radio and for newspapers and magazines. Most features were sympathetic and some, like the one by Paul Kimmage in *The Sunday Times*, were themselves outstanding pieces of work.

The one side effect of publication that pleased me more than any sales figures or publicity for me were the many instances where people contacted me directly or wrote or called newspapers and TV/radio stations to say that because of reading or hearing about my book they had been able for the first time to tell someone about similar instances that had happened to them. I did not set out to make the revelation with a view to helping anyone else. I did it for my own reasons and felt compelled, more than anything, to tell my story. As such, I do not deserve credit for helping the people who found the wherewithal to tell their stories, but it was something from which I think I can take a little pride. I know just how hard it was for each and every one of these people to summon up the courage to make their revelation and I am honoured to have been part of what can now become a healing process for them.

The first few interviews were almost as much of an ordeal as the original revelation. I approached them with a nervousness bordering on dread, and at points was close to tears, if not actually so. However, just as the sharing of the story enabled me to write about it, talking it through made subsequent discussions incrementally easier, to the point where I was able to talk fluently without breaking down, though I was never unemotional when the topic was broached.

Well over a hundred people contacted me, via my website, through the *Daily Telegraph*, the Rugby Football Union, and my publishers or via the newspapers and radio and TV stations which covered the topic, to tell me that they had suffered similar experiences. You would recognise some of their names immediately, and what this showed me was that paedophile crime is not the province of any particular class, walk of life or type of person. That so many took the trouble to find a method of direct contact undoubtedly means that at least a similar number, if not many times more people, made the first step to recovery as a result of the publication of my book.

Through the times that I discussed the book and the subject of abuse, I came up with a phrase which I think encapsulates the relief that can come when a victim finds the strength to speak about his or her experience for the first time. It may not be original, but I believe it to be true: once you find the wherewithal, for whatever reason, to share with someone the fact that you have been abused, from that point onwards, you will never be alone; you may still be lonely, but there is a huge difference between the two.

As a result of the book's high profile, I received several invitations to become patron or be otherwise involved in one of the many charities in Britain that tackle the issue and consequences of sexual abuse, male and female, adult and child. At the time I was not in the right frame of mind to take on any responsibilities because I was and am still coming to terms with my own experiences. However, I was humbled and flattered to be invited by such worthy organisations, and in time I will join one or two. At this point, my charitable energies have been channelled into work for the NSPCC and CEOP (the Child Exploitation and Online Protection centre), on top of the charities which I try to help outside the issue of abuse.

I suppose that nothing could have altered the fact that the vast majority of the media scrutiny and comment was about the abuse issue. Unfortunately, what this concentration did was all but obscure other parts of the book and the fact that, or so I thought, some parts were genuinely quite, if not outright, funny.

There was some attention given to the chapters that updated the fact that I had been adopted and had traced my birth mother and full brother and sister. This had been included in the first autobiography but had only just happened when it was published.

After more than fifteen years since meeting my birth mother and siblings, I again felt able to put some perspective on to the issues around my adoption. Unfortunately, my thoughts were not universally positive but I felt I had to tell the story and define its effects without trying to put a favourable shine on things. I was aware that it might cause upset but then again, it had also caused me a great deal of angst in the past and had affected me badly. Having to keep the thoughts to myself had been part of the problem and, in doing so, I had not been able to get into a position where I could start to address the effects.

As with the first book, the comments on adoption led to a number of people contacting me. This time, when I was asked for advice on the subject, I felt more confident in giving firm advice about two aspects because my own experience and that of several other adopted people reinforced two thoughts.

The first is that I strongly believe that anyone contemplating tracing a birth parent should do so only if they effectively feel compelled to do so. The reason for this is because you cannot unknow something you discover, and however little you think it has affected you, it is a powerful subject and it will have a far greater effect than you realise or can predict.

Secondly, in so far as it is possible, a person so seeking must do so with as few expectations of what they will find as possible. It is said that an expectation is a disappointment waiting to happen, and the fewer the expectations, the smaller the chance of disappointment. This does not extend to trivial things such as what a person looks like or how successful they might have been in life. It can also ward against the real possibility that the parent might react with hostility or refuse to have any contact at all.

It would be disingenuous to pretend that I am not pleased that the book sold well for reasons other than it being read by more people that it might help. I am a competitive person and wanted the book to outsell my first autobiography, which it has done comfortably. But when it came to the critical reaction to the book, I craved acceptance of the book from reviewers who reviewed outside the sporting genre. One of the effects of my childhood experiences has been a deep-rooted lack of self-esteem, and wanting this validation was another manifestation of this. As it turned out, I got this confirmation from every review of the book bar one. General literary critics from *The Times*, *Daily Telegraph*, *Sunday Times*, the *Independent* and other publications reviewed the book well.

At the time my book was included on the long list of entries, I did not realise that the William Hill Sports Book of the Year was the pre-eminent award in sports writing. In fact, I wasn't even aware that Simon and Schuster, my publisher, had put it forward. But by the time it came to announcing the short list, I was a good deal more informed and when it made the short list my insecurities came pouring out.

I looked at the short list, which was described by William Hill as the strongest they had ever had for the award, and was overawed by the talented authors who had also been chosen. At no point during the writing of the book had I expected to be in this position. The truth is that I had not even considered the possibility. My fellow nominees included a twice former winner, Duncan Hamilton – whose two winning books I had read and enjoyed enormously – for his book *A Last English Summer*; the award-winning sports journalist Matthew Syed's book, *Bounce*, was listed, as was *Open*, Andre Agassi's autobiography, written in collaboration with the Pulitzer Prize-winning writer J.R. Moehringer; the list was completed by fascinating books by Catrine Clay on the goalkeeper Bert Trautmann, *Trautmann's Journey*, and Luke Jennings' *Blood Knots*, on angling.

Things got worse when it was announced that the awards lunch, due to take place on 30 November at Waterstones, Piccadilly, was to be covered live on the Gabby Logan show on Radio 5 Live. Among the judges was John Inverdale, my friend and BBC colleague. I thought about contacting John to make a point. I never had any doubt that John would review my book professionally and that he would not give it any extra weight because he knew and worked with me. However, I was afraid that in trying to demonstrate his independence he might look upon it less favourably. I wanted to tell him that I expected no favours, but on the other hand I didn't think that our association should count against me. In the end I decided it would be wrong to question his professionalism. He has been a judge of this award for quite some time and is an honest and straight-dealing man. He did not need me to make a point of which he was well aware.

I went to the awards lunch with my wife, my editor and a number of people from Simon and Schuster, all of whom were a good deal more optimistic and good-natured than me. I told my wife in the car on the way to the lunch that I just wanted to get the disappointment out of the way, do the interviews and then go home.

When we got to the event, gigantic posters of each short-listed author stood out around the room. I nodded nervously to John and Gabby, all the while feeling sick and not wanting to be there.

John prefaced the award by giving a short speech about it and the way it had grown from its inception to be recognised throughout the literary world as the top prize in sports writing. He also mentioned the fact that the original intent of the award – to establish sports writing as a respected genre in the world of publishing – had been achieved, noting that each of the books short-listed stood out as a piece of literary work, irrespective of their subject matter.

As John began to describe the usual arguments about which book should win, I suddenly got a surge of hope that came from I know not where. He continued, saying that this year's winner had not been the source of too much disagreement before its unanimous election as winner, and he started to set out the characteristics that made it deserving of its title. The more he said the more apparent it became that I had won, and I had to stamp down an urge to shout and jump about in celebration.

When he announced that *Beware of the Dog* had won the William Hill Sports Book of the Year 2010, I closed my eyes and thought of my father, a man with whom I had had a difficult relationship, but who had always loved books and was extremely well read and articulate. I thought about the many people whose lives had touched mine over many years and also in the course of writing the book. I walked on to the small stage and said thank you. I had not dared to plan a winner's speech because firstly, I did not think I needed to and secondly, I thought it would be tempting fate. As an aside, this makes me wonder about winners' speeches made at Oscar, Bafta and other ceremonies and which are obviously rehearsed. Either the recipient must be supremely confident or at least have an inkling that he or she will win. If these speeches are prepared on the off chance, then all I can say is that the contender must be an unusual person and/or a born performer.

After receiving the prize, I went round the corner of the large room where Radio 5 Live were waiting to interview me live about winning. As Gabby Logan put questions to me I welled up and was, for one of the few times in my life, unable to think of any-thing meaningful to say. I gibbered a few thanks and muttered about being honoured and so on. The truth was that I was in a state of shock at the magnitude of the achievement, bearing in mind that this was my first book.

The feat became a bit more real when I returned to the now beaming group of people with whom I had stood pessimistically half an hour earlier. After talking to a few more journalists and giving a round of interviews, we went round the corner to a pub just off Jermyn Street. Everyone else got stuck into the celebratory drinks but I was still a bit numb and sipped and smiled. My wife and I received numerous texts congratulating me and many asked what we were doing as a celebration that night. As it was, we had planned nothing, because I was so sure I was not going to win that I had planned to take a car home and my wife was going to return to work that afternoon. We had not booked a baby-sitter and therefore had to be home by 6 p.m. to look after our young daugh-ter. So the celebration consisted of a takeaway curry and a quiet toast at home. In its way, that celebration was more real and appropriate because it was shared with the person, my wife, who had to put up with the excessive mood swings that accompanied my writing and with all the things that happened post-publication. I could not have done it without her, and the recognition bestowed by the award belonged to her as much as to me.